Persistent Peoples

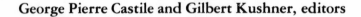

George Pierre Castile and Gilbert Kushner, editors

Contributing Authors

William Y. Adams

N. Ross Crumrine

Timothy Dunnigan

Charles J. Erasmus

Frederick J. E. Gorman

Vera M. Green

William B. Griffen

Robert C. Harman

Mark P. Leone

Janet R. Moone

John van Willigen

Willard Walker

Persistent Peoples

Cultural Enclaves in Perspective

UNIVERSITY OF ARIZONA PRESS

Tucson, Arizona

THE UNIVERSITY OF ARIZONA PRESS

This book was set in 11/12 V.I.P. Garamond

Library of Congress Cataloging in Publication Data

Persistent peoples.

    Bibliography: p.
    Includes index.
      1. Ethnic groups — Addresses, essays, lectures.
2. Ethnicity — Addresses, essays, lectures.
I. Castile, George Pierre. II Kushner, Gilbert.
III. Adams, William Yewdale, 1927 —
GN495.4.P45   305.8   81-10476

ISBN 0-8165-0744-9   AACR2
ISBN 0-8165-0750-3 (pbk.)

For
Edward Holland Spicer
Teacher, scholar, gentle man

¡Viva El Ned!

Contents

TABLES

FIGURES

About the Editors and Authors

GEORGE PIERRE CASTILE has studied the Tarascans of western Mexico, focusing on the problems of adaptation to outside forces. He has also done fieldwork among reservation Indians of the southwestern and northwestern United States, with special emphasis on the ethnohistory of northwestern groups. His publications include *North American Indians: An Introduction to the Chichimeca* and *Cherán: La adaptación de una comunidad tradicional de Michoacán.* He became associate professor of anthropology at Whitman College in 1978.

GILBERT KUSHNER has conducted research in Israel focused on directed change in an administered community of immigrants from India. His research in the United States has been concerned with ethnic identity and applied anthropology. He is the author of *Immigrants From India in Israel: Planned Change in an Administered Community* (University of Arizona Press, 1973). Professor of anthropology since 1970 at the University of South Florida, he became chairperson of the department in 1971 and was associate dean of the College of Social and Behavioral Sciences from 1972 to 1978.

WILLIAM Y. ADAMS has been field director of a number of major archaeological excavations in Egypt and the Sudan since 1959. Prior to that time he carried on extensive ethnological and archaeological investigations in the American Southwest. Since 1966 he has also been professor of anthropology at the University of Kentucky. His books include *Shonto: A Study of the Role of the Trader in a Modern Navaho Community* and *Nubia: Corridor to Africa*.

N. ROSS CRUMRINE has studied the Mayos since 1960. During two years of resident field research he assisted in Mayo rituals and ceremonials. His publications include *House Cross of the Mayo Indians of Sonora, Mexico* and *The Mayo Indians of Sonora: A People Who Refuse to Die* (University of Arizona Press, 1964 and 1977). Associate professor of anthropology at the University of Victoria, British Columbia, since 1968, he has also done field research in coastal Peru and Guam.

TIMOTHY DUNNIGAN has done fieldwork among the Lower Pimas of northwest Mexico and has published linguistic and ethnolinguistic studies of Dakota Sioux, Ojibwa, and Laotian Hmong. He joined the faculty of American Indian studies at the University of Minnesota in 1970 and has been associate professor there since 1974.

CHARLES J. ERASMUS has focused on preindustrial work patterns and problems of socioeconomic development in his studies of groups in Mexico, South America, Haiti, Ghana, Tanzania, Israel, and western Europe. His publications include *Man Takes Control: Cultural Development and American Aid* and *In Search of the Common Good: Utopian Experiments Past and Future*. He has been professor of anthropology at the University of California at Santa Barbara since 1962.

FREDERICK J. E. GORMAN has done fieldwork on the prehistory and ethnology of the Mohave and other Indians in the southwestern United States. An assistant professor of anthropology at Boston University since 1974, he has also done research on the historic and industrial archaeology of the northeastern United States.

VERA M. GREEN has done research in central Mexico, Puerto Rico, the Netherlands Antilles, south India, and the United States. The author of *Migrants in Aruba* and coeditor of *International Human Rights: Contemporary Issues*, she has been especially interested in applied approaches to anthropological research. An associate professor of anthropology, she has been director of the Latin American Institute at Rutgers University since 1976.

WILLIAM B. GRIFFEN has conducted research in northern Mexico, especially ethnohistorical work in the area of the modern state of Chihuahua. His books include *Culture Change and Shifting Populations in Central Northern Mexico* and *Indian Assimilation in the Franciscan Area of Nueva Vizcaya* (University of Arizona Press, 1969 and 1979). He has been professor and chairman of the department of anthropology at Northern Arizona University since 1964, except for three years as associate professor of anthropology at Saint Louis University.

ROBERT C. HARMAN has conducted research among the highland Maya of southeastern Mexico and the Navajo of the United States. His publications include *Cambios médicos y sociales en una comunidad maya tzeltal*. He joined the anthropology faculty at California State University, Long Beach, in 1969 and has been associate professor there since 1974.

MARK P. LEONE has done ethnographic work among Mormons and has studied the meaning and use of the past in contemporary American culture. He is the author of *Roots of Modern Mormonism* and has been associate professor of anthropology at the University of Maryland since 1976.

JANET R. MOONE has done ethnographic fieldwork in western Mexico and the southwestern United States among both rural and urban peoples. Her focus has been on contemporary cultural and social structural problems in situations of pluralism and change. Her publications include *Desarrollo tarasco: integración nacional en el occidente de México*. She has been a member of the anthropology faculty at the University of Colorado at Denver since 1969.

JOHN VAN WILLIGEN, formerly director of community development for the Papago tribe of Arizona, has been associate professor of anthropology at the University of Kentucky since 1974. He has done fieldwork among Papagos and Pimas in Arizona, Japanese managers in rural Wisconsin industry, and rural Kentuckians. Among his publications are the books *Predicting Socio-cultural Change* (coedited with Susan Abbot) and *Anthropology in Use*.

WILLARD WALKER has done ethnographic and linguistic research among the Oklahoma Cherokees, the Great Whale River Cree, the Passamaquoddies in Maine, and at Zuni Pueblo. He has been professor of anthropology at Wesleyan University since 1977.

Overview

The Analysis of Enduring Cultural Systems

Issues in the Analysis of Enduring Cultural Systems

George Pierre Castile

What is a people? By studying persistent peoples from around the world and raising questions of why and how they have endured, this volume attempts to define a people and examine the conditions of their persistence, starting with highlighting the principal issues that arise in the study of persistent cultural systems. In the definitive book *The Yaquis*, Edward H. Spicer frames his final analysis in the context of a "human type—the enduring peoples of the world" (1980:362). Since it is Spicer (1966, 1969b, 1971, 1976, 1980) who previously has contributed most to the identification and analysis of the phenomenon of persistence, his concepts will form the matrix of this discussion of the themes raised in the various chapters.

In order to define a people it is necessary to avoid simplistic definitions which confuse the issue. The notions which swirl about the amorphous term *ethnic*—ethnic group, ethnic identity, ethnicity, and the like—need to be disassociated from the concept of a people. The same ethnic label has been used to refer to co-religionists, racial isolates, linguistic groups, castes, and persons of common national origin, a range of meaning so vast as to be useless. We intend the term *people* to label a limited and clearly defined social type.

Studies of ethnicity frequently tend to take what De Vos (1975) has called the "psycho-cultural" point of view, a perspective which is reviewed in terms of "ethnic identity" by Clark et al. (1976). Such approaches concern themselves primarily with problems of the individual and his retention or loss of identification with a group — in other words, with persistent persons, not persistent peoples. In broad terms this aspect of persistence is a subcategory of acculturation best labeled *assimilation*, while the problem and process of the persistence of entire peoples *as groups* is properly called *enclavement* (Spicer 1966). Although structural mechanisms for controlling individual choice-making, such as the indoctrination of the young stressed by Erasmus, need to be considered, the source of enclaved peoples and collective identity systems should be approached from a culturological rather than psychological point of view.

The ethnic label has become heavily overlain with suggestions of race. Is a people to be regarded as an endogamous population? There is no denying that some of the peoples considered in this volume maintain some degree of breeding isolation voluntarily or involuntarily from the dominant majority populations. The Solubba, discussed by Adams, like other pariah peoples such as the Eta of Japan, have little choice in the matter, while others such as the Jews seek consciously to maintain endogamy for religious or other reasons. It is obvious, however, that the isolation is only one of degree and is never absolute over any prolonged period of enclavement. The range of physical types acceptable as members of a people can be truly enormous without compromising the sense of common identity or altering the recognition of the group as a separate entity by outsiders. Where the visible variation between populations within a nation-state is extreme, as Adams notes for the Nubians in Egypt or Green for the blacks in the United States, the separate identity is not easily lost. The Nubians in the Sudan, where they are racially less visible, become easily assimilated, while in the northern areas such as Egypt their visibility contributes to their isolation whether they wish it so or not. The primary significance of race for many enclaved peoples is found not in their genetic history but in their "belief in a unique racial beginning" (Spicer 1980:340). Attempts to define the group may often turn on some myth of origins and purity. Spicer cautions that "We must take the beliefs into consideration as sometimes important in the value scheme by which people live, but we cannot regard them as referring to any biological reality" (1980:340).

Like ethnicity, the concept of the plural society tends to intrude into the definition of a people. *Pluralism* "refers to a property, or set of properties, of societies wherein several distinct social and/or cultural groups coexist within the boundaries of a single polity and share a common economic system that makes them interdependent, yet maintain a greater or lesser degree of autonomy and a set of discrete institutional structures in other spheres of social life, notably the family, recreation and religion" (Van Den Berghe 1973:961). This notion seems to make room for classes and other social units as well as for entire peoples. The persistence of peoples is probably best thought of as a special case of pluralism in which groups maintain significant symbolic as well as — or sometimes instead of — institutional separation.

Another popular notion besides racial purity that attaches to many persistent peoples is the possession of a homeland. It seems obvious that every people must once have possessed a localized territorial base of its own in order for the group to have taken shape in the first place. However, many groups, such as those Adams calls "diaspora" peoples, have endured in spite of being scattered among many lands. The homeland obviously need not be controlled or even occupied by the peoples for their identity systems to persist. The Cherokees, for example — as Willard discusses in this volume — maintain important sentiments about their lost lands but these are, like most American Indian lands, truly and irrevocably lost. Some peoples retain footholds in their homelands for part of their populations, but it appears that the myth of the homeland is only another important symbol around which identity differentiation can coalesce to help define the people in opposition to "the others." If Adams is correct in his assessment of the Gypsies of the Middle East, then separate identity can be maintained without *any* knowledge — historical or mythological — concerning a homeland, but such a geographically detached identity system is surely the exception rather than the rule.

A separate language distinguishable from that of the majority population is a third popular criterion for defining the separate identity of persistent peoples. Like the other criteria it has some element of reality since many if not all of the peoples have at one time in their history had a distinctive language. However, as with the sacred homeland the language may disappear entirely, be confined to small segments of the total population, change from one tongue to another (for example, from Hebrew to Yiddish or Ladino), or otherwise vary in actual use. The necessity of coping with the "others" has virtually compelled enclaved peoples to practice bilingualism, but efforts promoting linguistic assimilation, such as those directed toward the American Indians by the reservation systems, can destroy even this level of linguistic differentiation.

The "true" language of a people is probably no more than another of the symbols by which groups reinforce their sense of themselves. In almost all of the cases discussed here the peoples themselves will accept as members ("real people," to borrow Willard's Cherokee phrase) persons who are not fluent in the symbolic language. Some groups, such as Leone's Mormons, of course, have never made use of language as a symbol of identity differentiation at all. American blacks comprise the descendents of speakers of a wide variety of African languages — not a single language at all — but very often attempts are made to identify some African components in the black variations of standard American English. Language, like race and homeland, is not a sufficient explanation of the persistent identity systems we are labeling *peoples*, though like the other criteria it is a frequent component of the symbol systems with which the peoples define their identities.

A fourth popular notion is that a people must have an unchanging culture. The history of those groups clearly demonstrates, however (as Harman stresses in his discussion of adaptation and fusion among the Maya, or Castile shows in his treatment of the Tarascanness of the Tarascans), that no such frozen lifestyle persists. Any cultural entity must change if its ecological situation alters, and peoples are no exception. Even intentional societies such as the Hutterites and the Israeli kibbutzim are susceptible to outside influences, as Erasmus shows.

It would seem that *the* defining characteristic of a persistent people is a continuity of common identity based, Spicer suggests, on "common understandings concerning the meaning of a set of symbols" (1980:347). What are these symbols that allow for an identity system that can persist through enormous change and in the face of domination by outsiders? Spicer suggests that "the continuity of a people consists in the growth and development of a picture of themselves which arises out of their unique historical experience" (1976:11). This image of collective identity is made up of "the symbols which a people develop, together with their meanings, concerning their experience as a people....Thus the persistence of a people rests on a set of meanings about actual events of history, as uniquely experienced by the people and stored as it were in a stock of symbols" (Spicer 1980:347). The symbol set need not be historically "real," it need only be believed in, in some ideal sense. The symbols may in fact change, as does all else in the adapting entity, but, as long as a continuity is maintained in the symbol system sufficient to define a collective identity separate from that of surrounding peoples, endurance occurs. "The persistence or stability of a people lies in the consistency of the successive interpretations with one another. If together they make up a single interrelated set of meanings through many generations then the phenomenon of the enduring people emerges" (Spicer 1980:356).

Gorman, in his examination of the Mohave, shows how a people may redefine their identity as the surrounding social environment changes.

The symbols may be highly variable, as the examples in this volume suggest, but it is apparently necessary that they include specific mechanisms to maintain the boundaries between the people and the "others." It follows then that this separation is the one absolutely vital area that the peoples must sustain if they are to endure and escape a loss of membership amounting to destruction. Both the source and the continued existence of a people appear to lie in an "oppositional process," that is, "a continued conflict between these peoples and the controllers of the surrounding state apparatus" (Spicer 1971:797). Obviously the enduring peoples are those who have developed some successful mechanisms to resist the efforts of the larger society to incorporate them, and their special characteristics are directly related to this boundary maintenance or oppositional process.

The degree of opposition is a critical variable in the survival of the enclaved peoples. Too much opposition can stimulate the majority population to undertake pogroms, exile, forced apostasy, and, in the ultimate case, genocide. Too little opposition and the membership may be absorbed into the larger society through an inability to define a group identity distinguishable from that of the dominant population. Erasmus considers some of the problems of the latter case in regard to the survival of intentional communities as has Leone in his consideration of the Mormons. The instances of "too much" are obvious in history. Oppressive opposition may help to strengthen a people's sense of identity, but only if it is not carried to the point of destruction.

The mechanisms and structures of maintaining opposition are varied. Voluntary withdrawal from the dominant society into an isolated community is a method often only temporarily sustained. A variation of voluntary enclavement is the ethnic specialization discussed by Adams: in some nation-states there are economic niches — both pariah occupations and high-status professions — available to minority peoples which the majority will not or cannot occupy themselves. Outsiders may establish themselves in a monopoly of these niches, voluntarily accepting subordinate political status and isolation from their homelands to do so. In some cases, at the other end of the spectrum, the enclavement of a people is insisted on by the larger society, which prevents ethnic apostasy even if the members of the minority seek it; the Irish Tinkers, discussed by Erasmus, exemplify this unsought form of opposition. The impoundment of minority peoples on reservations provided a structure for opposition even though that was not their purpose; these administered communities are notable for their ability to prevent absorption while seemingly intended to achieve it

(Kushner 1973). Green suggests that the common experience of racial discrimination, as a form of opposition between the majority population and the blacks of the United States, has made one people out of many and created a persistent identity system.

For many peoples, ritual serves as the mechanism for maintaining opposition and thus becomes their focus for identity. Crumrine points out that ritual dramatizes opposition by separating believers from nonbelievers on the basis of their participation in ceremonial activity. Dunnigan appears to take the view that the ritual displays of the Pima serve to reinforce the hostility and opposition between the enclaved peoples and the dominant majority, while Crumrine stresses the extent to which ritual defuses such conflict. Leone's discussion of the Mormon pattern of "peculiarity," in which ritual and belief shift to maintain conflict and therefore separation from the larger society, appears to combine the two views. Stress or surface tension is an aspect of boundary maintenance, and ritual creates tension at the same time that it promotes internal solidarity. Whatever its form, it defines "us versus them" as "believers versus nonbelievers." Harman's discussion of the Protestant Maya as "centrifugal" seems to argue that penetration of the ritual system by outsiders, even if other symbols of the people remain intact, can lead to disruption and possible dissolution of the group. Sometimes ritual is seen by the dominant society as less threatening than a political structure; the Cherokee curing/conjuring complex, for example, the central symbol of Cherokee identity, was allowed to survive, but the Cherokee "nation" as a separate entity was not.

The ultimate question in our examination of the persistent peoples is, Why do they persist? It is clearly demonstrable that many if not most of the enclaved peoples are in a disadvantageous status in whatever state has incorporated them. By very definition they are locked in an opposition to a nation-state in which they are subordinated and denied access to power. Some of the contributors have raised moral questions regarding the continued persistence of such enclaves. Spicer obviously tends to see in them much that is admirable as does van Willigen, who seems to equate enclavement with self-determination. Adams and Leone take a more negative view with Leone in particular suggesting that enclavement is equivalent to disadvantageous subordination and exploitation. A consideration of how and why enclaves have persisted must eventually come to some terms with these issues of apparent dysfunction. What adaptive advantage has their resistance gained them other than sheer survival?

To a large extent, in an evolutionary perspective the answer "survival" is sufficient explanation for any organic or superorganic system. Life is in the business of staying in business and to survive is by definition to be successful. The niches that the enclaved peoples fill are obviously not the most desirable in their nation-states but they are viable ones. In some of the value judgments expressed in this volume and elsewhere there seems an unwillingness to accept the fact that the heterogeneity of states may involve something other than a harmonious "separate but equal" condition, as Adams suggests. Subordination, I suspect, is deplored by many American anthropologists simply because of our own egalitarian ethos, which we, as Green's treatment of the American blacks or any of the discussions of Native Americans illustrate, have never sustained. The enclaves do not outrage adaptive logic by occupying less than ideal economic and social niches but they do outrage some widely held political beliefs. Looked at in terms of the survival of the group as a group, enclavement is a viable strategy, but is its human cost significantly higher than that of other adaptations?

The matter of cost brings us back to the distinction between persistent persons and persistent peoples. Willard and Castile both introduce some notions of expanding and contracting membership in the enclaves. The membership will fluctuate (where it is possible to do so) as the costs exceed those that particular members will accept. The thing that survives and must survive is the identity system itself, and this system must maintain a minimal structure and a minimal membership. The enclave may lose many, even most, of its members, but as long as a core endures to preserve continuity the people remains. Membership can always resurge if the core is intact, but if *all* structures are broken and *all* membership dispersed the people ceases to exist.

Once a society in the process of being politically dominated by a territorial state generates resistance or opposition to absorption, what would cause its failure? For those who have worked in applied anthropology the constant failure of state-sponsored change programs to achieve any end, including assimilation, is familiar. Destruction of the enclaves is achieved but usually only under extreme circumstances bordering on annihilation. The history of states is one of constant fluctuation; many if not most of the peoples have out-persisted two or more states. Perhaps it would be more appropriate to ask why states have been so ineffective at absorption of the peoples or even why states are so fragile compared to peoples.

In this introduction, indeed in this volume, we have obviously succeeded only in raising issues regarding the concept of an enduring people without resolving them. Larger questions are at stake, such as those explored in Moone's chapter attempting to link the persistence of peoples with the overarching problem of change and persistence in cultures. Perhaps continued explorations of this kind can function to illuminate the

xxii   *Analysis of Enduring Cultural Systems*

larger issues of change through the examples of the persistent peoples. Examination of their lengthy existence under a variety of sociocultural environments may tend to expose the mechanisms of adaptation more clearly than the study of simple cultural isolates that has formed the backbone of past anthropology. Perhaps they may be "a window for other peoples on the general human purpose" (Spicer 1980:362).

Part One

Regional Plural Interrelationships

| 1 |

Dispersed Minorities of the Middle East

A Comparison and a Lesson

William Y. Adams

In the Middle East cultural enclaves are probably more numerous and surely more persistent than anywhere else in the world. In some of history's earliest cities, those of the Sumerians in Lower Mesopotamia, Semitic immigrants had already formed a sizable minority and controlled certain areas of commerce in the third millennium B.C. (Hawkes and Woolley 1963:385). In the second millennium the rather mysterious Hurrians (the biblical Horites) were even more widely dispersed through the Hittite, Mitannian, and Babylonian empires, as well as in Palestine, though for most of their history they apparently controlled no state of their own (Hawkes and Woolley 1963:370–375; Gadd 1971:624–5). By the first millennium B.C. Jews and Canaanites had spread over so much of southwestern Asia that Aramaic — not Persian — became the *lingua franca* of the far-flung empire of Cyrus and Darius (Frye 1963:128). Greek mercenaries formed the backbone of Pharaoh's armies and controlled most of Egypt's foreign commerce long before the coming of Alexander (Wilson 1951:294), and other Greek entrepreneurs were to be found wherever salt water would carry them in the Mediterranean and the Black and Red seas (cf. Boardman 1964). Some of these peoples have inevitably disappeared with the passage of centuries, but an extraordinary number have not.

While enclaved minorities are a common phenomenon wherever indigenous peoples have been overrun or surrounded by more powerful invaders, a uniquely distinctive feature of Middle Eastern society is the dispersed or diaspora minority, living in tiny, widely scattered enclaves far from its ancestral homeland. For some, like the Gypsies, the homeland itself has been forgotten; for others, like the Jews and Armenians, it remains a great unifying memory and hope; for a happy few like the Greeks (and Jews since 1948) it is also a practical if distant reality. Whatever mythology may assert, however, the dispersal of these peoples can in no instance be attributed purely to external pressures.

The seven dispersed minority peoples of Southwest Asia and North Africa to be considered here — the Greeks, Armenians, Jews, Gypsies, Solubba of Arabia, Chaamba of the western Sahara, and Nubians — represent only a tiny sample of the total roster of dispersed minorities in the region. They have been selected partly because some data is available on them and partly because each exemplifies a somewhat different combination of ethnic distinctiveness and minority adaptation.

SEVEN DISPERSED MINORITIES
OF THE MIDDLE EAST

Greeks

Considering that the Greeks are the largest non-indigenous minority in Egypt (Wilber 1969:51), and are also present in substantial numbers in other Mediterranean countries, the literature on overseas Greeks in the Arab world is infinitesimal. It is, however, common knowledge that they are overwhelmingly associated with nearly every aspect of maritime trade, not only as shipowners but as customs brokers, operators of stevedoring firms, shipping agents, travel agents, maritime insurers, and the like. For these reasons Greeks are heavily concentrated in the port cities of the Mediterranean and Red Sea, although Greek companies also maintain offices in many inland cities. Since the traditional cuisine of the Middle East is largely of Greek origin, it is also not surprising to find Greeks as restaurant, delicatessen, and bakery owners in the more cosmopolitan cities of the Arab world. Greeks, Armenians, and Christian Arabs are also in control of most wholesale and retail liquor distribution, a trade which is forbidden to proper Moslems. Lastly, some educated Greeks are to be found in the medical, legal, and teaching professions.

The Greek colonies of Alexandria, Tripoli, and a few other Mediterranean ports have been in existence since ancient times, but a great deal of Greek dispersal probably dates from the period when both Greeks and Arabs were subjects of the Ottoman Empire (c. 1453–1918). Some overseas Greeks may also be refugees deported from Turkey under the Treaty of Lausanne in 1923.

Armenians

The situation of Armenians in the Middle East is parallel in many respects to that of the Greeks. Both are heavily involved in the export-import trade, though the Armenians are proportionately more active in the financial and merchandising ends of the business (Vreeland 1969:61; Wilber 1969:95) and much less in actual transport management than are the Greeks. Hence, they are not heavily concentrated in coastal areas; the majority of Armenians are in fact found in the inland towns and cities of Iran and the Arab countries. In addition to their entrepreneurial activities Armenians have become dominant in certain trades requiring manual and technical precision, such as bookbinding (Wilber 1969:96), auto repair (Harris 1958:43), and photography. Because of the high value they place on education, there are also disproportionate numbers of Armenians in all the learned professions and in the arts (Wilber 1969:96); their situation in this regard may be compared to that of Jews in the United States.

The historic Armenian homeland was in eastern Turkey and on the south slope of the Caucasus (now the Armenian Republic of the U.S.S.R.). Virtually all Armenians were expelled or fled from Turkish territory (except Istanbul) following a series of massacres in the late nineteenth and twentieth centuries, and their wholesale dispersal through the Arab countries and Iran undoubtedly dates from that time (Harris 1958:43; Zeltzer 1969:29). Nevertheless there were Armenian colonies in Syria (Zeltzer 1969:29), in Palestine, and in Egypt (Evetts and Butler 1895:1–12) as far back as the Middle Ages.

Jews

More than nine-tenths of the Jews formerly resident in the Arab world have been resettled in Israel or in the United States and Canada since 1948. Before that date their situation was generally comparable to that of both Greeks and Armenians in that they were an overwhelmingly urban minority engaged in various forms of entrepreneurship and certain manual trades. As in medieval Europe they had a virtual monopoly on moneylending, a profession forbidden to Moslems and Orthodox Christians alike.

Because of various legal and social disabilities, however, there were pro-portionately fewer wealthy Jews than there were Greeks or Armenians, while the number of marginal shopkeepers and artisans was much larger. In northwest Africa the metalsmithing and carpentry trades were very largely in Jewish hands (Briggs 1958:67–68).

The Jewish colonies of Mesopotamia and Syria may date all the way back to the traditional diaspora following the Babylonian captivity; those in northwest Africa apparently coincide with the Roman persecutions and the destruction of Judaea in the first and second centuries A.D. (Briggs 1958:68; Briggs and Guède 1964:10). After 1492 northwest Africa also became a refuge for the Jews expelled from Spain by Ferdinand and Isabella (Coon 1964:250). Although not systematically persecuted, Jews in the Arab world have been subject to more social and legal restrictions than have other religious minorities (cf. Briggs 1958:68; Briggs and Guède 1964:10; Sweet 1971:216), and many of them in the present cen-tury lived in circumstances of extreme poverty (Briggs and Guède 1964:17–21; Shiloh 1969:73; Wilber 1969:78; Zeltzer 1969:32).

Gypsies

Gypsies have been scattered through the Middle East for at least a thousand years (cf. Sykes 1930, II:11), yet almost nothing has been writ-ten about them, in contrast to the rich folkloristic literature on European Gypsies. According to Coon (1964:65) they " ... move about through all the countries north of the [Arabian] peninsula and east of Suez." In the nineteenth century there were also several small Gypsy tribes in Egypt (Lane 1908: 393), and I saw one small band in the northern Sudan in the 1960s. Many Gypsies are free-wandering, but some are permanently at-tached as clients to the nomad tribes of Iran and Iraq (cf. Barth 1961:91–92). There are also settled Gypsies in Iranian cities (English 1966:72, 78), and in Cairo (Lane 1908:394). The available literature suggests that the part played by Middle Eastern Gypsies differs in no essential detail from that traditional among European Gypsies: they are tinkers and smiths, itinerant small traders, entertainers, fortune-tellers, and beggars.

Solubba

The Solubba (the singular form is *Sleyb*) of Arabia offer many parallels with the Gypsies. They may even be of Gypsy origin, since they are reported to speak among themselves a non-Arabic patois (Patai 1967:262). They are, however, regarded in the broadest sense as a part of the Arab tribal hierarchy, although occupying one of its lowest rungs. Unlike other "pariah" groups of the peninsula they have no memorized genealogy and not even the fiction of tribal organization (Lipsky 1959:67). *Solubba* is not, nevertheless, merely a synonym for "low-caste"; these people are considered both by themselves and by their neighbors to have ethnic and not merely hierarchic or occupational identity.

The Solubba appear to be exclusively desert dwellers. Groups of them are attached as clients to most of the more powerful bedouin tribes of the Arabian Peninsula and to others in Jordan and Syria (Patai 1967:251). Like the Gypsies they serve as tinkers, leather workers, entertainers, and prostitutes (Lipsky 1959:67; Patai 1967:260). There are also a few free-wandering Solubba bedouin groups; by common consent they are exempted from the general pattern of raiding and territorial competition in which nearly all other bedouin tribes are involved (Patai 1967:255). Paradoxically, in spite of their reputation for cowardice and servility, the Solubba are respected for their prowess as desert hunters and trackers and are frequently employed as caravan guides (Lipsky 1959:67).

Chaamba

An Arab group standing in marked contrast to the Solubba are the Chaamba of Central Algeria, a powerful bedouin tribe occupying a sizable territory to the south of the Atlas Mountains. Outside their tribal homeland, Chaamba are also to be found in most of the towns and cities of the western Sahara, interspersed among the indigenous Berber and Negro peoples (Briggs 1958:115–17; Briggs 1960:201–4; Miner 1953:20–21, 66–68, 140–50). Their dispersal presents interesting parallels to that of the Greeks, for, as the latter have specialized in maritime trade through their command of nautical technology, so the Chaamba have specialized in caravan trade as a result of their expertise with camels (Briggs 1958:115–16). Sedentary Chaamba act as caravan agents in the oasis towns and cities, while migratory groups (who may be compared to the crews of Greek ships) carry on the actual trade between them, paying for that privilege a fee to the Touareg, who are the indigenous overlords of the western Sahara (Coon 1964:208). Dispersal of the Chaamba has not been halted by the recent decline of caravan trade, for most of them have simply turned shopkeeper. In 1937 it was estimated that 80 percent of all shops in the southwestern part of the Sahara were owned by Chaamba (Briggs 1958:116).

Nubians

The Nubians are an African Moslem people whose traditional homeland was the valley of the Nile in the far south of Egypt and the adjoining part of the Republic of the Sudan. Since much of that region has been flooded by the Aswan Dams, more than half the Nubian population has been obliged to find new homes in Egypt and in the Sudan. Long before their forced evacuation, however, there were Nubian colonies in Cairo, Alexandria, and elsewhere. In the seventeenth century Nubians were described as dominating the guilds of construction workers, watchmen, and slave dealers in Cairo (Adams 1977:613). More recently Nubians have become predominant in various kinds of domestic service (Wilber 1969:50); there are also large numbers of Nubian taxi drivers in Cairo and other Egyptian cities. Educated Nubians find some employment in the Egyptian civil service and in small trade.

In addition to all the above groups, some displaced Nubians have bought or been granted agricultural lands to the north of Aswan and have established new peasant villages there. They are the only minority group considered in this chapter who are engaged to any extent in tilling the soil. It is doubtful, however, that the Nubian peasants of Upper Egypt should be considered a dispersed minority in the same sense as the other groups I have discussed, for they have merely attempted to re-create their traditional homeland as near as possible to the destroyed original (much as have the Armenians of the Armenian S.S.R.). These people may therefore be designated as *resettled* rather than as *dispersed* minorities; it is, I believe, an important distinction.

CRITERIA OF IDENTITY

Each of the seven groups described above recognizes itself, and is recognized by others, as in some sense distinctive, yet the criteria of distinctiveness are far from uniform in the seven cases. Table 1.1 shows some of the characteristics that may serve as foci of identity for the dispersed minority peoples of the Middle East.

Religion

Events in Lebanon in the 1970s have demonstrated all too painfully that sectarian differences are still the most fundamental of all cleavages in Middle Eastern society. They are not, however, a consistent focus of identity for dispersed minority peoples, as can be seen in Table 1.1. Of the seven groups considered here, only the Jews are an absolutely exclusive religious community. It is true that Armenians and only Armenians are members of the Armenian Orthodox and the Armenian Catholic churches, but these sects are different only in liturgy and not in doctrine from other eastern Christian confessions. Greeks are even less doctrinally exclusive; although nearly all are members of the Greek Orthodox or the Greek

TABLE 1.1

CRITERIA OF IDENTITY OF DISPERSED
MINORITIES OF THE MIDDLE EAST

	Greeks	Armenians	Jews	Gypsies	Solubba	Chaamba	Nubians
Religion	±	+	+	±	−	−	−
Sacred language	+	+	+	−	−	−	−
Vernacular language	+	+	(−)	+	+	±	+
Sense of history	+	+	+	−	−	?	+
Traditional homeland	+	+	+	−	−	+	+
Occupational specializations	+	+	+	+	+	+	+
Race	−	−	−	−	−	±	+

Key: + Yes − No ± Yes and no (−) Not usual ? No data

Catholic sects, they are actually outnumbered in both these denomina-
tions by Christian Arabs (cf. Berger 1964:235; Gulick 1967:26, 42–44;
Zeltzer 1969:40).

Both Gypsies and Solubba have a kind of negative religious identity.
The former are generally looked upon by both Moslems and Christians as
having no religion, though they themselves profess lip service to whatever
is the dominant faith of their neighbors (Gropper 1975:108–9). The
Solubba are accepted in the broadest sense as Moslems, but the laxity of
their regard for religious niceties is a subject of general disparagement
(Patai 1967:259–60). The Chaamba and Nubians likewise adhere in principle to the same faith as the surrounding populations but differ to some
extent in practice. According to Briggs (1958:67) the Chaamba in the
Berber town of Ghardaia are " . . . socially beyond the . . . pale because of
differences in religious doctrine"; on the other hand the Nubians are
considered both by themselves and by their Egyptian hosts to be more
devout than the Egyptians themselves.

Language

All seven of the peoples covered in this survey are linguistically distinct from their neighbors in one sense or another, yet, for all that,
language has never been a focal point for ethnic identity or for ethnic

hostility in the Middle East to the same extent as it has in Europe or in India. For one thing, nearly all Middle Eastern minority peoples are fully bilingual and speak the language of the dominant majority as fluently as they do their mother tongues. Many of their indigenous languages are moreover unwritten and therefore unassociated with traditional or sacred literature. At the opposite extreme are archaic languages like Hebrew, Old Armenian, and Byzantine Greek, which, because they enshrine sacred texts, are of tremendous symbolic importance even though no one speaks them and few can understand them (except in the case of the revived Hebrew language of Israel).

Greeks, Armenians, and Jews are all theoretically identified by a modern as well as by an ancient and sacred language. All Middle Eastern Greeks can in fact speak modern Greek, and most Armenians can speak Armenian; on the other hand the majority of Sephardic Jews knew little or no Hebrew prior to the time of their resettlement in Israel. In daily discourse they used either Spanish or local dialects of Arabic (Shiloh 1969:75; Zeltzer 1969:32). Gypsies, Solubba, and Nubians each have a distinct spoken language but no written language; to the extent that they are literate, they use the language of the dominant majority. It may be because of this limitation that language does not appear to be important as a focus of ethnic identity for any of these groups. The Nubians, for example, assert their difference from the Egyptians on the basis of possessing a separate tribal pedigree and a separate homeland, not on the basis of the distinctive African mother tongue whose importance they largely discount (cf. Adams 1969:284).

Historical Perspective

Not surprisingly, those minority groups with their own written languages and sacred texts — the Greeks, Armenians, and Jews — have also the strongest sense of their special place in history. There is not much evidence that the Middle Eastern Gypsies have a sense of historical identity, while the Solubba lack even the tribal pedigree which is the charter of historical identity for most other Arab tribes (cf. Adams 1977:563–68).

The Nubians present an interesting case study, for they, like the "People of the Book" (as Arabs refer to the Christian and Jewish minorities), have a strong sense of their separate history. It is not, however, rooted in any genuine understanding of their pre-Islamic past, which included some quite glorious episodes, but rather in the possession of a wholly spurious genealogy which is their charter of membership in the

Arab social system (Adams 1977:563). The Chaamba assuredly also have such a pedigree, though whether it contributes to their sense of identity and separateness has not been recorded.

Ethnic distinctions can be reinforced by external as well as by internal mythology. The Solubba, for example, are widely believed by other Arabs to be descended from Crusaders, though apparently they do not assert this claim themselves (Lipsky 1959:67; Patai 1967:262). The Nubians are looked down on by some Egyptians as the descendents of slaves (cf. Wilber 1969:50), a belief which contains only a grain of truth, and which the Nubians indignantly deny.

Traditional Homeland

Five of the seven groups considered here have either the myth or the actuality of an ancestral homeland to which they or their descendents hope some day to return, and for at least four of them (Greeks, Armenians, Jews, and Nubians) it is also a quite realizable goal. Many well-to-do Greeks retire finally to the ancestral shores (though they may have been born and spent their entire lives abroad), and since 1948 more than three-fourths of all Middle Eastern Jews have resettled in Israel (Berger 1964:235–36; Gulick 1967:42–44; Sweet 1971:216; Wilber 1969:78). Armenians, however, can return to the new Armenian homeland in Russia only if they are willing to live under socialist rule, a prospect that has generally been repugnant to this highly individualistic and entrepreneurial people. The hope of rebuilding a truly independent Armenia, including the former ancestral territory in eastern Turkey, nevertheless remains strong for many. No such prospect exists for the Nubians, most of whose ancestral land is now beneath the waters of Lake Nasser. In their imagination, it is now remembered as a kind of lost Eden (cf. Adams 1977: 661–62).

Closely associated with the memory of an ancestral homeland is another tradition which might be called the myth of forced dispersal. In somewhat different forms it is found among Jews, Armenians, and Nubians. The historic reverses suffered by these peoples are of course real enough, yet in each case, as we have seen, their dispersal from their native lands began long before the supposed date of their expulsion. But the same tradition which idealizes the memory of the homeland must also insist that only misfortune could impel them to leave it, and thus, when misfortune is overcome, they will reclaim it. Even Nubians who had emigrated at a much earlier date can now be heard to assert that "but for the dam, no man would have left his village" (Geiser 1973:189).

In contrast to the foregoing cases, it appears that the Gypsies and the Solubba retain neither the actuality nor the memory of a homeland, even though the historical linguist has no difficulty in tracing the Gypsies to their place of origin in India (cf. Gropper 1975:1–4).

Occupation

Of all the differences associated with minority status in the Middle East, none appears to be quite so consistent as that of occupation. Differentiation in this respect is of course far from absolute; some trades are followed by members of several groups, and a few may even be followed by all of them. It is nevertheless true that each of the seven groups considered here exhibits a different complex of occupational specializations; even more importantly, each group exercises a monopoly or a dominant position in one or more key occupations within the area of its residence. These "ethnic specializations" include maritime trade for the Greeks; caravan trade for the Chaamba; international trade in various commodities (e.g., carpets) as well as certain technically skilled crafts for the Armenians; moneylending, the jeweler's trade, and various manual crafts for the Jews; tinkering and entertaining for the Gypsies and Solubba; desert tracking and guiding for the Solubba; and domestic service for the Nubians. Whether occupational differentiation is a cause or an effect of ethnic differentiation, and whether it is voluntary or enforced, will be considered later.

Race

Due to the high degree of endogamy among all Middle Eastern minorities, members of each of the groups discussed here may at times exhibit distinctive phenotypic characteristics which make it possible to say, "That man is surely an Armenian," or, "She must be either an Arab or a Jew." More commonly, however, individuals do not clearly proclaim their ancestry by their appearance. The one significant exception to this regard is the Nubians, whose ancestry is conspicuously though not exclusively Negroid (cf. Adams 1977:45–46.) They are thus the only consistently visible racial minority among the groups considered here, although there are comparable groups in other parts of the Middle East (cf. Gubser 1973:65–66; Lipsky 1959:29).

It goes without saying that the Nubians do not prize their racial visibility, or even acknowledge it, since Islamic society is by no means free from racial prejudice (cf. Gubser 1973:65–66; Lipsky 1959:29; and especially Lewis 1971). In their own reckoning they are the offspring of Arab fathers and African mothers, so that, in the context of a strictly patrilineal society, their African blood is of no account (Adams 1969:284). (It is this same "accident" which results in their possessing a non-Arabic mother tongue, since children are taught to speak by their mothers.)

It is nevertheless probably true that being in a disadvantaged and largely inescapable racial category has contributed both to the desire and to the ability of the Nubians to maintain a separate ethnic identity vis-à-vis the Egyptians. The situation of Nubians who have emigrated southward instead of northward provides an instructive contrast in this regard, for in the Sudan they are not visibly distinct from the rest of the "Arab" population. As a result the Nubians of the Sudan make no special effort to keep up their indigenous language or the memory of the homeland; they are in fact being quite rapidly and fully assimilated into the general population (Adams 1977:650–51; Barclay 1964:10).

PATTERNS OF ADAPTATION

It remains now to consider how the dispersed minority peoples of the Middle East have adapted to their physical surroundings and to the larger socioeconomic framework of which they are a necessary part. Table 1.2 shows the various patterns of adaptation.

Rural Versus Urban Residence

The peoples considered in this study, and most other dispersed minorities, exhibit two sharply distinct patterns in regard to residence. The Greeks, Armenians, Nubians (exluding those resettled near Aswan), and Jews are almost exclusively urban dwellers, though Jews are to be found in some fairly small towns as well as in major cosmopolitan centers. At the opposite extreme, the Gypsies are largely rural and the Solubba exclusively so. Only the Chaamba exhibit both adaptive patterns: some are resident as commercial agents in towns and villages, while others conduct the caravan trade across the intervening deserts. There appears, however, to be a quite sharp distinction between these two groups, with no back-and-forth exchange of members.

So far as Middle Eastern dispersed minorities are concerned, rural and urban can be read as synonymous with nomadic and sedentary, respectively. The one adaptation which is lacking among all groups is that involving sedentary rural life, or, in other words, peasant farming, though this is the normative occupation of more than two-thirds of all Middle Eastern dwellers (Patai 1967:268). (The Nubian peasants resettled near Aswan are here excluded from consideration.) Two observations may be

TABLE 1.2
PATTERNS OF ADAPTATION OF DISPERSED MINORITIES OF THE MIDDLE EAST

	Greeks	Armenians	Jews	Gypsies	Solubba	Chaamba	Nubians
Residence							
Urban, sedentary	+	+	+	*	−	+	+
Rural, nomadic	−	−	−	+	+	+	−
Education							
Highy educated	+	+	+	−	−	−	−
Literate, but not highly educated	+	+	+	*	−	+	+
Generally illiterate	−	−	*	+	+	+	+
Occupational specializations							
Learned professions	+	+	+	−	−	−	−
Financial entrepreneurship	+	+	+	−	−	*	−
Transport	+	−	−	−	−	+	*
Petty trade	+	+	+	+	?	+	+
Technically skilled crafts	−	+	−	−	−	−	−
Manual crafts	−	−	+	+	+	−	−
Domestic service	*	−	−	−	−	−	+
Restricted and despised occupations:							
Moneylending	−	−	+	−	−	−	−
Liquor trade	+	+	+	−	−	−	−
Despised crafts	−	−	+	+	+	−	−
Entertaining and prostitution	−	−	−	+	+	−	−
Economic status							
High	+	+	+	−	−	−	−
Intermediate	+	+	+	−	−	+	+
Low	*	−	+	+	+	+	+
Endogamy							
Selective	+	+	+	−	−	+	+
Enforced	−	−	−	+	+	+	+

Key: + Yes − No * Occasional ? No data

made on this point. First, under traditional Islamic law non-Moslem landholders were liable to a heavy tax (Levy 1965:48), and Jews were sometimes forbidden altogether to own land (Briggs and Guède 1964:10; Sweet 1971:216). Second, since land pressure is not severe in most parts of the Middle East, it has seldom been necessary for peoples to migrate very far from their homes in search of tillable soil. Those who have scattered widely abroad have almost surely done so not to pursue the peasant's destiny but to escape from it.

Education

Dispersed minorities of the Middle East exhibit enormous variability in the level of education which is normal for their male members. In this regard a significant difference exists between "People of the Book" and other minorities, both Moslem and non-Moslem. In principle, Greeks, Armenians, and Jews have always prized education; members of all three groups are usually literate and frequently highly educated. This was somewhat less true for Jews than for Christians, since many Middle Eastern Jews lived in small and isolated communities under very impoverished circumstances (Shiloh 1969:73; Zeltzer 1969:32–33). Some degree of literacy is also a practical necessity for other urban minorities, the Chaamba and some Nubians, who are engaged in trade. On the other hand no very advanced schooling has been available to these peoples, and it is not uncommon to find wholly illiterate individuals among the Nubian cooks and house servants of Cairo and Alexandria. The nomadic life of the Gypsies and Solubba, and some Chaamba, virtually assures the perpetual illiteracy of these peoples.

We may, then, offer a summary generalization that "People of the Book" are usually literate and often highly educated; other urban minorities are frequently literate but rarely very well educated; and rural, nomadic minorities are almost invariably illiterate.

Occupational Specializations

The consistency with which particular occupations are associated with particular minority groups has already been noted. In the following discussion, occupational specializations are considered in order of decreasing prestige and profitability.

Learned professions and the arts. There can be no doubt that the value placed on education by "People of the Book" is substantially greater than in the case of most Moslems; hence the number of Greeks, Jews, and above all Armenians in learned professions (such as medicine, law, teaching, and engineering) and in the arts is far out of proportion to their numbers throughout the Arab world. For these peoples education unquestionably has been and remains the primary means of escape from the disadvantages of minority status. By contrast, almost no members of Moslem minorities are to be found in the learned professions. Those doctors, lawyers, judges, and other professionals who are not "People of the Book" are drawn from the dominant Arab or Persian majorities.

Finance and entrepreneurship. In a largely illiterate society a high degree of education is almost automatically a ticket to affluence, and in a society in which commerce is the lifeblood, the appropriate use for wealth is to create more wealth through entrepreneurship. Thus we find throughout the Middle East that the educated minorities — the Greeks, Armenians, and Jews — are almost as disproportionately represented in the upper levels of finance and commerce as they are in the learned professions. The dominant position which these groups enjoy in international trade is further enhanced by the far-flung network of communication, sometimes reinforced by kinship and intermarriage, which extends from one Armenian community to the next and from one Greek community to the next throughout the Middle East and beyond. In the western Sahara the Chaamba exhibit the same phenomenon, though on a much more modest scale. It is their literacy and their communication network which gives them a commercial advantage over the largely illiterate Berber and Negro peoples among whom they have settled.

Transport. Since commerce is the lifeblood of the Middle East, economic advantage accrues not only to the wealthy and educated, but also to those with special expertise or resources in the field of transport. This is particularly conspicuous in the case of Greeks in the maritime trade and of Chaamba in the caravan trade. On a much humbler scale the otherwise despised Solubba also benefit from their unparalleled knowledge of desert terrain, which affords them a measure of livelihood as caravan guides.

Petty trade. The least exclusive of all occupations in the Middle East, petty trade carries higher prestige than tilling the soil but requires little education and little capital. Not surprisingly, whatever their other specializations may be, all of the groups considered in this study except (possibly) the Solubba engage to some extent in petty trade.

Technically skilled crafts. Requiring a combination of formal and theoretical training and manual dexterity, technically skilled crafts have been and remain the special province of the Armenians. Why this should be so is something of a mystery. It seems to be primarily a modern phenomenon, inasmuch as the photographer's and auto mechanic's trades are less than a hundred years old. Perhaps — whether by accident or adaptive design — the subculture of the Armenians places a high value on accuracy and precision in a part of the world where, for many purposes and in many circumstances, inexactness is considered a virtue.

Domestic service occupations. Various kinds of domestic service are preeminently the domain of the Nubians, though in Egypt some Greeks are similarly employed, especially in hotels (Wilber 1969:96). It might be supposed that the Nubians are condemned to servile occupations by their racial "inferiority" (in Egyptian eyes), and there is some historic truth in this view (cf. Baer 1964:39). On the other hand in Middle Eastern society domestic service occupations are generally more highly regarded than are a good many manual trades, and especially those which dirty the hands (Baer 1964:33). Hence the Nubians, despite their racial disadvantage, are by no means confined to the lowest occupations on the social ladder, as are the Gypsies and Solubba (see below). They have, moreover, made a virtue of necessity by cultivating a reputation for cleanliness and honesty, so that their special qualification for domestic service is reinforced by positive as well as by negative considerations (Wilber 1969:50).

Manual trades. Since they require little formal education, manual trades are in general very poorly regarded in the Middle East; unlike any of the callings thus far discussed they carry less prestige than does tilling the soil (cf. Lutfiyya 1966:32–35). Consequently, persons with the resources or education to avoid them almost invariably do so. Only three of the seven groups described in this study (the Jews, Gypsies, and Solubba) include significant numbers of artisans, yet for all of these groups the control of certain menial trades has been the mainstay of economic existence at times and in places. At the same time it has been responsible for their confinement to the lowest positions in the Middle Eastern social hierarchy. To understand this relationship it will be necessary to consider in somewhat more general terms the phenomenon of restricted and despised occupations in the Middle East.

Restricted and despised occupations. There are some occupations which are either repugnant to proper Moslems or are actually forbidden to them by the strictures of their faith. Historically, these callings have offered unique adaptive possibilities to both low-caste Moslem groups and non-Moslem minorities. Although universally disparaged on social grounds, the restricted and despised occupations are not always poorly rewarded.

At the top of the hierarchy of low-status professions, from the standpoint of remuneration, would surely be that of moneylending. Since it was traditionally forbidden to Moslems and Christians alike, this calling was virtually monopolized by the Jews. Next in order of reward would probably be wholesale and retail liquor distribution, which is permitted to Christians but not to Moslems. This trade is controlled in some areas by Greeks, in some by Armenians, in some by Jews, and in some by Christian Arabs. Further down the scale of disparaged occupations might be included the various forms of domestic service in which many Nubians are employed, although these are not actually forbidden to other Arabs or even consistently avoided by them.

Near the bottom of the social and economic ladder are a number of manual trades which, though not actually proscribed, are nearly always avoided by self-respecting Moslems as well as by eastern Christians. Foremost among them are the metal-working trades, and above all blacksmithing and tinkering (cf. Briggs 1958:59–60; Lipsky 1959:67) — perhaps because these trades result in the dirtiest hands (cf. Baer 1964:33). Wood- and leather-working fall into the same general category (Briggs 1958:60). From end to end of the Moslem world these trades are in the hands either of non-Moslem minorities or of the lowest-status Arab tribes: the Gypsies in Iran, the Solubba in Arabia, the Jews in northwest Africa, and innumerable others elsewhere (cf. Briggs 1958:67).

Also far down the list of despised occupations are most forms of public and private entertainment, and especially those involving music, dancing, and prostitution (cf. Baer 1964:35–37). Almost everywhere these callings are relegated to the same "pariah" groups who practice smithing and tinkering: the Gypsies, Solubba, and others. The Jews of northwest Africa, however, are an exception to this generalization; apparently they do not serve to any extent as entertainers.

Economic Status

We usually rank Americans and other Western peoples in a hierarchical scale in terms of something we call socioeconomic status, but this double-barrelled concept will not serve in the Middle East, where social status and economic status are not inseparably linked. In the traditional fabric of Islamic society all non-Moslems occupy a lower status than do Moslems (Levy 1965:67), but it is conspicuous that in our sample of seven minority peoples the three avowedly non-Moslem groups (the Greeks, Armenians, and Jews) enjoy substantially greater prosperity than do the other four, of whom two (the Chaamba and Nubians) are universally accepted as Moslems. Table 1.3 emphasizes the differences between social

TABLE 1.3
Social and Economic Ranking
of Dispersed Minorities of the Middle East

Social*	Economic
1. Chaamba	1. Armenians
2. Nubians	2. Greeks
3. Greeks	3. Jews
Armenians	4. Chaamba
4. Jews	5. Nubians
5. Solubba	6. Gypsies
6. Gypsies	7. Solubba

*According to Islamic tradition

and economic status by arranging these seven peoples into two hierarchical rankings, one on the basis of Moslem social tradition and the other on the basis of estimated per capita income.

A glance at Table 1.2 is enough to show that the groups considered in this study fall into two sharply distinct economic groups. On one side are the "People of the Book" (Greeks, Armenians, and Jews), whose economic status is generally middle to high; the average per capita income of these groups is in fact higher in most places than that of the dominant Arab and Persian populations among whom they live. (Some of the Jews in Morocco and Iraq are clearly exceptions to this generalization.) In an altogether different category are the remaining four groups: their economic status is medium to low (probably about comparable to that of the general population) in the case of the Chaamba and Nubians, and consistently very low in the case of Gypsies and Solubba.

Endogamy

All minority peoples are more or less endogamous by definition, but there is significant variation both in the extent to which endogamy is enforced and in the reasons for it. The Jews are the only exclusively endogamous group among the seven considered in this survey. The Greeks and Armenians also practice religious endogamy, but they are not forbidden to marry members of other, doctrinally similar Christian sects, and in fact a certain number do. It is apparent in the case of all these groups, at all events, that their endogamy is selective and voluntary; it is dictated by their own exclusiveness more than by proscription on the part of the dominant majority.

At the opposite extreme from the aforementioned groups are the Gypsies and Solubba, who might conceivably wish to marry outside their tightly restricted and disadvantaged societies, but who are prevented from doing so by the repugnance of their hosts. "No Arab man can marry a Solubba girl. He would be killed by his people if he did, and she also," Patai (1967:258) reported. Some intermarriage does take place between these people and slaves, who are considered more or less as their social equals (Lipsky 1959:67).

The Nubians and the Chaamba probably exhibit a combination of selective and enforced endogamy, though in slightly different ways. There is a mutual antipathy between Nubians and Egyptians which inhibits, though it does not wholly forestall, the desire for intermarriage on the part of either group (Wilber 1969:50). The Chaamba, on the other hand, are differently situated with regard to different neighbors. In Timbuctoo and other Saharan towns they are at the top of the social heap, and their endogamy here — which applies only to first marriages — is evidently a matter of preference (Miner 1953:181). In the Berber city of Ghardaia, however, the Chaamba minority are "socially beyond the pale" (Briggs 1958:67).

IMPLICATIONS OF PLURALISM

In Bernard Shaw's play *Man and Superman* the brigand Mendoza is heard to observe, "Abnormal professions attract two classes: those who are not good enough for ordinary bourgeois life and those who are too good for it. We are dregs and scum, sir: the dregs very filthy, the scum very superior" (Shaw 1904:81). Stated in more objective and less objectionable terms, that dichotomization would seem aptly to characterize the dispersed minority peoples of the Middle East — not only those covered in this survey but also most others. Among the variables included in Table 1.2, it is easy to recognize two sharply distinct trait clusterings. In one group are the urban, educated, middle- to upper-class minorities who are disproportionately represented in high-status occupations, and whose endogamy is largely voluntary. At the opposite end of the social scale are the predominantly rural or small-town-dwelling, illiterate "pariah" groups, practicing despised occupations and enforced endogamy. Between these two extremes there appears to be very little middle ground. The Greeks, Armenians, and many Jews belong to the first group, as do the Chaamba within their particular habitat. Other minorities, not included in this survey, who exemplify the same pattern are the Italians (Wilber 1969:51), many Christian Arab groups (Hourani 1947), and the Hausa in the southern Sahara (Works 1976). To all such groups Abner Cohen (1971) has applied the term "trading diaporas."

In the low-status group of minorities are the Gypsies, Solubba, some Jews of northwest Africa and Iraq, and many other "pariah" groups of the Islamic world. Concerning these people, Briggs (1958:60) has offered a collective characterization:

> Groups of gypsylike people ... are found scattered clean across the Moslem world, from the Atlantic Ocean to Baluchistan. ...Throughout all this vast area their economic function and social position remain essentially the same....Their history is always obscure....
>
> The smiths have a monopoly of the local production of iron, copper, and brass ware, and of the manufacture and decoration of articles of wood. They are the jewelers, tinkers, tanners, and makers of sandals too, and their womenfolk turn out fancy leatherwork. As is often the case with smiths and tinkers throughout the world, there is something faintly yet frighteningly supernatural about them: they are makers of amulets and charms, brewers of insidious concoctions and casters of powerful spells. They are the hunters in the Tibesti and Borkou. Despised and also feared, they live apart from the community, but come and go as they please. They fight rarely if ever, and no one dares molest them. They usually speak the language of the group with which they are in most frequent contact.

In a broad sense the Nubians also belong in the inferior group of minorities, though unlike the others they are predominantly urban, and their cultivation of special qualities has enabled them to find an adaptive niche somewhat above the bottom of the economic ladder.

The Jews are decidely unusual among Middle Eastern minorities in exhibiting both high-status and low-status adaptations (cf. especially Zeltzer 1969:32). This probably reflects the fact that they have been longer and more widely dispersed than any other group, and as a result have had to adapt to a greater number and variety of environmental and historical circumstances. The profound social and cultural gap between upper- and lower-status Jews has created an enduring headache for the state of Israel, which seeks to assimilate both groups into a new, classless Jewish society (cf. Eisenstadt, Yosef and Adler 1970:305–427; Weingrod 1965).

From a narrow viewpoint of cultural materialism, both of the recurring minority syndromes discussed in this chapter may be regarded as adaptive. Minority status gives to its members a special access to occupations which are either above the reach of the dominant majority or are beneath its dignity; in either case it provides a rationale of sorts for the maintenance of ethnic boundaries. We have already noted too that, whatever mythology may assert, the dispersal of all Middle Eastern minorities has been to a considerable extent voluntary and deliberate.

If minority status is indeed adaptive in the Middle East, we are bound to ask why it is not more popular in other complex societies; why many ethnic groups elsewhere in the world have accepted or even deliberately sought assimilation rather than struggling to maintain their boundaries and identity. The answer, I think, must be sought in the special and anomalous nature of Middle Eastern society. That society offers a kind of standing contradiction to the theories of Durkheim (especially 1933), Tönnies (1957), and Redfield (1941:338–61), insofar as it combines "organic solidarity" in the economic sphere with "mechanical solidarity" in the social sphere. The former is attested to by a high degree of economic differentiation and interdependence, the latter by the continued maintenance of ethnic and kinship boundaries. Sjoberg (1960) has long insisted that this anomaly was historically characteristic of all pre-industrial cities, but his own examples suggest that it was nowhere so highly developed or so persistent as in the Middle East. Horace Miner clearly pinpointed the special quality of Middle Eastern society a generation ago when he characterized the inhabitants of Timbuctoo as "city folk" (Miner 1953:267–82; cf. also Briggs 1958:57–76; Briggs and Guède 1964).

Dispersed minority status, then, reinforces the economic security and the social solidarity of particular religious and ethnic groups by giving them privileged access to certain occupations over a wide area. It also provides an opportunity for growth and adaption by permitting minority members to follow their specialized callings into new areas. That observable covariance in the economic and social spheres is perhaps sufficient for the theoretical needs of cultural materialists (cf. especially Harris 1968:643–87), but it hardly addresses the question of causality for those of us who believe, with Spicer (1971:796), that motivation must be considered. Do members of Middle Eastern minorities dominate certain trades because of their insistence on maintaining ethnic boundaries, or are they forced unwillingly to maintain a separate identity because of their occupational pursuits — or both?

In the case of economically advantaged minorities — the Greeks, Armenians, Chaamba, and some Jews — it is easy to accept the primacy of economic motivation if we wish. Obviously it is the cultural and social circumstances of being Greeks, Armenians, and so on, with all that it implies about educational and communicative advantages, that allows these peoples to dominate highly lucrative areas of commercial and professional life; for them the economic advantages of minority status may be assumed to outweigh the social disadvantages. (We should not, nevertheless, underestimate the persecution and privation to which all of these peoples have been intermittently subjected throughout their history.)

In the case of the Nubians the economic advantages of minority status are much less apparent. Their adaptation to the dominant society seems to show, paradoxically, aspects both of compulsion and of volition. Racial prejudice has confined them to the lower end of the economic ladder; subject to that limitation, however, they have established a claim to the highest-status occupations to which Egyptian society will admit them and have developed the special skills and personal qualities necessary to dominate those occupations.

It is the Gypsies and Solubba—and countless others in the same adaptive niche—whose situation is both theoretically and morally troubling. Minority status gives these peoples a guaranteed access to despised and generally unremunerative occupations which no self-respecting Moslem or Christian would touch; at the same time and by the same token it excludes them from almost any other occupation. Is that an advantage or a disadvantage? Could these peoples escape from the prison of "pariah" status if they shed the visible symbols of their ethnicity—and would they be better or worse off if they did?

There can be no doubt, on one hand, that the Gypsies and Solubba are the victims of enforced endogamy, and thus cannot escape from their despised position through intermarriage. Yet nothing obliges them to retain their non-Arabic and non-Persian languages, or to neglect the few and simple religious observances which would be sufficient for their full acceptance as Moslems. Should the patois languages and special customs of these peoples be compared to the counter-culture of American ghetto dwellers, perpetuated because to lose them would be to lose all sense of group identity and self-respect, and gain nothing in exchange? Or are they self-imposed barriers standing between the Middle Eastern "pariah" peoples and a fuller and richer life? These questions, I submit, are of more than theoretical importance, for they reflect upon the viability of cultural pluralism as a blueprint for our own future society.

The moral dilemma posed by Middle Eastern minorities is brought closer to home when we consider two groups whose dispersal has carried them into our own Western world: the Jews and the Gypsies. Under the assimilative pressures—and opportunities—of the industrial Western nations, both groups have lost some measure of ethnic distinctiveness and solidarity, yet both have stubbornly and to a large extent successfully resisted complete assimilation. Can their boundary- and identity-maintenance be regarded as adaptive in Western as well as in Middle Eastern society? In the case of the Jews one might perhaps again argue that their predominant position in certain areas of commerce, the professions, and the arts is enhanced by the maintenance of ethnic boundaries and ties.

In the case of the Gypsies, however, the adaptive advantages of separateness are hard to perceive. They have been subject to all the same assimilative pressures as have the Jews, and have just as tenaciously resisted (cf. Gropper 1975:1). It sometimes appears that they will suffer any privation or indignity for the sake of remaining poor, illiterate, dirty, diseased — and free from external control. This last might be the key to the riddle of Gypsy motivations; certainly it has a broad appeal to much of the disaffected youth of the 1970s and 1980s. Yet it seems chiefly to be Western romantics, not the Gypsies themselves, who extol the freedom of Gypsy life in song and story.

European opinion once attributed the non-assimilation of the Gypsies to their own cultural incapacity (cf. *Encyclopaedia Britannica* 1929, 11:43–44). Modern scientific theory makes any such view untenable but can apparently offer no convincing alternative. Indeed, the two most sympathetic students of American Gypsies in the 1970s (Gropper 1975; Sutherland 1975*a* and *b*) both seem baffled as to whether their persistence should be attributed to external or to internal compulsions. Another student (Miller 1975) asserts that Gypsy exclusiveness proceeds from an ideology of ritual impurity (as applied to non-Gypsies) which they have carried as part of their cultural legacy since they left India more than a thousand years ago. As a general explanatory principle this "doctrine of survivals" seems to carry us all the way back to Tylor (1958:70–159).

Having shifted the discussion from the persistence of minorities in the Middle East to their persistence in our society, I think it is appropriate to consider the lessons which the Middle East may offer for us. Many Americans — especially anthropologists — are now disillusioned with the "melting pot" ideal of our forefathers and prefer instead the vision of a diversified society involving permanently stable cultural differences. There has been nothing of the sort in our past experience, but for historical precedents we can surely look to the Middle East, where the "mosaic society" has been the normative human condition for several thousand years (cf. Coon 1964:1–9).

One must hasten to acknowledge that in the Middle East ethnic pluralism has always coexisted with social stratification, and — as this survey clearly demonstrates — the two have reinforced each other. Obviously no one dreams of such a future for America; the hope is rather to achieve cultural diversity within a framework of social and legal equality. Yet a landmark decision of the United States Supreme Court, hailed by all enlightened thinkers, asserts that "separate but equal" is an inherently contradictory doctrine. While this was addressed specifically to the issue of racial segregation, the wider implication is clear: social differentiation is inseparable from hierarchic ranking. The experience of minorities in the Middle East certainly tends to confirm this point of view.

The American founding fathers envisioned, though of course they did not achieve, a genuinely classless and egalitarian society; in other words a society that would finally do away with the principles of social and legal stratification, basic to all civilizations up to that time. Social policymakers ever since have assumed that the founders' ideal of equality could best be achieved through processes of social assimilation and cultural homogenization. The fact that we are still far from equality does not prove to me that their vision was wrong; on the contrary, the historic experience of the Middle East suggests that it was right. If so, then we will someday have to choose between "separate" and "equal" as our primary goal for the American future. To my mind the first is acceptable only if we decide (as some minorities apparently have) that the second is unattainable.

Even more disturbing to me is the prospect that an ethnically divided society without economic disparities — if such a thing could ever be achieved — would still not diminish intergroup tensions. On this question I think it behooves us to ponder deeply the tragic example of Lebanon. No Middle Eastern country was thought to be more "modern" and "westernized," and none was more often cited as a successful example of cultural and ethnic pluralism (cf. Khuri 1975; Salem 1973; Smock and Smock 1975). As recently as 1975 the Smocks (1975:104) could write that the "... Lebanese exhibit a will to live together and to make their multisectarian experiment a success. The extreme outward show of politeness to members of other religious groups constitutes one element in this determined effort to avoid tension ... this commitment to good relations comprises one of the most significant factors in the Lebanese experience and is also the element least exportable to other fragmented societies."

Alas, it is sadly apparent in retrospect that Lebanon had nothing to export to other fragmented societies; beneath the illusion of harmony the level of interethnic tension was if anything higher than in neighboring and more overtly stratified countries. It was only a "balance of tensions" that maintained some sort of equilibrium, and the external pressure exerted by Palestinians and Israelis was enough to upset that fragile balance. It is of course possible to blame the Lebanese disaster on extrinsic factors — the Palestinians or the Israelis or the aftereffects of French colonialism — but the cultural historian looking beyond the immediate past is confronted with a similar record of interethnic violence extending back through all history (cf. Zeltzer 1969). Unless we in America can find a better way of organizing cultural diversity than the Middle East has been able to do in 5,000 years, I think we are safer sticking to the egalitarian and assimilationist ideals of our forefathers.

| 2 |

The Question of Enclavement in Colonial Central Northern Mexico

William B. Griffen

In the early years of Spanish colonial occupancy, which began around 1560, the northern part of the province of Nueva Vizcaya, which falls roughly within the present-day Mexican state of Chihuahua, was a culturally heterogeneous region. The main tribal groups inhabiting the area were the Conchos of the Conchos River, and their eastern, desert-dwelling extension, the Chizos, over to the Big Bend area of present-day Texas; the La Juntans and other Jumano-speaking people of the lower Conchos River and its confluence with the Río Grande and some distance down the latter; the Sumas, Janos, Jocomes, Mansos, and Apaches in the northwest part of the modern state of Chihuahua; desert-dwelling Conchos and Chinarras between the northwestern groups just mentioned and the peoples of the Conchos River drainage; Toboso-speaking peoples, such as the Cocoyomes and Coahuiltecan-speaking groups, from the eastern desert area and lapping over into the present-day state of Coahuila; the Tarahumaras in the southwest part of modern Chihuahua; and various groups who inhabited the Laguna district in the present area of Torreón and Parras. People like the Tepehuanes, who originally lived around the Parral district, will not be mentioned since so very little is known about them.

Shortly after the arrival of the Spaniards a number of processes of acculturation were begun, as previously autonomous cultural groups were placed in a subordinate position to a social system whose power structure was based on a fairly rational or conscious manipulation of human and natural resources. The handling of such resources occurred on two levels. One was on the level of the political state with a rational bureaucracy and state policy aimed at managing subordinate groups for their betterment, protection, and eventual incorporation into the main society. The second was on the local level, where colonists, many of whom made up a local elite, controlled and used these resources for their own benefit and profit, and in a way which very often was in conflict with the goals of the colonial government. This often confounded the policy for cultural change of the Crown and, together with the locally varying conditions, set into motion processes of culture contact which led, in different directions and at different rates of acculturation, to the eventual assimilation or extinction of many groups.

TYPES OF NATIVE SOCIETIES
AT THE TIME OF CONTACT

The native societies which existed at the time of Spanish contact can be grouped together in slightly differing categories on the basis of extant data that includes local geographical resources and assumed subsistence types. Since the major social differences that might have existed are not known, the typology is not based initially on them. It does, however, hint at differences in subsistence orientations of the different native groups, and these were major variables in the contact process. Because this chapter is based entirely upon historical data,* a certain amount of inference must be carried out regarding what the local Indian cultural systems were like, since the documentary sources are never very clear or complete concerning the native peoples. However, the principal advantage of using such sources is their "longitudinal" data, which can give information on differ-ent rates of local adaptation of the native groups, and varying lengths of time during which there existed identifiable, subordinate native societies.

Such classification, however necessary, is sticky business since a read-ing of the data seems to indicate no sharp cultural boundaries among most aboriginal groups at contact time. Those who lived along water courses

---

*Since the data for this chapter have come largely from my own research, I have not referenced the resulting works on each occasion they are referred to in the text. These sources are listed in the bibliography.

and at the higher elevations were more often reported to practice some horticulture, while those dwelling in the desert regions were said to practice no or little crop-growing. Hence, at the time of contact, societies exhibited a range of variations in their dependence on horticulture and hunting and gathering. Fishing was done where possible along river courses such as the Conchos and in lake areas such as at the Laguna de San Pedro.

PROCESSES OF CULTURAL CONTACT

Spanish society consisted of several overarching institutional contexts in which the different local native societies were met. These were the mine, ranch, mission, and military units. The Parral district (beginning with the Santa Bárbara mines in the 1560s), the central river valleys of the Conchos and other major stream courses, and later, around the 1700s, the district of Chihuahua City, were the hub of Spanish power and acted like a magnet, bringing in different peoples from a number of far-flung regions. These people included Indians from the west coast (the present-day areas of Sonora and Sinaloa); from New Mexico to the north; from the nearby desert regions to the north, east, and from the mountains to the west and south; as well as Indians (Nahuatl and Otomi speakers), Spaniards, mestizos, and even some Negroes from central New Spain in the more distant south. Consequently, there was a great mixing of peoples with a resulting detribalization of many and a reworking of cultural elements. However, the several types of native communities existed for varying periods of time, and they were dealt with by the Spaniards as more or less isolable units.

Spanish institutions had varying influences in the development of colonial Indian social types. The principal attraction and central support of the area for the Europeans was the extraction of metals. Directly and indirectly, the mines needed great amounts of labor, in large part supplied by native Indians. Workers were needed for digging ore, lumbering and woodcutting, transportation of supplies and ore, and other facets of the mining process. The food and transportation support systems were focused upon agricultural holdings of farms and ranches. Here crops for food, and animals for both transportation and food, were raised. These enterprises also needed great amounts of labor during at least certain times of the year.

The other two institutions, the military and the missions, had a different, and — from an economic standpoint — a generally more peripheral, role. As the Spaniards settled into the region, a considerable amount of raiding and warfare was directed toward them. Friendly or "good" Indians often formed a major portion of the Spanish punitive forces. Since these natives were invariably from a number of different ethnic groups, a context for some detribalization and cultural change was set up.

By and large, the mission system, run by Franciscans, does not seem to have been as important a contact institution in this central region as it was in some other areas, such as the west coast or the Tarahumara country, where missionaries (Jesuits) were some of the prime immediate determiners of historical events. In the central river valley hub zone a number of local or autochthonous groups were placed with missionaries, under whose care their energies were required for labor in economic pursuits and for military duties as auxiliary troops, such activities being a regular feature of mission life. As the colonial period progressed, local peoples disappeared either through assimilation or actual biological extinction, and other groups from somewhat further away were brought in. However, by the end of the period, the number of local missions and their satellite parishes decreased as the overall native American population diminished.

From the earliest days of missionary activity, more than one ethnic or "tribal" group often was located at a single mission. This was true along the Tarahumara and Concho border; in the borderlands of the Conchos, Sumas, and Janos and Jocomes in the northwest; and at the centrally located missions such as Atotonilco and Santa Cruz de Tapacolmes. Different tribal groups were mixed together in order both to put "wild" and unsettled Indians with the more peaceful and sedentary peoples who could serve as a good example for the former and to keep the dwindling population of the missions up to a reasonable level. Clearly, the development and continuation of ethnic groups with strong institutions of social organization and shared sentiments would be, under these circumstances, rather difficult.

As Spaniards penetrated and settled the region, they set up processes of cultural contact leading to the cultural assimilation or the biological extinction of native American groups. While Indians from outside the immediate area formed small settlements at mines and ranches, including Opatas and Yaquis from Sonora, who in the eighteenth century made up small garrison communities of auxiliary troops, these were usually quite short-lived. The most permanent settlements occurred with local native groups, not with displaced Indians from outside Chihuahua.

The Spaniards themselves developed their own categories of native communities. In the early years they clearly recognized those natives who were part of the Spanish social system, that is, who were under direct Spanish control at haciendas, missions, or in Spanish towns such as the Valle de San Bartolomé. In contrast, there were the "wild" (*salvajes* or *bravos*) Indians not under Spanish control who stayed in the hinterland away from Spanish society and who often fought Spaniards and raided their holdings. The Spaniards also recognized a third, essentially inter-mediate, category of people who were basically friendly to the Spaniards, who often would work on Spanish holdings, but who otherwise were not too well controlled by them and hence were said to be "half wild." The latter seem to have frequently lived in somewhat nucleated settlements (such as some of the more distant Concho and Jumano settlements) in contrast to the more nomadic desert-dwellers. While they may have attacked Spanish settlements on occasion and stolen animals, they were not deemed to be the permanent hostiles that many of desert-dwelling Tobosos, Coahuileños, and Janos-Jocomes were.

As time wore on, several processes came about as a result of Spanish contact. One of these was the diminution in population of the hinterland nomads (who mostly lived in the northern and eastern deserts). Those people remaining (Tobosos, Coahuileños, Chizos, and later Apaches) had adapted well to the Spanish presence by specializing to some extent in raiding and living off Spanish holdings. This success was largely due to the integration of the horse by the natives into their own exploitative systems, increasing their range of activities with wider traveling and better striking power.

A second process was the disappearance of the middle group or "half-wild" Indians. A number, probably the majority, moved in closer to Spanish holdings and became permanently "peaceful" people, while some, often as individuals, joined the more nomadic, desert-dwelling, perma-nently hostile raiders. This was not a smooth process, however, and there was considerable movement back and forth between Spanish and native camps during many decades of the colonial period.

Finally, a third process was the increasing detribalization of those natives living as part of Spanish society. As they ceased to identify them-selves with existing ethnic groups, they came to form the lowest stratum (caste or *casta*) of Spanish society, which continued to be called "Indian" (*indio*) and apparently contained many pan-Indian elements. These people gradually lost their languages and all specific ethnic identity and ceased to constitute separate cultural groups.

PROCESSES OF ENCLAVEMENT

The old province of Nueva Vizcaya was, then, during the colonial period, a multi-ethnic society. This multi-ethnicity and its corresponding variety of cultural elements changed over the years. In the early years (*ca.* 1560 to 1600) there were few Spaniards, and Spanish culture was rep-resented at only a handful of locations. There existed a great many different Indian settlements and tribal groups, many of which were contacted in some fashion by representatives of Spanish society (mineral explorers or *gambusinos*, slave-raiders, ranchers, missionaries, or the military). The period from around 1600 to 1700 saw an expansion of Spanish settlements with many Indian groups living in or adjacent to them. Following this period, the last hundred years or so before Mexican Independence in 1821 saw the disappearance of most of the identifiably distinct cultural groups, except for the Tarahumaras in the southwest, the Apaches in the north (some of whom were still living in the peace-settlements, the *establecimientos de paz*, established for them in the late 1780s), some Sumas at El Paso, and a few other remnant or refugee groups at some of the old towns and missions.

The question arises, then, to what extent can processes of enclavement be identified during this period of 260-some years? First, the processes of enclavement are not counter to the processes of cultural evolution (Spicer 1966). Rather, they exemplify these processes as being the results of specific adaptations to certain conditions.

Spicer states that an enclaved society is "a culturally distinct subsociety" which "becomes a stimulus to wider forms of integration in the whole." The "necessity for reconciling and accommodating the different cultures within the whole" serves as a "stimulus to higher forms of sociocultural integration" (Spicer 1966). This is one of the results of the processes of cultural change which clearly occurred in northern Nueva Vizcaya. The "higher integration" can be witnessed in the development of the missionary and military systems, and in the management of governmental processes in general. The question arises, then, did this integration occur because of enclavement or for other reasons?

Enclaved societies are characterized by several key attributes. First, an enclavement is always a whole society, not just part of a society such as "a group of occupational specialists or co-religionists." In other words it is a "culture-bearing unit" which carries out basic cultural tasks such as enculturation, economic processes, religious activities, and the like. Second, an enclavement must consist of cultural elements, regardless of their origin or specific characteristics, that are organized in a way distinctive from those of the dominant society, so that feelings and sentiments can be focused on the group's being recognized as a separate entity with its own tradition, a factor which may be of great importance in maintaining the specific subculture of the subordinate society. The cultural elements, of course, may be and often are the result of fusions of elements from both of the societies. In addition, at least in the early stages, a group must have a separate territory with which it identifies part of its cultural symbolism, although, with continual opposition to the dominant groups, a separate territory becomes unnecessary. A concept of moral superiority is also developed by the enclaved group (Spicer 1966, 1971).

The two essential characteristics, then, are a recognized difference in cultural elements and a clear difference in identification by the enclaved group, in which there is a maintenance of sentiments of solidarity and a regulation of contacts and interaction with outsiders. Enclavement is "dependent on the growth of vigorous and exclusive forms of social organization" (Spicer 1966, 1971).

It would seem that none of the societies of the northern Nueva Vizcaya area actually fit the definitions of enclavement as here outlined. In the first place, although the processes set in motion by the Spaniards took place over a span of years and in a conquest state, both of which factors are necessary conditions for enclavement, northern Nueva Vizcaya was an entirely nonindustrial state. The social systems of nonindustrial states are quite different from those of industrial states with regard to many sociocultural features, too numerous to detail here. A few of these differences, however, are found in the nature and extent of capital and capital accumulation, and the need for labor; the range of communication and transportation networks; the use and effectiveness of different kinds of mechanisms of social control; the frequency, viability, and function of extended family and other large kinship organizations; the kind of social stratification; and the power, size, and diversity of bureaucratic administrative organizations. Nonindustrial and industrial states constitute two different types of event systems in which different kinds of events can occur and certainly different degrees and frequencies of the same kinds of events (Bohannon 1963: 359–60). While this statement should be, with respect to enclavement, treated as a hypothesis on which more research is needed, it would be reasonable to expect that the totality of these differences would make for a difference in the results of enclavement processes in nonindustrial and industrial state systems.

Spicer (1966), studying the Yaquis, Lowland Mayas, and Tzotziles from the colonial period to the present, notes that by the 1920s enclavement was well established. Early processes of enclavement for these groups seem to have been established in some degree during the colonial period at least for the Tzotziles and apparently also for the Yaquis (but not for the Lowland Mayas). However, it was not until the twentieth century, apparently, that such enclavements became clear cut and well developed. This appearance of better development may be a problem of inadequate data, since the historical sources need much more analysis than they have yet received. It was in the later stages of enclavement, in both industrializing Mexico and the United States, that enclaves became recognized by the respective governments as social realities and were dealt with as such on a positive basis (rather than as a bizarre, anomalous, or perverse situation needing correction by eradication), that is, by recognizing the enclave as a legitimate cultural entity (with some degree of self-determination), including its language, and bringing it into closer contact with the national society and culture.

Another aspect of this appearance of better development that should be kept in mind is that of our present vantage point. Looking back on the colonial period in the Chihuahua area, we can infer that enclavement, if it occurred, never progressed very far, since the societies in question no longer exist (except for the Tarahumaras). However, if a synchronic or cross-sectional view of, say, 1680, 1700, or even 1730 had been adopted by an investigator living at these times (with better data, of course, than we now possess), it might very well seem that some of the societies had been enclaved and would have persisted as such indefinitely. Possibly the pueblos at La Junta would have appeared to be an enclaved society.

SELECTED EXAMPLES OF NORTH MEXICAN SOCIETIES

The Raiding Indians

The groups of raiders were all primarily hunting and gathering peoples at the time of Spanish penetration into the area. They reoriented a portion of their hunting patterns to the acquisition of Spanish domestic animals, crops, and other items, and thus intermittent or rather regular raiding of Spanish holdings then became built into the economic systems of these groups.

Those nomadic raiders who seem to have been somewhat more peripheral to the Spanish system were the Janos, Jocomes, Sumas, Mansos, Chizos, and Apaches, in the north. While these peoples had varying kinds of contact with Spaniards, including being under mission domination for short periods, this contact does not seem to have been as intensive as it was for some of the groups who lived farther south.

The more southern peoples were known in the later phases of their adaptations as Cocoyomes (Toboso-speakers) and Coahuileños. Almost all of the members of the first group and a great number of those of the second were finally rounded up and deported from the province in the early 1720s, and another large group of the Coahuileños, called Cabezas, had surrendered to the Spaniards in 1690 and settled down at the town of Santa María de las Parras. All of these groups were amalgamations of a number of small bands whose existence was first recorded when the

Spaniards arrived and began to report on the area. In the latter years of their history, before these peoples fell under direct Spanish control, they lived in highly composite groups which appear to have exhibited some of the processes necessary for the development of cultural enclavement.

The destinies of these southern peoples were the result of more intensive contact than that experienced by the northern groups (such as the Janos), because they lived closer to the main Spanish mining, ranching, and mission settlements. For a hundred or more years before their demise these more southern nomadic raiders were in and out of missions (often missions especially set up for them) and Spanish holdings such as haciendas, where they were laborers, usually for rather short periods of time. They had more continual contact with the Spanish in negotiating for peace and settlement, in fighting against them, and in serving as auxiliaries and scouts for punitive forces (all of which also occurred, although to a much lesser degree, with the more northern groups).

It can be interpreted that, in the overall adaptive picture, these peoples were in effect incorporated into Spanish society and occupied a niche created by the structure of that society itself, a niche similar to that of a group of non-indigenous bandits (a common structural phenomenon in preindustrial and slightly industrialized European societies, including the nineteenth-century American West) who had become highly dependent upon Spanish society. The great number of constant raids during the 1600s and the first two decades of the 1700s tends to support this interpretation, as do testimonies taken from Cocoyome groups in 1715 which indicate that these people had regular and institutionalized sentiments of opposition to Spanish society, sentiments which were by this time a part of the regular enculturation process. As in other parts of the frontier border country, trading of stolen goods and captives was a common feature. It is also clear that the Indians by then had institutionalized their version of the Spanish peace-negotiation process, a regular frontier practice since the latter part of the 1500s, which they had learned to work to their own advantage with delaying tactics, by obtaining additional handouts from the Spanish authorities, and in other ways that kept them in a good, if not always superior, bargaining position. Thus it is possible that some of the raiding groups were at least incipient enclaves of Spanish society. Obviously, more research is needed before definite conclusions can be drawn.

The La Juntans

The La Juntans comprised a group of village dwellers who lived in and around the confluence of the Conchos River and the Río Grande. These people were missionized sporadically, but their main contact with Spaniards was of a different nature. Men from these pueblos for many years (from 150 to 200, depending on how the documentary record is interpreted) served as temporary, seasonal laborers on Spanish haciendas and other holdings, especially at harvest time. Some, apparently at times with their families, spent longer periods of time working for Spaniards. A number of the towns in their home territory maintained a separate cultural identity until the 1760s, although for more than a century some families and larger groups had been moving southward and taking up residence closer to the major Spanish settlements (such as at the mission towns of Julimes and Santa Cruz de Tapacolmes, and the Spanish town of Valle de San Bartolomé). Indeed, the separate cultural identity of the inhabitants of these places can be noted from several sources, including in their banding together for uprisings and hostile "disturbances." However, it was constantly noted by Spanish observers that these were intensive revolts, and different from the regular raiding pattern of the desert nomads. It appears from the evidence that is available that these non-nomadic, settled groups sometimes exhibited certain coordinated although temporary leadership, most notably in 1644, 1684, and 1718–1720. It would seem from the meager historical data that these villages could easily be a candidate for an enclaved society (or societies) until the 1760s or so, when, as a group, reduced in number from the more than 3,000 souls earlier reported, the La Juntans finally left their homeland and moved closer to Spanish settlements, reportedly motivated in large part by Apache attacks. After this, they apparently rather rapidly lost their identity and cultural distinctiveness (at least they do not seem to have been heard of again).

During the above-mentioned revolts at least two nativistic religious prophets arose (in 1644 and 1684), preaching anti-Spanish doctrines to these La Juntan peoples, demonstrating some kind of essential unity among them during the seventeenth century, as well as common opposition to the Spanish way of life. Some of the cultural separateness at this time may have been maintained by the Spanish development of a distinct administrative district with an Indian governor over the Indian settlements along the Conchos River, to and including all of the towns of the La Junta district. This Indian governor acted as intermediary between the various Indian settlements and the Spaniards in keeping the peace and in recruiting laborers to work on Spanish holdings. Furthermore, the constant traveling back and forth by native Americans for several generations between Spanish-held territory and the La Junta towns as part of the migrant labor force tended only to keep alive and reinforce the cultural differences and, no doubt, the ambivalent feelings between Indian and non-

Indian. Some of the groups called Conchos should also be included here as part of the La Junta pattern.

The Mission Groups

A number of native groups were brought into the Franciscan and Jesuit missions of the central river valley area. The Jesuits managed the Tarahumara missions, the short-lived Santa Ana de Chinarras east of Chihuahua City in the early 1700s, and Santa María de las Parras, established in 1598 and terminated in 1646. The rest of the area was controlled by Franciscans. With the possible exception of the Tarahumara country, it seems that enclavement processes never really got started in the several mission groups.

At the majority of the missions (the Tarahumara excepted) there seems to have been rather constant replacement or turnover of population of different ethnic groups, and, especially at those missions near Spanish settlements, there was a great amount of ethnic heterogeneity at any one time. Frequent replacement of population also occurred at the Jesuit mission at Parras; many of the people from this multi-ethnic population, or their descendants, later formed part of the Coahuileño raiding group, specifically the Cabezas, mentioned above. The composite band of Cabezas, some fifty years later, settled at the town of Parras, the site of the ex-Jesuit mission. Judging from the extant parish records kept especially for this group, these Indians had lost their separate ethnic identity within some 30 years.

The Tarahumaras

Except during times of revolts the colonial Tarahumaras were organized into (as they are in the twentieth century) a number of loosely integrated communities or neighborhoods which functioned as the culture-bearing local groups, but which had little or no overall sentiments or tradition as a single entity. During the colonial period two processes occurred among the Tarahumaras. First, a number of Tarahumaras were attracted to and acculturated into the Spanish empire. Second, many became disaffected and developed strong feelings of de-identification with the dominant Spanish society, and they took refuge in the western mountain fastnesses far into the back country. These processes could have led to elimination of the more marginal personalities and to the formation of a close-knit group of Tarahumaras in the hinterland, a group with strong in-group feelings and hence possibly beginning on the road to enclavement. However, they did not become enclaved, at least not for long, in part because the geographical terrain forced a kind of pocket agriculture and dispersed settlement pattern on these people who remained identified as Tarahumara. Consequently, what was formed was a "zone of refuge," to use Aguirre Beltrán's terms (1967), but not a true enclavement; they possessed a tribal culture in the traditional sense in a particular territory outside of effective control of Spaniards or Mexicans (until the twentieth century), but nothing more.

EXTENT OF ENCLAVEMENT IN NORTHERN NUEVA VIZCAYA

It does not appear that enclavement occurred to any extent in the area of northern Mexico under consideration here. In some cases, processes of acculturation that began with the European conquest of the area were never continued long enough or intensely enough for true enclavement to occur. At best, what took place was the development of zones of refuge for remnant tribal populations, all of which, with the exception of the Tarahumaras, eventually disappeared.

Spicer (1966) notes that cultural pluralism cannot develop in the absence of enclaves, that is, that the formation of enclaves is actually a subprocess of the larger process of pluralization. A plural society consists of "a political entity which contains two or more groups making separate identification from one another in ethnic terms" (Spicer 1972:16). But groups which make such separate identification are enclaved societies with a long tradition of having developed their own internal sentiments or sense of superiority in opposition to the larger political state or political environment they have found themselves in. This process of enclavement involves developing a common "language of opposition" and special symbols, including folk history, which form the common identity system and persistent cultural system of the enclaved society (Spicer 1971, 1972:21–76). In northern Nueva Vizcaya conquered peoples became subordinate ethnic groups for a period of time, but the necessary processes of enclavement either never occurred or were aborted early on. What can be seen as the development of wider or higher forms of social and cultural integration (Spicer 1966) during the (especially early) part of the colonial period would seem to stem from the conquest of previously independent societies which were manipulated into extinction or assimilation, and not because of any well-developed enclavement process.

Such evidence, then, would indicate that northern Nueva Vizcaya was not actually a plural society but rather a multi-ethnic and culturally heterogeneous one. Enclavement and pluralization were actually prohibited because of the way the Spaniards moved the Indians around for purposes of labor and defense; because of the nature of the organization of the agricultural and mining holdings, with their large demands for labor — including *encomienda* and other slave-like labor arrangements; and because of the management of the mission systems, especially that of the Franciscans, which resulted in very impermanent populations or in communities with a high ethnic mix, with strong paternalistic control by the missionaries. In effect, Spanish policy as practiced was formulated specifically to extirpate or prohibit enclavement. In the policy of secularization of the missions, for example, it was clearly assumed officially, although not always carried out in fact, that Indians were capable of making enough progress toward "civilization" (hispanicization and Christianization) that this frontier social unit and its associated culturally distinct population would eventually disappear. The twentieth-century policies of Mexico and the United States in part accept and foster cultural differences by recognizing Indian languages and history as legitimate (the Jesuit order had done this to some extent in the sixteenth and seventeenth centuries). Such a thrust may be largely a product of the nation-state of the twentieth century (which has increasingly included an acceptance of the principle of self-determination for minority or subordinate peoples) rather than a view which was ever a part of the Spanish nonindustrial conquest state of the colonial period.

Consequently, the processes of enclavement in the twentieth century would be expected to be different from those in nonindustrial conquest states. In the latter the tendency was, among other things, for communications systems to be less well organized and extensive, for the division of labor to be less differentiated, for the population density and the energy consumption per person to be much less, and for there to be fewer competing demands on governmental or societal resources than in modern states. As a result, the processes of enclavement in nonindustrial societies were correspondingly different. At the same time, as least in the Spanish colonial system, the ideal was an authoritarian system with little tolerance for cultural diversity and ambiguity and a strong emphasis on paternalism toward the lower classes and Indian groups. This policy insured that, even if some groups with different cultures were moving in the direction of enclavement, processes of acculturation were aimed at turning all the subordinate groups into units like those that already existed in the society. In modern societies, even though there is a "melting-pot" folk philosophy, the much higher per capita and total-society energy budget and the greater integration (more highly functionally interrelated parts) means there is much more specialization and therefore greater diversity than in nonindustrial states. This diversity, then, sets the stage for the development of more sharply defined processes of in-group/out-group feeling and hence more easily identified enclavement. Consequently, given the characteristics of nonindustrial societies as well as the specific policy implemented in northern Nueva Vizcaya, these subordinate ethnic groups in effect represent the maximum expectable amount of enclavement possible under Spanish colonial conditions. Further research into the nature of the enclavement process in different societies as well as elsewhere in colonial Latin America will help make such judgments clearer.

Part Two

Opposition
and Persistence

| 3 |

The Persistent Identity of the Mohave Indians 1859–1965

Frederick J. E. Gorman

In order to trace the efforts of the Mohave Indians to retain their collective identity in contrasting cultural environments over the past three hundred years, I have adopted the analytic framework developed by Spicer (1971) to study persistent cultural systems.

The Mohave are assigned membership in an ethnohistoric culture complex that has been labeled both "Lower Colorado" (Kroeber 1939:42) and "River Yuman" (Castetter and Bell 1951:40; Forbes: 1965:15). They shared this distinction on linguistic and ecological grounds with neighboring tribes, such as the Quechan ("Yuma"), Maricopa, Halchidhoma, Kohuana, Kamia, Kohima, Halikwami, and Cocopa, who also lived on or near the lower Colorado River. It is difficult to determine precisely the spatial boundaries of the River Yuman complex, because, like others, it existed in the face of an overlapping of different cultural characteristics. For example, all of these member tribes exhibited aspects of theology and social organization of kindred that linked the River

Yumans to southern California groups rather than with those to the east (Forbes 1965:42). The River Yumans also shared elements of cosmogony, tribal organization of occupational status, and aspects of material culture with certain cultures in the Southwest and Mexico (Forbes 1965:42). The Mohave, Quechan, and Maricopa are held to be the archetypal representatives of the River Yuman complex, for the specialized aboriginal way of life that developed along the Colorado River is thought to have been manifest earliest among these three tribes (Forbes 1965:35).

MOHAVE IDENTITY AS A PRODUCT OF THE OPPOSITIONAL PROCESS

Persistent identity systems are the product of continuous conflict between a "people" and the "controllers of surrounding state apparatus" over "issues of incorporation and assimilation" into the large entity (Spicer 1971:797). The implication is that this "oppositional process" is necessary for the formation and maintenance of persistent identity groups, and that several "conditions of opposition" are involved (Spicer 1971:797).

Spanish and Mexican Attempts to Incorporate the Mohave

The Mohave are known to have been located in the northern region of the lower Colorado River for at least three hundred years (Castetter and Bell 1951:44; Stewart 1969a:259), and the tribe has outlived two state organizations. Like the Navajo (Spicer 1971:797), the Mohave were never actually incorporated into either the Spanish Empire or nineteenth-century Mexico. The Mohave allegedly participated in the successful Quechan Revolt of 1781 against the Spanish (Forbes 1965:200), but they were too remote from settlements of the latter to have been affected directly (Stewart 1969a:259).

Later, the Mohave were "technically incorporated" by Mexico, although the Lower Colorado region was ineffectively controlled during the early nineteenth century (Stewart 1969a:259). This tribe, together with the Quechans, thwarted Mexican attempts to maintain land routes to California (Forbes 1965:241; Forbes 1973:22; Stewart 1965:188). In sum, the Mohave maintained their independence throughout the hispanic period (Stewart 1969a:259) largely because of their peripheral location and their formidable military reputation.

During the following years, 1820–1859, the Mohave harassed Anglo-American pioneers and U.S. military expeditions even though they were preoccupied with intertribal warfare (Stewart 1969a:262). Anthropologists (Castetter and Bell 1951:72; Stewart 1965:187) have defined

Mohave warfare in this period as a semireligious, identity-promoting activity (Devereux 1961:492) that has persisted into this century in the form of contentious, pantribal sentiments of militant nationalism. The Quechan and the Mohave are each thought to have maintained a distinct group of part-time professional warriors (Forbes 1965:16, 42, 75; Fathauer 1954:102–11; Stewart 1947a:260–67) to engage in organized combat with their occasional allies (the Yavapai and Cocopa) against other River Yumans, principally the Kohana, Maricopa, Halchidhoma, and Cocopa. They are also known to have fought non-Yumans, such as the Northern Chemehuevi, Ute, Apache, Southern Paiute, Diegueno, Pima, and Papago (Castetter and Bell 1951:44; Stewart 1968:10). The Mohave in particular exhibited military spirit to the point where they functioned as a unit (including women when necessary) in offensive and defensive operations, and they were venturesome to the extent that they raided and traded from the Hopi mesas to Los Angeles (Castetter and Bell 1951:40–44; Devereux 1961:428; Forbes 1965:61; Forde 1931:138; Stewart 1947a:261).

Mohave relations with other River Yumans during this period exhibit another aspect of Spicer's (1971:797) oppositional process. There is some evidence that the Mohave attempted to dominate the Kohuana by forcing this tribe to reside with them for five years after expelling Kohuana allies, the Halchidhoma, from the Colorado River Valley around 1829 (Stewart 1969a:265).

Incorporation of the Mohave began after the tribe was soundly defeated by a sizeable contingent of the United States Army in 1859 (Forbes 1965:338; 1973:22; Stewart 1965:188), and a military post (later named Fort Mohave) was established immediately thereafter in the Mohave Valley. The outcome of this confrontation might have been different and incorporation delayed had the Mohave not lost a substantial number of their infantry two years earlier in a disastrous battle with the Pima and Maricopa near Tempe, Arizona (Devereux 1961:427; Stewart 1969a:261).

U.S. Incorporation Pressures and Mohave Responses, 1859–1890

The Mohave experienced three historical phases of economic and political pressure for cultural assimilation into the United States between 1859 and 1965. Less is known about the pressures that were exerted upon the Mohave during the first phase of their incorporation, 1859–1890, than about those which occurred during later periods (cf. Stewart 1969b). The tribe does seem to have experienced nondirected changes (Spicer 1961b:521) in its aboriginal subsistence economy from 1859 to 1890 which were of no particular interest to United States military and civil authorities. Like other River Yumans, the Mohave traditionally practiced a transhumant subsistence strategy in which scattered rancherías were moved from the lower Colorado River flood banks to the mesas and back according to a seasonal schedule of riverine farming and fishing alternating with upland hunting and gathering (Castetter and Bell 1951:70; Forbes 1965:100; Forde 1931:140; Kirchoff 1954:530). Argricultural production among the Yuman tribes began to decline between 1852 and 1877 as transportation wage labor (Castetter and Bell 1951:73; 84) grew in response to the establishment of U.S. military posts along the Colorado River. These installations were supplied by naval transport vessels, and numerous individuals from several River Yuman tribes (notably the Cocopa, Quechan, and Mohave) were engaged as riverboat pilots, crewmen, and woodcutters (Dobyns, Stoffle, and Jones 1975:163; Sherer 1965:1–12). Many of those who were committed to a cash economy by 1877 shifted to farm wage labor in commercial irrigation agriculture projects that were being organized in the Yuma and Imperial valleys after the Southern Pacific Railroad replaced naval transportation of military supplies in that year (Dobyns, Stoffle, and Jones 1975:163). Others chose intermittent work as railroad hands, saloon porters, or small cash market farmers (Bee 1963:210; Devereux 1961:66).

The political pressure to change was direct, however, for U.S. military sanction was immediately applied to curtail Mohave warfare (Stewart 1973:323). This military action contributed to the formation of a permanent split in the tribe between 1862 and 1865, which occured when a peaceful faction (Fathauer 1954:117) moved from the Mohave Valley south to Parker, Arizona, on the newly established Colorado River Reservation to take advantage of agricultural opportunities there (Stewart 1969*a*:268). The less pacific segment of the tribe remaining in the Mohave Valley was probably responsible in 1865 for the two-year expulsion of the Chemehuevi from the Chemehuevi Valley which separated both Mohave factions (Stewart 1969*a*:265).

Both groups of Mohave thereafter maintained their common identity through interaction over the eighty-mile distance between them by means of intermarriage, shifts of residence, visitation for ceremonial purposes or for shamanistic curing, or hospitalization and schooling (Devereux 1961:84, 111, 143, 191, 199; Fathauer 195 l*a*:91; Stewart 1969*a*:263).

Between 1870 and 1890 the Mohave were exposed to disease and poverty (Stewart 1969*a:*263; 1973:323), but they did not resist incorporation through participation in the nativistic cults that were popular elsewhere during these decades. The most common themes of such revitalization movements — restoration of ancestors and their property — were anathematical to Mohave values (Devereux 1961:319). Rather, they intensified native patterns that were incompatible with Anglo-American values, as did the Navajo (Vogt 1961:326). The Mohave appear to have increased their preoccupation with the statuses of warrior and shaman, the ceremonial practice of funeral cremation, and perhaps mythology. After the curtailment of warfare, warriors began to gratify their ambitions through sexual conquest and shaman-killing actions which represented an exaggeration of basic, traditional themes (Devereux 1961:327, 519). Shamans were frequently assassinated for allegedly causing epidemics of unfamiliar diseases or crop failures, but these killings were no longer the tribally organized, public events they once had been (Devereux 1961:399, 406, 521). Mohave belief in malevolent witchcraft and the practice of shamanism may have increased in these decades (cf. Stewart 1973:323). The Mohave also developed a "contempt" for the "all-absorbing" Anglo-American interest in property which they consciously expressed through funeral immolation of a deceased individual and all of his property, including the residence (Devereux 1961:317). This ritual destruction prevented the accumulation of capital, and a mythology was developed initially to rationalize the contrast with funeral practices of Anglo-Americans (Devereux 1961:190) and later to exclude them from the ceremony itself.

Mohave Adjustment to the Reservation System of Incorporation, 1890–1930

Incorporation pressures intensified during the second phase, 1890–1930, when the reservation system was designed to produce homestead communities (cf. Spicer 1961*b*:528), and the Mohave experienced cultural disorganization that was manifested primarily in terms of "declining family cohesion" and "chaotic sexuality" (Devereux 1961:477). The Mohave retained their collective identity, however, by shifting emphases on membership in Mohave clans and on the statuses of warrior versus shaman while further intensifying their funeral practices. A systematic American attempt was made to alter Mohave identity by redefining native education, naming, and settlement practices. In 1890 Fort Mohave was converted to an industrial boarding school which functioned as a mechanism of forced acculturation (Sherer 1965:10) through compulsory attendance of Mohave children. The Indian Agency School established on the Colorado River Reservation (Devereux 1961:482) served a similar function.

In 1905 all Fort Mohave Indians (Sherer 1965:49), together with those on the Colorado River Reservation (Devereux 1961:131), were required to take English surnames (according to their membership in a lineage and not a clan) in order to provide the basis for land allotments. The Mohave resorted to compartmental usage of English names; that is, they continued to use clan names among themselves (Sherer 1965:49). Several ethnographers (Bee 1963:225; Fathauer 1951*a*:131; Kroeber 1925:732; Sherer 1965:16; Spier 1952:324), noting the lack of ritual and visible symbolism that characterized membership in Mohave and Quechan clans, have been led to think of these as relatively unimportant. Clan membership is thought to have regulated exogamous marriage within most of the River Yuman tribes (Bee 1963:222; Devereux 1939:53, Fathauer 1951*a*:129; Forbes 1965:36; Forde 1931:145; Spier 1953:325), and it is systematically related to the custom of addressing females by their clan names (Devereux 1961:130, Forbes 1965:38, Kroeber 1925:732; Sherer 1965:65). The Mohave were unable to relinquish clan naming because it was an important internal characteristic of the process by which they maintained their collective identity, as will be shown later.

In 1911 the Fort Mohave Reservation was established for the Mohave Valley group (Stewart 1969*a*:263). The land allotment system was employed by the Department of the Interior to partition extended families on Mohave rancherías into nuclear families; these were to become the new units of autonomous land use (cf. Devereux 1961:68). This transition may have been accepted by the Mohave with a minimum of adjustment since few of their rancherías had been local corporate groups in the past (Spier 1953:325), and perhaps because their wage-based economy in non-agricultural pursuits at this time might have made it easier to maintain the nuclear family without continuous cooperation of relatives, as Bee (1963:214) has observed among modern Quechans. Those agricultural Mohave on both reservations who later found that farming by nuclear families was unprofitable compared to land-lease arrangements with out-side farmers may have leased their lands and regrouped into extended family households as did the Quechans (Bee 1963:212). Retention of the warrior status in this period is evident in the eagerness of middle-aged males to serve in the First World War (Devereux 1961:520). The assassi-nation of shamans by warriors began to decline around 1890 on the Colorado River Reservation and after 1905 on the Fort Mohave Reserva-tion (Devereux 1961:407). Witch-killings were reported up to 1925, but the trend may reflect a decline in the incidence of epidemics attributed to them and Devereux's (1961:521) assertion that it no longer provided the "morale-building aggression of warfare." Legal sanctions were instituted in an attempt to end witch-killing on both reservations by the end of this period (Stewart 1973:320). Shamanism may have become an important symbol of opposition on the Colorado River Reservation after 1910. It became common practice for shamans to treat Mohave patients before or after hospitalization on the reservation despite the fact that adequate native health care was provided from this date onward (Devereux 1961:174, 478).

Tribesmen intensified their "ceremonial transfer of Mohave property to the land of the dead" as early as 1903, when they reportedly began to purchase American manufactured goods expressly to destroy at funerals as an expression of "antagonistic acculturation" (Devereux 1961:317, 349, 521). Funereal destruction was no longer restricted to the property of the deceased alone.

Redefinition of Mohave Identity, 1930–1965

During the third and final phase under consideration, 1930 to 1965, the Mohave experienced both directed and nondirected changes. The latter affected not only the political and economic status of the tribe but their settlement as well, and these changes seem to have been readily absorbed. In 1931 the boarding school was closed and a substantial number of families moved from the Fort Mohave Reservation across the river to the public school area of Needles, California (Sherer 1965:10). Public education of the Mohave Valley faction thereafter was apparently effective, because all but the aged possessed an elementary education and could speak, read, and write English by 1965 (Sherer 1965:12). This goal may have been attained by the Indian Agency School one or two decades earlier on the Colorado River Reservation (cf. Devereux 1961:232).

Completion of the Parker Dam in 1938 caused Lake Havasu to flood the farms of those who remained on the Fort Mohave Reservation, and they too moved to Needles or to the Colorado River Reservation (Stewart 1969a:263). By 1965 about 70 percent of the Fort Mohave Indians had regrouped at Mohave Village in the Mohave Valley (Sherer 1965:12). The Chemehuevi were forced to abandon their Chemehuevi Valley Reservation that was also inundated by the flood of 1938, and this tribe moved south to reside permanently with the other Mohave faction on the Colorado River Reservation (Stewart 1969a:262). The availability of work on the Park Dam project coupled with wage and agricultural price inflation during these years made manufactured goods more accessible to the Mohave, who were regarded as "acculturated in most *external* ways" (Devereux 1961:111, 222, 506; italics mine). At the end of this phase the Mohave and Chemehuevi began to profit from leases of reservation land to outside commercial farming interests and later from the tourist development of their Bluewater Marine Park (Stewart 1969a:263).

The trend toward material acquisition was accelerated by an economic sanction that was directly applied to compel the Mohave to accumulate capital. In the 1930s families continued to impoverish themselves periodically through massive destruction of personal property at funerals, despite their awareness of property inheritance among whites (Devereux 1961:449, 450, 453). The government began to interfere with this process by withholding house-construction loans from the Mohave, but any residence owned outright by them was still burned at the death of its adult inhabitant during this decade (Devereux 1961:453). Property destruction gradually became limited to the personal effects of the deceased (Fathauer 195 1a:124), as was the case with the Quechans (Bee 1963:221), but among the Mohave some of it still had considerable value (Devereux 1961:453).

Continuation of the law against shaman-killing had an uncertain impact on the incidence of Mohave witchcraft during the third phase. Many natives believed that witchcraft had increased to the extent that "the tribe was threatened with extinction" (Devereux 1961:197), although Devereux (1961:316) thought the law had the opposite effect of reducing its incidence. Mohave belief in witchcraft and the practice of shamanism is still very much alive in the late twentieth century, particularly among older adults, although the young and the highly acculturated participate to a lesser degree (Devereux 1961:234, 320; Stewart 1973:322).

The status of warrior appears to have been retained by the tribe during this period. Braves believed to be potential shaman-killers were identified on the Fort Mohave Reservation in the late 1930s (Devereux 1961:149). Some of these may have dispatched their victims by more subtle means than previously or induced their suicide through severe physical punishment; at least one outright killing known to have occurred during these years (Devereux 1961:398–99, 402, 412). Many middle-aged males attempted to enlist in the armed services during the Second World War as they had in the First (Devereux 1961:520).

Mohave Resistance to an Aspect of Political Incorporation

I am unable to present information on the oppositional aspect of Mohave political incorporation in terms of the conditions mentioned by Spicer (1971:97), because the extent to which the reservation system of political organization contributed to the oppositional formation of Mohave identity remains unstudied. The Mohave are known to have exercised control over ethnic membership in their polity, however, despite attempts by the Department of the Interior to redefine this membership. The Mohave allegedly resented wartime internment of Japanese-Americans on the Colorado River Reservation, because these Nisei had come against their will (Devereux 1961:319). This resentment was expressed again in 1952 to successfully end the postwar transplantation of landless Hopi and Navajo to that reservation (Stewart 1969a:263). In sum, the Mohave developed reasonably well defined symbols of identity — funereal cremation, warrior and shaman statuses, and clan naming and affiliation — that differentiated the tribe from the Anglo-Americans who sponsored or endorsed the reservation programs that the Mohave opposed.

THE MOHAVE IDENTITY SYSTEM

Mohave Symbols of Collective Identity

The first component of two that define the Mohave identity system consists of a set of collective identity symbols of the oppositional type that embody common beliefs when displayed alone or in association with other symbols. These collective identity symbols are meaningful in that the Mohave persistently identify themselves by reference to them, and they assume these were also held by their ancestors (cf. Spicer 1971:796). The Mohave remain highly conscious of their tribal identity and their unity (Devereux 1961:521), unlike a number of other River Yuman groups in the late twentieth century (Kroeber 1920:482; Dobyns, Ezell, and Ezell 1963; Kelly 1972). Two of the three Mohave collective identity symbols are not materially visible nor are they often ritually or liturgically displayed (Devereux 1961:319; Fathauer 1951a:72).

Mohave clan affiliation and naming is the first collective identity symbol because it constitutes the basis of their marriage system, the institutional means by which they maintain their identity (cf. Spicer 1971:799). In order to understand the extreme importance of clan affiliation in Mohave thought about marriage (Fathauer 1951a:131; Spier 1953:324), it is necessary to define the different marriage patterns that are recognized by them. Most persistent identity groups, like the Mohave, use a marriage system that is partly, rather than completely, closed. This condition implies that there are two marriage patterns in these societies: marriage within the group and marriage outside of it. To understand how marriage embodies common belief about Mohave identity, the variety of rules that characterize their marriages must be accounted for, rather than simply assigning one marriage pattern to the tribe (Adams and Kasakoff 1975:168). A description of marriage within the tribe requires that clan exogamy be distinguished from clan endogamy. Marriage outside of it entails a difference between two alternative forms that depends on the sex of the Mohave spouse involved. In effect, the tribe employs rules for making four kinds of marriage (cf. Devereux 1961:142).

Clan exogamy is the preferred form of marriage among the Mohave themselves, for it is considered to be an expression of "nationalism" (Devereux 1939:510). This practice systematically perpetuates their collective identity in a way that will be discussed later. Descent among the Mohave is the basis for clan exogamy, because patrilineal membership in a clan provides the orientation for initiating this first type of marriage; that is, the clan itself is the exogamous unit (Devereux 1939: 513; Kroeber 1925:732). This observation was contradicted later by Fathauer (1951a:138), who inferred that lineages within clans were the exogamous units. This discrepancy will be examined later. The Mohave do not mention the fact that clan exogamy is and has been a highly informal union that is practically devoid of ritual. For the most part, this kind of marriage simply involves the establishment of a common residence by the couple after a casual affair, regardless of the previous marital status of either spouse (Devereux 1961:358). Despite the rigor with which they reckon partners, each Mohave marries, on the average, three times and has numerous sexual relationships with various partners who are permitted to do so from puberty to maturity (cf. Fathauer 1951a). Females usually take the initiative in forming or dissolving both marriages and extramarital relationships. Both spouses retain the right to divorce, and the union can be dissolved at will by either partner. I do not know if this form of serial monogamy has been discouraged among the Mohave through the increased marriage license and divorce fees that have made temporary marriage among the Quechans (Bee 1963:225) costly. The offspring of clan-exogamous unions are called "real Mohave," and all adult statuses later become available to them (Fathauer 1951a:124).

Clan endogamy is considered to be a form of "incest," that is "anti-nationalistic" (Devereux 1939:529). This practice entails the "social death" (Devereux 1961:357) of the bride through forfeiture of her membership in her lineage and her clan. Thereafter she is regarded by her kinsmen as "no longer one of them" and simply as "the wife of her husband" (Fathauer 1951a:137). Endogamy imposes an additional punishment, for each spouse loses the right to divorce, and permanent union is expected in contrast to casual exogamous marriage (Devereux 1961:360; Fathauer 1951a:137). The offspring's access to all of the varieties of adult status is not restricted in principle, but it seems to have been in practice, for the children of endogamous marriage were regarded by the Mohave as likely to practice shamanism by adulthood (see the case studies in Devereux 1961). It seems possible (although unlikely) for the Mohave to engage in this type of marriage outside of the tribe with spouses who are affiliated with specific Quechan, Cocopa and Yavapai clans that the Mohave consider to be equivalent to certain of their own (Devereux 1961:131, 144, 207).

The third and fourth types of marriage were made outside of the tribe, unlike the first and second which occurred among the Mohave themselves. For the most part, the Mohave regard tribal exogamy as miscegenation which threatens the tribal marriage cycle (Fathauer 1954:108) and erodes their collective identity (Devereux 1961:443). Although both forms of marriage within the tribe are mythologically foreordained (Devereux 1961:363), Mohave marriage with aliens is not. This suggests that tribal exogamy is of comparatively recent origin and reflects cultural adjustment to historical factors, such as warfare, which may have been stimulated by the Spanish colonial slave trade (Stewart 1965:188), and acculturation, which characterized Mohave relations with Americans after 1850 (Stewart 1973:263).

The Mohave distinguish two types of tribal exogamy according to the cultural identity of the male spouse. Marriage between a Mohave male and an alien female appears to be the more tolerable form, because it extends patrilineal membership in the clan to offspring and access to all adult statuses (Fathauer 1951*a*:88). Prior to 1850 this type of union involved concubinage in which female war captives were given to aged, single Mohave males. The reluctance of young and middle-aged Mohave males to engage in war-captive concubinage largely negated the possibility of divorce from this type of union (Fathauer 1954:100). The reason for this will be given later. The less tolerable type of tribal exogamy involves alien males and Mohave females. While the right to make a union of this kind is not formally recognized by the tribe, the right of the Mohave female to divorce is emphasized by her kinsmen. Lack of patrilineal membership in a Mohave clan formerly marked the offspring of these marriages as victims of infanticide (except in the rare instance in which the father happened to be a member of a Quechan, Cocopa, or Yavapai clan that has its counterpart among the Mohave, as previously mentioned). Since the tribe does not possess a mechanism of adopting the offspring of unions with alien males into the Mohave mother's clan, the children were called "not real Mohave" (Devereux 1941:578; 1961:131; Fathauer 1951*a*:88). This situation has been summarized succinctly:

> In brief, both adults and children are asked to think of the child first and foremost as a link in tribal continuity. By contrast, children whose fathers refuse to recognize them belong to no gens and therefore do not qualify as individuals capable of ensuring social and tribal continuity. Hence, such children can be destroyed without a biological loss to the tribe. . . . By contrast, the full-blood defective, whose paternity was not in dispute was, at least in principle, viewed as a bonafide link in tribal continuity . . . who could not be killed without violating a major value of Mohave culture (Devereux 1961:258–59).

These marriage patterns suggest that the persistence of Mohave identity depends to some extent on the biological continuity of the tribe; note that Spicer (1971:796) does not consider this to be an essential characteristic of identity maintenance.

Mohave shaman and warrior statuses constitute the second collective identity symbol because the activities of each either promoted the tribe's sense of well-being or disrupted it. In addition to their self-appointed task of defending the tribe in aboriginal times, warriors benefitted the Mohave by killing malevolent witches; certain shamans performed this latter task as well (Devereux 1⁹ .45–46, 246, 265). The shamans' ability to cure unfamiliar diso⁻ ¹⁾rs   ct er than those which they cause) is also recognized as a common ⌐enefit (Devereux 1961:179, 339). On the other hand, both shaman-killing warriors and shamans are believed to practice malevolent, disruptive w⌐ chcraft (Devereux 1961:45). Shaman-killing warriors and shamans are also similar in that both are believed to practice clan endogamy and vicarious suicide (Devereux 1961:46, 285, 472).

The third identity symbol is the funeral rite; both its configuration and its meaning have been studied from the perspective of ethnopsychiatry by Devereux. This ritual expression of collective identity among the tribe embodies a mythologically foreordained set of common beliefs about relations between living and dead Mohave. For example, mythological precedent is invoked to contrast their funeral behavior — emotional intensity that is followed by forgetting the dead — to that of the Anglo-Americans — emotional control and remembrance of their deceased (Devereux 1961:190).

The Mohave attempt to sever all connections with their dead in three ways. First, mention of the names of all deceased relatives and ancestors is prohibited. This practice is rigid to the extent that its violation is regarded as the cultural expression of insanity among them (Devereux 1961:190).

Second, the Mohave believe that those who predecease them pass through a sequence of metamorphoses which make them elusive to mourners who wish to join them unless they too die shortly thereafter. This provides the mandate for the ritual attempt at suicide by close relatives of the deceased on his funeral pyre (Devereux 1961:432, 435; Stewart 1947b:147). Devereux (1961:363) noted that the only other type of ritual suicide in Mohave culture occurred at the celebration of clan endogamy. This was the only formal marriage ceremony among the Mohave, who occasionally celebrated it as a mock funeral with a pyre during the nineteenth century. Its purpose was to convert the consanguineal tie between the couples' families to an affinal linkage. This involved the observance of the mourning ritual (including the destruction of the groom's property) by both sides as an expression of the social death of each spouse prior to their assumption of their new married status (Devereux 1961:309, 358, 363—64, 369; Fathauer 1951*a*:137).

Third, the Mohave are strongly linked to their dead through property that had been loosely shared, such that the "difference between ownership and use . . . is minimal" (Devereux 1961:446—47). Severance of this material connection has been discussed earlier as an aspect of the oppositional process. Belief in the necessity of property destruction by the principals involved and also of appropriate behavior by funerary officials and observers is enforced by fear of a particular type of insanity that is said to result from noncompliance (Devereux 1961:179, 190; Stewart 1947*b*:148).

Spheres of Participation in the Mohave Identity System

The second component of the Mohave identity system is more complex than the first. The Mohave maintain their collective identity by participating in two and perhaps three of the spheres of common understanding that have been isolated by Spicer (1971:799).

The Mohave participate in the *language sphere* through their use of a "terminology of opposition" (Spicer 1971:799) by which they maintain a boundary between themselves and the dominant group. Their common modes of reference have changed, however, during each historical phase of their·incorporation. From 1859 to 1890, for example, the Mohave appear to have verbally distinguished themselves from Anglo-Americans, whom they labeled *apen kutctha:ny* ("beaver eater"), which probably identified these "most foreign and dangerous of aliens" as the source of "foreign disease" (Devereux 1961:45, 135).

During the subsequent phase, 1890 to 1930, the Mohave expanded their terminology of opposition by referring to both whites and blacks as *hi:ko* (a term of unknown meaning). Inclusion of the latter group probably resulted from exposure of the tribe to a black regiment of federal cavalry that was stationed on the edge of the Colorado River Reservation at the turn of the century. In contrast to their attitude toward whites during the period, the Mohave were not thought to be prejudiced toward blacks, although this label may possibly have identified them (and whites) as sources of venereal disease (Devereux 1961:135, 456).

The Mohave again expanded their oppositional terminology during the most recent phase, 1930 to 1965. The younger and more acculturated tribesmen adopted into their native language the labels by which the dominant group referred to itself, namely, "American" or "white." Continuing opposition is evident, however, in the fact that these Mohave readily accepted friendly whites but expected them to conform to Mohave standards of behavior. The highest praise bestowed on a conforming individual occured when he was considered to be "really a Mohave and not a white man at all" (Devereux 1961:135, 137, 523).

Participation in the *moral sphere* may be the most important means by which the tribe maintains its identity. Mohave dreaming, stereotypy, and xenophobia express three respective sets of values that pertain to ideal behavior among themselves versus that which they attribute to others. The Mohave believe that every human activity has a mythological precedent (Devereux 1961:53). Their culture hero Mastamho established this precedent by teaching the Mohave how to dream of power that is necessary to successfully conduct all daily activities, especially those of reproduction and survival (Devereux 1961:47, 161). Dream power does not change in the form in which it is given to Mohave who seek it from one generation to the next, a fact which reflects the essentially static nature of their cosmology (Devereux 1961:12; Fathauer 1954:98). Myths also remind the Mohave that their acquisition of power by means other than dreaming is a cause of insanity among them, and also that insanity will result from an individual's refusal to use dream power once it has been acquired (Devereux 1961:53, 57). The degree to which an individual is able to modify Mohave "dream culture" depends on his ability to convince fellow tribesmen that his dream power is genuine, and also upon the extent to which his dream is congruent with the traditional patterns (Devereux 1961:141).

The Mohave have a stereotypic view of ideal behavior among themselves. During one historical phase, however, the values that underlay this stereotype appear to have been transferred from association with one collective identity symbol to another; this will be discussed later.

Xenophobia or fear of strangers is a major moral theme that conditions Mohave relations with all other ethnic groups — including their former allies, the Quechans. Intimate physical contact with non-Mohave that involved combat, sexual intercourse, food-sharing, or handling of material possessions was perceived by the Mohave to cause their most basic psycho-physiological disorder, which they termed either "enemy" or "foreign disease" (Devereux 1961:129, 132; Fathauer 1951a:90). Foreign disease is mythologically foreordained as the prototype of all disorders among the Mohave, who also believe that foreign disease and witchcraft have been the two most prevalent forms of disorder among them (Devereux 1961:32, 135). A third type of contamination, that resulting from Mohave dream interaction with deceased relatives, is termed "ghost disease" (Devereux 1961:21–24; Fathauer 1951c:607; 1954:104). This internally directed form of xenophobia structures another dimension of ideal behavior among the Mohave themselves.

The *political sphere* of identity maintenance among the Mohave is less well known. Its aboriginal form has been partially reconstructed in relation to Mohave social organization (Fathauer 1951a), clan affiliation and naming (Sherer 1965), and the reservation system of incorporation (Stewart 1969b). The fragmentary and inferential nature of this information suggests that Mohave participation has been a less important means of identity persistence than the development of common understanding in the areas of language and morals. This imbalanced emphasis is a plausible and effective way to maintain collective identity, according to Spicer (1971:799).

MAINTENANCE OF MOHAVE IDENTITY

Spicer (1971:799) defined the maintenance process in terms of "varying participation [in the language, moral, and political spheres]" and as "fluctuations in the intensity of [participatory] sentiments that are associated with the [collective identity] symbols." His definitions can be made operational to understand Mohave identity maintenance during an incorporation phase by specifying the way that each sphere of participation articulated with each collective identity symbol. Although the Mohave share knowledge of these articulations, not all of them take the form of sentiments that they express as codified statements (cf. Kasakoff 1974:156).

The Reconstructed Maintenance Process, 1859–1890

Mohave sentiments that articulated participation spheres with collective identity symbols during the initial incorporation phase of 1859 to 1890 are largely inferential in the sense that they were remembered by aged informants during the subsequent phases (Devereux 1961:5, Fathauer 1951a:127, and Sherer 1965:3 provide examples).

Mohave participation in all three spheres appears to have been linked by the symbol of clan affiliation and naming. Articulation is evident in the moral sphere through the practice of dreaming, for the tribe perceived its *common* welfare to depend on reservoirs of dream power that were possessed by each clan and which its members gained by dreams of a totemic nature (Devereux 1961:90). Clan exogamy among the Mohave is thought to increase the access of the offspring to clan reservoirs of dream power through bilateral filiation (Fathauer 1951a:90). Fathauer (1951a:90) identified this desire to "perpetuate biological bonds with the ancestors" as the sentiment of "biological and mystical continuity" in Mohave culture. These two threads of continuity were regarded by the Mohave as being intertwined, since there was a tendency to regard certain clans as likely to produce certain offspring who would have certain power dreams (Fathauer 1951a:90). Clan exogamy is thought to have been the predominant form of marriage among the Mohave during this period (Kroeber 1925:732).

Mystical continuity was threatened by the alternative form of marriage within the tribe. Clan endogamy was perceived not only to limit access to dreams (Fathauer 1951b:274), but also to invert dreampower, and the consequence of this inversion was the practice of malevolent shamanism by either spouse or by their offspring (Devereux 1939:529; 1961:65, 87, 96). These individuals prepared for shamanism by deliberately contracting an endogamous marriage, according to some Mohave informants. Other Mohave believed that the permanence of endogamous marriage inadvertently prompted one spouse to resent the other. This animosity was manifest when the dissatisfied partner became a shaman in order to bewitch and murder his or her spouse and children (Devereux 1961:59, 87, 199, 285, 373). Clan endogamy is implied to have been rare during this period (Devereux 1961:411, 509).

Mohave stereotypes of behavior among themselves or Anglo-Americans are not known from this period. Xenophobia was strongly articulated with clan affiliation and marriage in terms of moral sentiments about disease. Clan endogamy was said to invoke ghost (?) disease upon all members of two clans which permitted marriage between cross-cousins, for example, or on the lineages within one clan that allowed parallel cousins to marry (Devereux 1961:17, 87, 140, 149,.358, 366; Fathauer 1951a:137). Tribal exogamy was associated with foreign disease (Devereux 1961:21, 24, 136; Fathauer 1951c:607, 1954:104), and for this reason it threatened the persistence of Mohave mystical identity because it was said to "weaken the blood" and "disturb continuity with the ancestors" (Fathauer 1951a:90). Marriage outside of the tribe that involved Mohave males and alien females exposed the former to foreign disease that was not inevitably debilitating or fatal (Devereux 1961:137). Nevertheless, this type of union appears to have been restricted to old males, who (being unafraid of the malignant influence because it developed slowly) received female war captives, since young and middle-aged Mohave males were reluctant to contract foreign disease by this means (Devereux 1961:129; Fathauer 1954:100, Stewart 1947a:271). Although the children of aged Mohave fathers and alien mothers possessed membership in Mohave clans, they inherited foreign disease from their mothers (Fathauer 1951a:90). The incidence of these marriages is unknown. Tribal exogamy between Mohave females and alien males exposed the women and her clanless offspring to foreign disease that was implied to have been debilitative or fatal. From 1859 to 1890 halfbreed children of this sort were usually buried at birth to conceal the evidence from the reservation authorities (Devereux 1961:139, 142, 143, 262, 519, 578; Fathauer 1951*a*:88). The implication is that this type of union was fairly common, perhaps more so than among the Quechans (cf. Bee 1963:224).

The common mode of reference to "real Mohave" children of clan-exogamous unions versus "not real Mohave" halfbreeds, who were unacceptable clanless offspring of Mohave females and alien males, expressed sentiments that articulated the language sphere with clan affiliation. This terminology of social separation probably helped to maintain the internal solidarity of the tribe (cf. Spicer 1971:799).

There is weak evidence for clan-affiliated participation in the Mohave political sphere during this phase. As among the Quechans, there seems to have been a prestige-ranking of clans that may have been related to hereditary political positions (cf. Bee 1963:218). Among the Fort Mohave faction, the hereditary great chieftainship is said to have been in possession of the Malika clan, while the Neolge supplied tribal orators, Oach and Gottah provided tribal singers, and so on (Sherer 1965:51). An all-male tribal council is implied to have been in existence on the Colorado River Reservation toward the end of this period (Devereux 1961:189), but whether participation in it was also structured by clan affiliation is unknown. This sphere clearly warrants more study before confident inference can be made.

There is some evidence that the statuses of warrior and shaman were articulated with the moral sphere of participation during this phase, particularly in terms of sentiments that pertained to dreaming and xenophobia. The constructive and destructive potential of both these social types was derived from power dreams (Devereux 1961:304; Fathauer 1951*a*:102; 1951*b*:274; Stewart 1947*a*:257). Not only was dream power requisite for the possession of either status (Fathauer 1954:99), but the variety of all available statuses was predetermined in Mohave cosmology; thus "in each generation certain individuals automatically occupied statuses that comprised the social system, but the system itself remained unchanged" (Fathauer 1951*b*:274). The allegedly high incidence of malevolent witchcraft coupled with the rarity of clan endogamy during this phase suggests that the latter was not the predominant source of inverted dream power necessary for shamanism. Two other possibilities are likely. One native theory ascribed shamanism to a child's dreams during its foetal stage. These dreams and the consequent power which they engendered were not remembered until its adolescence (Devereux 1961:60; Stewart 1973:317). During the maturation period, both parents observed the child's behavior to detect clues about his or her future status.

The effect of this parental monitoring process was thought to guide the child toward shamanism (Fathauer 1951a:274, Stewart 1973:316). A competitive native theory of shamanism held that individuals simply acquired certain dream powers which eventually deteriorated and turned against their owners, making them embark behaviorally and psychologically on a course which caused them to be murdered (Devereux 1961:56). In this view, individuals drifted toward shamanism by singing semi-shamanistic songs through which they became healers and eventually witches (Fathauer 1951c:605). The Mohave noted that a shaman often brought about his own death by inciting his victim's relatives to kill him. During the phase in question, these avenging relatives were usually members of the elite group of suicidal mallet-club warriors (Fathauer 1954:104; Stewart 1973:319). It should be recalled that these shaman-killers also tended to practice endogamous marriage and malevolent witchcraft.

The xenophobic sentiment expressed as enemy disease may have intensified between 1870 and 1890 among the warrior segment of the tribe. Combat, the source of enemy disease, was now forbidden to the Mohave until 1917, when they would enlist in the armed forces to serve in France during the First World War. In the absence of violent physical contact with aliens, the Mohave apparently became susceptible to enemy disease by merely dreaming about such encounters (Devereux 1961:43).

The funeral rite was strongly articulated with all three dimensions of participation in the moral sphere. With regard to dreaming, the Mohave believed that they could interact fearlessly with the ghosts of their deceased relatives until the funereal destruction of property, which occurred five days after death. After this day, ghost-dreaming became dangerous (Devereux 1961:139, 177, 186, 192, 452). The stereotype of postmortem behavior among the Mohave dead was (and is) directly related to the funereal destruction of property. The Mohave altered their image of the deceased from a previously beloved and generous relative to that of a dangerous and acquisitive ghost. The destruction of the material possessions of the dead was believed to satisfy the desire of the deceased to accumulate property, and it prevented the ghost from returning to claim what belonged to it (Devereux 1961:187–88, 445–46). The material possessiveness of the dead was regarded as aggression against the living, and the intense hostility felt toward the dead was manifest in this phase by the tendency to mourn an individual (including placement of his body on the funeral pyre) before death actually occurred (Devereux 1961:446, 452).

Failure to severe all relations with their dead exposed the living to any one of the three kinds of ghost disease that were potentially fatal manifestations of their xenophobia. Contamination resulted from the efforts of their deceased spouses or relatives to lure the living through dreams to the Mohave afterlife (Devereux 1961:21–22, 128, 137–39, 180–83, 440, 446).

These were, and continue to be, the basic elements and relationships that compose the Mohave identity system. Subtle but important adjustments occurred during the succeeding historical phases of incorporation that affected the efficiency of the maintenance process, however, and these warrant examination.

Fluctuations in the Intensity of Moral Sentiments, 1890 – 1930

The reservation system of incorporation may have altered Mohave moral participation in the marriage system of clan affiliation and the funeral rite. The intensity of sentiments about dream power through clan exogamy seems to have declined to the extent that the increasing incidence of clan endogamy among the Mohave was becoming known to other River Yuman tribes by the end of this phase. Simplification and eventual obsolescence of the destructive clan-endogamous wedding ceremony during the period may have progressively weakened the sanction against this type of marriage (Devereux 1961:322, 366, 370). Clan exogamy however, remained the predominant practice (Devereux 1961:411; Kroeber 1925:732). The intensity of xenophobic sentiments about the clanless halfbreed offspring of Mohave females and alien males began to decline; this tendency was reflected in isolated instances in which such children were informally permitted to use (but not adopt) their mother's Mohave clan name (Devereux 1961:131, 143). The fear of foreign disease from this course remained strong, and infanticide was "still an effective barrier to miscegenation, since as late as the 1920s, the reports of the commissioner of Indian Affairs listed fewer halfbreeds among the Mohave and the Yuma [Quechans] than among many other tribes" (Devereux 1961:135). The weakening of this sentiment in regard to clan affiliation may have originated around the turn of the century when the Mohave began to neutralize their fear of foreign disease by pretending that certain likeable whites and other aliens were "really . . . Mohave" (Devereux 1961:134). This practice however, does not seem to have been frequent.

The statuses of shaman and warrior continued to be articulated with the moral sphere in terms of xenophobic sentiments during the second phase. As carriers of foreign disease, those clanless halfbreed offspring who were spared from infanticide were still considered dangerous, and their adult status was usually restricted to the practice of shamanism (Fathauer 1951a:90). As for warriors, Mohave servicemen who returned to the reservations after the First World War were still considered to have been exposed to enemy disease (Devereux 1961:43).

The moral sphere of Mohave participation in the funeral ritual may have involved a stereotypic equivalence of aliens with the ghosts of their kinsmen in that the same kind of behavior was ascribed to each during this phase (Fathauer 1951c:607). For example, the Mohave viewed themselves as "warm" and "generous" to each other with native and white foods and money, although they did not represent themselves this way to Anglo-Americans, whom they viewed as "cold, unethical and grasping"; these violations of their value system were also attributed by the Mohave to their ghosts (Devereux 1961:179–81, 188, 312).

The intensification of property destruction at funerals during this phase may have been a symbol of Mohave opposition to incorporation, but it also has been linked by Devereux (1961:439, 446, 452) to a simultaneous decline in the incidence of suicide at funerals. Devereux thought that immolation of additional purchased property represented a "compensation to the dead for the mourner's failure to follow him into death." Since the Mohave believe that ghosts are sent to earth to obtain additional property when it is scarce in the "land of the dead" (Devereux 1961:442), it seems equally possible that intensification represented an attempt by the tribe to compensate for the previous scarcity of property available for immolation during the last decades of the preceding phase (1870–1890) when they were poverty-stricken.

In overview, the maintenance process in the moral sphere of participation in the Mohave identity system seems to have involved dynamic equilibrium. Although the symbolic aspects of clan affiliation probably played a lesser role in identity maintenance than before, this trend may have been offset by the intensification of the funeral rite.

Redefinition of Moral and Political Participation in the Mohave Identity System, 1930–1965

The Mohave increasingly committed themselves to the American cash economy during the third phase of their incorporation. Wage labor reduced the amount of leisure time that was previously available for participation in pantribal ceremonies, such as "Harvest" or "Memorial," which were important occasions for the ritual expression of their collective identity (Devereux 1939:529; 1961:317; Fathauer 1951a:134). These changes were accompanied by others of a less visible nature in the moral and political areas of common understanding among the Mohave. Pronounced fluctuations in the intensity of moral and political sentiments that were associated with clan affiliation and the statuses of warrior and shaman lead me to believe that the Mohave probably redefined two spheres of participation in their identity system during this third phase.

Sentiments about the acquisition of dream power that articulate the moral sphere with clan affiliation seem to have been altered. Kroeber reported in 1954 that the "dream core of Mohave culture" remained relatively intact despite "overwhelming acculturation pressures" (Devereux 1961:320). Apparently dream power did not fare as well among the Quechans under later, similar circumstances (Bee: personal communication). Also, Mohave clans appear to have continued their function as reservoirs of dream power that could be acquired or transmitted to offspring by means of marriage within the tribe (Devereux 1961:222). The Mohave were a highly homogeneous population as recently as 1950, and Fathauer (1951a:91) noted that individuals who were called "Mohave," and who were therefore unmixed with other groups, were approximately 95 percent fullblood. What seems to have changed are the kinship criteria that distinguished clan exogamy from endogamy. The traditional definition of clan exogamy given below was operative in 1939:

> Both father's and mother's kin are held to be blood relations, and sexual intercourse, including homosexual relations and sexual games among children, is prohibited between any ego and his ascendants, descendants, and cousins, including second cousins. Even if no blood relationship can be traced, a person should not have sexual relations with any other belonging to the same *gens* (Devereux, 1939:53).

Fathauer (1951a:130) could not confirm this practice by 1946, for some Mohave informants insisted that marriage of spouses having the same name was permissible, provided the relationship was more distant than third cousins on either side, a definition which approximates Quechan exogamy (Bee 1963:224). It would seem that clan affiliation was no longer a *jural* criterion of exogamy versus endogamy among the Mohave, but rather it simply became a *de facto* criterion that was likely to remain in effect due to the small size of the marriage pool.*

---

*For example, approximately 63 males and 76 females between the ages of 18 and 40 made up the active marriage pool of Mohave on the Colorado River Reservation circa 1945 (Fathauer 1951a:18). Every individual was affiliated with any one of perhaps twenty-two Mohave clans, a fact which implies that the number of potential marriage partners in each was small. For this reason, the likelihood of marrying a third or fourth patrilateral cousin who was also a member of the same clan seems low; that is, endogamous marriages were more likely to involve matrilateral cousins. The situation is less clear on the Fort Mohave Reservation during this phase. It is known that seven clans became extinct (with no replacement) between 1925 and 1961, leaving only two-thirds (15/22) of them to partition the marriage pool there (Sherer 1965 provides the list of clans). The effect of this diminishment upon a small, closed group of potential spouses would perhaps also bias endogamy toward the practice of marrying matrilateral cousins. My assumption may be untenable in both cases, because the tribal marriage pool on each reservation was not closed due to intermarriage between them. Frequent intermarriage might have offset these biases such that endogamy was equally likely to involve patrilateral relatives.

This alteration may have caused some confusion among the Mohave about how clan endogamy was to be defined, however, for "incestuous" marriage was rumored to have been frequent during the late 1930s on the Colorado River Reservation. Clan endogamy was not often recognized by the Mohave during this decade when it involved second cousins at least (Devereux 1961:136, 357, 509). The rise of clan endogamy can also be attributed to two other factors. After 1930 the groom's property was no longer destroyed at clan-endogamous weddings, a change which probably relaxed the sanction against this marriage practice (Devereux 1961:322). By 1946 most younger and more acculturated Mohave exhibited only partial understanding of their kinship system, and many middle-aged adults were unable to agree on kinship terminology. Moreover, some of the aged did not remember the nomenclature of distant kinship (Fathauer 1951a:127). The same trend was manifest among the Quechans during this phase (Bee 1963:216, 218).

Changes in the intensity and form of foreign-disease psychoses among the Mohave suggest that a relaxation of their xenophobic sentiments about tribal exogamy occurred during this time. Although marriage to non-Mohave continued to be discouraged as late as 1950 (Fathauer 1951a:87), tribal exogamy increased on the Colorado River Reservation during the 1930s and 1940s, while the incidence of foreign disease did not. This trend may reflect the receptiveness of the younger Mohave there to the newly arrived Chemehuevi in 1938 (Devereux 1961:136, 141, 355). It may also reflect the fact that tribal exogamy now also involved halfbreed Mohave who were believed to lessen the impact of foreign disease upon their fullblood spouses. This modification of sentiment was complemented by a continuation of the traditional belief that clan-affiliated halfbreed offspring of marriages between Mohave males and alien females exposed fullblood tribesmen to foreign disease that was not inevitably debilitating or fatal (Devereux 1961:131, 138). Diminished fear of foreign disease was especially evident in the successful effort of an internal reform movement to stop the infanticide of the clanless halfbreed offspring of Mohave females and alien males (Devereux 1948:136; 1961:131). While the Mohave began to deemphasize their susceptibility to foreign disease through physical contact with aliens, they may well have intensified their belief in contagion by merely dreaming about it (cf. Devereux 1961:137). This same dynamic balance also characterized the shifting intensity of enemy disease sentiment during the first phase of incorporation (1859–1890). The new dream emphasis on foreign disease may explain why it began to be manifested in association with the ghost disease: no longer did it appear as an isolated psychosis. By 1938 no Mohave shaman was known to have been able to cure foreign disease (Devereux 1961:128, 136, 141, 179; Fathauer 1951c:607).

There is some evidence that continuation of clan-affiliated member- ship in the tribal council on the Fort Mohave Reservation may have involved a redefinition of political participation around 1951. Specifically, women were now able to hold the hereditary offices of their clans (includ- ing the council chairmanship) if they were the sole surviving adults (Sherer 1965 provides examples). Women were also mentioned in an undefined but possibly similar political context on the Colorado River Reservation in 1933 (Devereux 1961:157).

The Mohave may have redefined a sentiment about dream power and also a stereotype that altered their moral sphere of participation in the statuses of shaman and warrior. The incidence of shamanism was alleged by the Mohave to have increased after 1945, and the status continued to be generally accepted through the 1950s (Devereux 1961:320). Yet in 1946 Fathauer (1951a:102) found that the average Mohave did not have power dreams of the sort necessary to become a shaman (or a warrior); instead, he dreamed of personal matters that were not tribal in scope. This discrep- ancy strongly suggests that traditional clan-based concepts of dream power were no longer relevant to the practice of witchcraft (cf. Devereux 1961:68, 287). In fact, Wallace (1947:256) observed that the accultura- tion of Mohave children in schools and hospitals interfered with their interest in shamanistic dreaming to such an extent that few members of the younger generation experienced power dreams of this sort by 1947. During these years, some of the shamans were likely to have been the clanless halfbreed offspring of Mohave mothers and alien fathers men- tioned earlier. This may account for McNichols's (1944:170) contempo- rary observation that Mohave mothers frequently conditioned the kinds of adolescent dreams that characterized future shamans through their own expectations and by reactions to their children's behavior. In other words, these shamans probably based their practice upon dreams of a personal sort. If shamanistic dream power was involved at all, it was likely to have been derived exclusively from matrilateral clan reservoirs and not from the traditional bilateral source.

The Mohave also redefined other moral sentiments that were asso- ciated with the status of warrior. During the previous phase (1890– 1930), the set of values about ideal behavior among Mohave males in- volved sentiments of warmth, generosity, strength, and silence. After 1930, however, males apparently began to view themselves as "sober," "stoical," and "stolid," qualities which they considered to be *military* virtues and which they ascribed to their nineteenth-century ancestors (Devereux 1961:299, 427, 514). Devereux (1961:299–300) has convinc- ingly argued that this new stereotype was absorbed by the Mohave from popular Western literature and film as an expression of their "antagonistic acculturation." He postulated that these newly constituted ideals were used by the Mohave not only to judge conformity among themselves, but also to successfully deceive whites into viewing the Mohave as unemotional after the tribesmen began to suppress the affective content of their communication with them. The new self-image was a symbol of Mohave opposition to incorporation.

Xenophobic sentiments associated with the status of warrior seem to have been relaxed insofar as no Mohave shaman was known to be able to cure enemy disease, even though tribesmen returning to the Colorado River Reservation from the Second World War were considered to have been exposed to it. This psychosis was treated in the reservation hospital or cured by a Quechan shaman (Devereux 1961:43).

The xenophobic sentiments of ghost disease that structured part of the moral sphere of Mohave participation in their funeral rites were similarly relaxed. As was the case with foreign and enemy diseases, no shaman was able to cure any of the ghost psychoses by 1938; victims had recourse to the reservation hospital alone (Devereux 1961:136, 142).

In sum, the dream-oriented framework of tribal identity persisted into the third historical phase, but the critical maintenance mechanism of dream power seems to have been activated less frequently. This is inferred from a decline in the practice of clan exogamy, which had programmatically enhanced the acquisition of dream power. Sentiments that promoted this pattern of marriage and discouraged the other forms were probably relaxed as the result of acculturation, as were Mohave sentiments against interethnic relationships. Although they remained susceptible to all of their xenophobic psychoses, the Mohave were no longer able to cure these themselves; instead they relied upon Anglo-American medical services or those of a Quechan shaman.

The clan-affiliated structure of political participation is known to have persisted on one Mohave reservation through redefinition of membership in its tribal council. Mohave belief in shamanism may also have persisted through redefinition of membership among practitioners of witchcraft. Finally, Mohave males altered their self-image to oppose further incorporation efforts. The persistence of this moral aspect of Mohave identity also involved a redefinition of membership because military ideals were applied to the behavior of all tribesmen, and not only to those who thought of themselves as warriors.

STRATEGIES FOR PERSISTENCE OF IDENTITY

The historical continuity of tribal identity among the Mohave is reasonably well-documented, and for this reason reflection upon it may yield insight into a typology of persistent cultural systems. I suggest that the Mohave possess a type of identity persistence that has diagnostic features. These are simply described below; no attempt has been made to compare or contrast them with criterial aspects of other types of identity persistence.

There are two outstanding external characteristics of the Mohave identity system. After their military defeat, the Mohave chose to resist initial American attempts at forced partial incorporation by exaggerating traditional behaviors associated with certain collective identity symbols instead of initiating a revitalization movement. According to Spicer's (1971:799) model, nativistic movements restore the political sphere of participation (in an identity system) which has disintegrated as the result of military defeat or repressive incorporation. Prior to such revitalization, however, Spicer believes that collective identity may persist through compensatory participation in the moral or language spheres. Intensification seems to be an alternative to revitalization when the moral sphere consists of values that are antithetical to the concepts of ancestral restoration found in revitalization movements. Intensification movements deserve more study (cf. Vogt 1961:326).

The second external characteristic of Mohave identity is the compartmental display and manipulation of the tribe's most important symbol of its collective identity — clan affiliation and naming. These practices were retained in opposition to the comprehensive program of forced, directed change that was instituted on both Mohave reservations during the second phase of their incorporation. The tribe's strategy of identity persistence has certain elements in common with the compartmentalization of collective identity symbols in the Eastern Pueblos (cf. Dozier 1961:175–78; Spicer 1961*b*:532–33).

The Mohave identity system also has several internal characteristics that may be diagnostic of its type. For the most part, Mohave collective identity symbols are not ritually or liturgically displayed. The least visible of these symbols — clan affiliation and naming — masked the institutional means of social relations (specifically marriage) by which the Mohave maintained participation in their system of meanings. Spicer (1971:799) noted that the institutional mechanism is a poorly known component of identity systems; I suggest that this is so because it is part of a collective identity symbol that is deeply embedded in one or more areas of common understanding. In the case of the Mohave, the relationship between marriage patterns and clan affiliation becomes clear only when the moral sentiments of dreaming and xenophobia are elucidated. It is possible that persistent identity systems of the Mohave type depend on biological continuity more than is realized; if this is so, then it would seem to be a critical weakness of the maintenance process. Tribal exogamy was no less responsible for the erosion of Mohave identity than the incorporation efforts of the reservation authorities.

Xenophobia may also be an integral aspect of moral participation in this type of persistent cultural system. Among the Mohave this mechanism remained unchanged longer than any other because of self-stabilizing fluctuations of dynamic equilibrium in the intensity of its various sentiments. That this insularity mechanism was the only focus of deliberate internal reform among the Mohave may be symptomatic of informal but extensive adjustments in other areas of this type of persistent cultural system. It is possible that super-stable mechanisms of this sort are likely to become dysfunctional; Mohave xenophobia, for example, ultimately increased the dependency of the tribe on the medical services of the incorporative group.

Certain facets of identity maintenance among the Mohave probably characterize other types of persistent cultural systems as well. For example, the two nuclear Mohave statuses of warrior and shaman were shown to have complementary and interdependent functions. From a systemic perspective, it seems inevitable that redefinition of membership in one would lead to a similar alteration of the other. Other examples of Mohave resistance to incorporation in the language and moral spheres of participation in their identity system might characterize other types. For example, when the Mohave adopted the language modes of reference that Anglo-Americans used to distinguish themselves from other groups, the tribe encoded these terms with ethnic stereotypes in their moral sphere that were not readily decipherable to whites unless they were already familiar with moral aspects of common understanding among the Mohave.

Certain aspects of Mohave stereotypy might also characterize other persistent identity systems. Especially noteworthy is the fact that the Mohave stereotype of the incorporating group differed according to the identity system context in which they projected it. In the linguistic context of common understanding, Anglo-Americans were implicitly identified as sources of disease. By contrast, the material acquisitiveness of Anglo-Americans was equated by the Mohave with the behavior of their deceased relatives in the context of the funeral ceremony. Finally, the Mohave seized upon a white stereotype of themselves when it could be used to maintain their psychological insularity. The dominant group had successfully altered technological, linguistic, and political aspects of Mohave life, but it had not yet deciphered Mohave personality. The tribe used this means to prevent it from doing so, and I suspect that this strategy is also to be found in other persistent identity systems.

| 4 |

Blacks in the United States

The Creation of an Enduring People?

Vera M. Green

Blacks in the United States, unlike subcultural groups formed by occupational similarity or an initial sense of "peoplehood," have developed a sense of collective identity because of the persistence of racism in the dominant society. The black ethnic group is made up of cultural, racial, occupational, and ideological "shreds and patches," although admittedly some shreds and patches are larger than others. However, there is a tendency to consider blacks as an ethnic group much the same as the Irish or the Greeks. Africa is referred to and often considered as a single national or cultural entity such as Holland, with about the same level of pre-World War II diversity. Scholars and laymen, black and white, often lament the fact that the same level of internal organization and cooperation does not exist among blacks as exists among other immigrant populations. Ignoring the possibility of noncooperation among Swedes, the English, or Italians, for example, this negative viewpoint equates the supposed lack of cooperation among blacks with a lack of unity. Cruse, for instance, referred to American blacks as members of a "detached ethnic bloc of people of African descent reared for three hundred years in the unmotherly bosom of Western civilization" (1968:49); "Afro-Americans produced a culture that is distinctly our own and, for the most part, American in general milieu" (Cruse 1968:52). It is within this context that he lamented what he considered the intellectual and cultural impasse found in the black community (1968:57). In addition, he found that "many rank and file Negroes have recently remarked ... that the Negro is a 'lost race' ... that the Negro has no unity" (1968:59). The latter view has also been reported by Muraskin (1975).

Attacking Cruse, Redding argued that the American Negro people are not a *people* in Cruse's sense of the word: "what has never been born cannot have a rebirth" (Redding in Cruse 1968:22). In a sense, both are correct. Cruse, however, was more concerned with what should be happening, what must necessarily happen. Cruse was a visionary crying in the wilderness, for it was during the events of the late 1960s and early 1970s that the various elements in the United States black population united for the type of fundamental action which he advocated.

The concept of *ethnic group* means a people considered distinct by external as well as by internal consensus (Barth 1969; Shibutani and Kwan 1965). The concept of *subculture* involves varying degrees of cultural and/or structural distinctiveness which are sufficiently noticeable to both outsiders and members of the group to warrant differentiation on an emic, or internally perceived, level.

Studies of cultural persistence generally deal with matters of cultural and historic continuity in whole societies or in parts of once viable nationalities or self-contained, sociocultural entities presently occupying subordinate positions within larger nation-states. Groups in this position belong " ... to the type we may call enduring people, who develop a persistent cultural system. As in the case of the Yaqui Indians, their continuity may not depend on genetic purity, or in the continuous possession of a homeland, in the maintenance of a particular language, or even in a whole way of life ... " (Spicer 1976:5). Spicer indicated that the crucial factor is the existence of a "coherent sense of collective identity," which is based on common cognitive and affective aspects of meaning (1976:6).

Who are the "American" blacks? What role has persistence played in their current status as either an ethnic or subcultural group or an enduring people? Herskovits (1966) heads the list of anthropologists who have stressed African cultural persistence among blacks in the United States. These themes have been revived, and one finds writers such as Shimkin, Louie, and Frate suggesting African historical connections for certain rural sections of Mississippi (1978:133). In a discussion of the sociology of the black American, Lyman (1972:182) exhorted sociologists studying blacks in America to " ... keep in mind the irregularities of situations, the chance and spontaneous elements in response," and, " ... in addition, the obdurate and recalcitrant nature of the world against which blacks move is of crucial importance. Rather than a unilinear march along a single track, black life in America might be likened to water poured on porous cement. Although the material appears impregnable, the different drops and streams find their own way through the interstices which are not apparent to the casual observer." In contrast to the regularity, order, and continuity of theory, discontinuity, "persistence punctuated by eruption, irregularities and lack of uniformity" are relevant in actual life (Lyman 1972:181). Reactions to the continuing crises which were inevitable under the circumstances, according to Lyman, resulted in "agonizing reappraisals of individual and group identity" (1972:181; Cruse 1968; Comer 1972).

It is my contention that the basis for separate ethnic or subcultural status of blacks lies in the persistence of the attitudes and the activities of the larger society as alluded to in Lyman's remark — that is, racism — not in genetic, linguistic, or national-cultural (i.e., Congo or Yoruba) purity. In the words of Comer: "Facing extreme racism with too much group division and too little power, blacks had a long row to hoe" (1972:187). In 1972 Comer announced: "A 'black people' is being born. Only now is the black community becoming an ethnic group comparable to the others in America" (1972:192). What are the strains which make up the black ethnic group? Why do authors like Comer and myself speak of blacks as an incipient ethnic group?

While recognizing the variations between the sections of Africa from which the majority of the American slaves arrived, Comer appears to have followed the general reasoning of authors (such as Herskovits) who see the broad similarities outweighing differences among members of various African ethnic groups. He has focused upon the contrasts between slaves and freedmen, house slaves and field slaves, slaves of the rich and slaves of the poor, and racially mixed and racially pure slaves (1972:186). Nevertheless, regardless of the grand level similarities, daily life revolves around the relatively small differences such as language use and meaning, relations to patrilateral in contrast to matrilateral kin, and food taboos. If the Africans were simply one great homogenous mass, why were tribal differences carefully noted and utilized by slave owners as well as purchasers? In certain areas, members of different African ethnic groups were sought to fulfill different occupational slots and were found desirable or not desirable because of different ethnic traits. At one time, for example, Ibos were banned from Louisiana and South Carolina due to their "suicidal proclivity" (Phillips 1928:44). Although the breeding of slaves was an important factor in the United States, research into the ethnicity of slaves prior to the development of slave breeding may aid our understanding of the unity, or lack of unity, among slaves, particularly those on large plantations. In any event, if Herskovits (1958) and Foster (1960) are correct in stating that the first groups to arrive were pivotal in the establishment of subsequent cultural patterns, the internal slave culture that resulted in different parts of the country would have reflected the variable African as well as European traits described by Arensberg (1955) and others. However, even if all the Africans were considered a homogenous mass, the subsequent interaction with different types of Europeans in different ecological zones from one hundred to three hundred years would necessarily result in some sharp distinctions.

In 1860, 4,441,830 Negroes were listed in the United States census, and of these 488,070 were free. While it was recognized that the free population was under severe restrictions, this did not mean that they were all in identical circumstances. Approximately one half of the free population was residing in the south. Let us simply consider the demographic aspects of the free blacks in a few southern states.

In 1840 in Mississippi there were 1,366 free blacks (DeCell and Prichard 1976). By 1860 the total free Negro population of Mississippi had dropped to 773 or 775, of which approximately 77 were slave holders, compared to 17 in 1830 (Wallace 1927:8; Wharton 1947). The free black population in Louisiana totalled 18,647, of which 212 from rural areas and 753 from cities were slave owners (Sterkx 1972). In Mississippi 25 blacks owned 20 to 75 slaves, and 50 blacks owned 10 or more slaves. In Louisiana 25 blacks owned more than 10 slaves, and 112 blacks owned 5 to 10 slaves. The combined free population of the Louisiana cities of Baton Rouge (468) and Algiers (250) almost equaled the total free population of Mississippi. Nevertheless, in Maryland in 1860 only one county had fewer than 1,000 free blacks. The free black population of that one county, Allegany, was more than half of the free population of the state of Mississippi (467). The total figures for the state of Maryland were 83,942 free black persons and 87,189 slaves (Brackett 1889:265). (Brown, however, 1972, reported the Maryland free total as 86,942.) In Delaware there were 19,829 free blacks and 1,798 slaves. The Virginia totals were 58,042 free and 490,865 slave; while in North Carolina 20,463 were free compared to 331,059 enslaved in 1860 (Brown 1972). Free Negroes in Baltimore totaled 25,680 compared to 2,218 slaves; in St. Louis 1,755 were free compared to 1,542 enslaved, while 11,131 free blacks resided in Washington, D. C., compared to 3,185 slaves. Texas and Mississippi were two of the few states with a decrease in free population. In Texas, for example, the number of free blacks declined from 397 in 1850 to 355 in

1860 (Barr 1973). The sheer weight of demographic facts indicates not only the possibilities of sharp differences between slave and free populations but also a basis for differentiation between communities in terms of structure and activities.

Within the slave population there was considerable variation. A variety of occupations was present, including laborers, domestics, and artisans, as well as professionals. Sometimes slaves were completely dominated by overseers, while in other instances they hired themselves out and paid their masters (Wade 1964). In a study of Yazoo County, Mississippi, variations of hiring out were reported. Certain masters received the wages directly, but in other instances slaves who were hired out were "permitted to keep some of their wages" (DeCell and Prichard 1976:114). In the area of Satartia, Mississippi, in 1850 slaves " . . . had small corn and vegetable crops of their own. They could go to town with a 'pass' on Saturday and sell any produce that they wished from this garden." The Negroes also sold wood to steamboats and kept the money for themselves. However, others residing in different counties did not necessarily have these opportunities, and thus a basis was laid for differentiation in exposure, experience, and even values (DeCell and Prichard 1976: Chap. 20).

In addition to geographical differences, such as those among blacks from the midwest, New England, "down east," and the border south, there were cultural variations. Some of those in sections of Illinois, Missouri (Harris 1904), and Louisiana (Sterkx 1972; Rousseve 1937) were culturally French. In addition, there were blacks in parts of the northeast (such as Massachusetts), sections of the south, and the southwest where traditionally there were close Indian connections. Many forget that in these areas there were both slaves and freemen associated with the Indian populations. Finally there were those, though few in number, who traditionally resided along the Mexican border where the Spanish influence was decisive (Green 1978:379).

In the case of free northern blacks, there were naturally numbers of persons of African descent left to their own devices. Consequently, they were responsible for their own schools and churches, as well as for their livelihoods. In Ohio there were 25,279 free blacks in 1850, 3,237 of whom resided in Cincinnati. Despite several riots and stringent black laws, by 1844 the Cincinnati community had "six schools of their own and before the war two well-supported public schools," and an orphan asylum (Woodson in Dabney 1926:45).

In Rhode Island, where as early as 1799 a masonic lodge was opened by the black community, an academy was established in 1836 which reportedly decreased illiteracy among the Negroes of Providence by 50 percent by 1840 (Bartlett 1954:38). There was also a mutual relief society and a social club for young men. In 1838 two-thirds of the black residents of Providence owned their own homes (Bartlett 1954:38). By 1910 approximately 40 percent of the black residents of Providence were employed as teamsters, laborers, janitors, servants, or delivery men (Bartlett 1954).

In one of the comparatively few studies of an all-black town, it was shown that all the institutions in Lawrence, Oklahoma, had been manned by blacks since the founding of the town in 1891. Whites who sought to settle there were denied permission during the early periods (Hill and Ackiss 1943:6). In the early 1940s, at the time the research was undertaken, the economy of the town was on the decline. Of the 100 families still residing there, 36 percent were unemployed or supporting themselves by odd jobs or seasonal labor such as picking cotton. Nevertheless, the community continued to enforce its own standards by socially isolating "those who don't do well," that is, those who·break the norms (1943:34). "So strong in fact has been the family sentiment that common law marriage has never been approved, and has been the exception rather than the rule" (Hill and Ackiss 1943:20). These attitudes appeared to have little to do with either the proverbial middle-class values or the economic situation but were, as Blake indicated for Jamaica, a function of local custom (1955). In Lawrence as in Boley, Oklahoma, another all-black town, a form of egalitarianism existed in the sense that the "leaders are as democratic in their attitudes towards the masses as they are toward one another" (Hill and Ackiss 1943:33). The authors indicated that neither education nor light complexions were the criteria for upper-class status and that, in effect, the "color question was simply non-existent" (1943:32). The attitude toward color and the enforcement of the local norms towards marriage and illegitimacy are in contrast to the situation reported for communities in other areas during the same time period.

Slaves in some states even paid taxes (Brown 1972:139). Some performed as concert artists for their masters (Southall 1969). Some spoke English, others French. At the time of emancipation at least 488,070 blacks were already free, and of these an estimated 6,230 (Hoetink 1967:27) were themselves slave owners. At the turn of the twentieth century there were black miners, cowboys, fishermen, doctors (two were even listed in the 1860 census for Louisiana), ranchers, planters, small yeoman farmers (Woofter 1930; Sterkx 1972), as well as tenant farmers, sharecroppers, and service workers.

The information presented above offers an idea of some of the types of differential cultural/ecological exposures which black groups in different areas of the country underwent in the past. It should serve to facilitate our understanding of the complexities of black communities in the United States if we realize that, given this type of variation in early experiences and lifestyles, it is difficult to expect any necessarily high degree of generally shared experience around which to build core values and expectations. These variable experiences and, more importantly, the isolation resulting in *the lack of awareness* of the total range of variability meant that without a catalyst a sense of peoplehood would necessarily be slow to develop. The catalyst was present in the racial attitudes of the majority community from the mid-1600s on, and it became even stronger from the 1830s through the 1950s. The net of segregation became consistently tighter even before emancipation. Segregation of churches, the means of travel and, more importantly, restrictions of occupations which blacks formerly held, such as craftsmen and artisans, occurred. All those with identifiable black ancestry were increasingly affected — the French as well as the English speaker, the standard as well as the vernacular speaker, the educated as well as the illiterate. Discrimination and segregation, like taxes, became a progressively greater burden. Persons of black-Indian or black European extraction, who did not wish to "pass" for white, and blacks from Maine to Mississippi in part began to share more of the same experiences. Riots occurred systematically during the 1900s in northern cities along with the use of lynchings in both southern and northern areas as a technique for intimidation and control. In addition, less violent means were constantly in operation. For example, in the 1800s free blacks in urban Rhode Island were harassed each Sunday going to and from church as part of the weekly amusement of the white locals. In Kentucky in 1834 the presence of sizeable numbers of free blacks in the counties — 600 in one — led to a recommendation to disenfranchise free Negroes (Patterson 1922:167).

The pressures from racism, segregation, and discrimination were therefore felt horizontally on three levels: geographically — throughout the United States; structurally — that is, across educational and income brackets; and phenotypically — across color boundaries; as well as vertically through time and cross-culturally, that is, across group lines such as the French-speaking blacks of Louisiana as well as the English, and the "Indian-connected" located in areas such as Oklahoma (Willis 1970:47).

The period of the late 1950s and 1960s has served to crystallize the unification process. Comer reported that "most blacks no longer want to escape their blackness" (1972:192). Many of those formerly doting on their white and Indian ancestry have now turned full circle to ignore obvious Indian and European connections. In any event, it cannot be doubted that blacks as a whole are beginning to consider themselves as a unit. Consequently, rather than engaging in criticism or allowing criticism from others for "not sticking together in the past," blacks must consider it an accomplishment that individuals who were isolated from their cultural origins and who suffered severe oppression were able to function together in the past as well as history indicates. This statement must not be regarded as a variant or a substantiation of the helpless-victim theory criticized by authors such as Harding (1976). For, as Harding suggests, total concentration on what was "done to" blacks or blacks as "recipients," with little effort to see how blacks were able to respond creatively and constructively within the existing limits, is simply another aspect of prejudice.

What does this approach mean in terms of an ethnic, subcultural, or enduring group identity? Given the definition of ethnic group outlined above, the simple recognition "by selves and others" is sufficient to fulfill the requirements of being an ethnic group. The issue of subculture, involving structural or cultural similarities and differences, is more complex. Historically, most black and white natives of the same locality, who occupied similar economic positions, were similar culturally but were treated separately in terms of structure (Gordon 1964). The type and degree of structural separation also differed in various sectors of the country. In some eastern areas there has been less legal or "public" segregation since the 1800s, but there has been a continuation of private segregation. If we look synchronically at one period — for example, 1945–1960 — we see that black groups in the same locality, especially in inner-city ghettos, differed from each other culturally and perhaps even structurally due to factors such as migration (Green 1978; Rose 1971). Such differences are naturally found on the national level as a result of the existence of black subcultures based on fundamental cultural variation (such as French-speaking or Indian-connected blacks), and subcultures less distinct from one another, which come about within basically similar populations due to interactions between distinct environmental and historical factors. For example, black informants in Houston distinguished between East and West Texas blacks, claiming that the former were more often group-oriented, farming types, while the latter were more individually oriented, "cowboy" or ranching types. Association patterns were primarily within each section rather than between sections. Church membership in Houston reflected this tendency, as most congregations consisted of either East or West Texans but not a conglomerate of both (Green 1970). Finally, there are subcultures which in a sense develop as a result of structural separations. The older black communities in the midwest or the colonial northeast, where, culturally, blacks were virtually indistinguishable from the whites of the localities but suffered varying degrees of structural separation, are in this category.

Subcultures originating from populations without much cultural variation may occur locally or regionally and thus may be envisioned as horizontal, while those with deep cultural differences can be seen as vertical. For example, within the category of French-speaking blacks, the existence of both Cajun as well as Creole French speakers suggests that within the broader vertical framework there is a horizontal continuum which allows for at least two divisions.

The existence of these cultural subdivisions, rarely discussed in the literature, in addition to basic definitional difficulties perhaps explains why there are a myriad of articles presenting potentially conflicting statements as to whether there are subcultures in black communities.

Are blacks an enduring people? I believe that the one universal all blacks share is a collective sense of identity based on historical factors of a generalized African ancestry, bondage (if not actual enslavement), and public and private harassment. While all three factors are translated into integrative symbols of identity, the latter is the most crucial. Other identity symbols may change through time or differ locally or situationally, but the meaning remains the same. For example, in the past, terms such as Hokaway and Ofay were used to refer to blacks and whites, respectively, in sectors of black communities in Chicago during the 1940s. However, even these terms were not universally understood and used in these localities during the same time period.

In the process of building the black identity systems, the consistency of the reactions to racial and color antagonism by whites served as a means of integrating those of varying degrees of African descent albeit in different ways. Therefore, not all are attached in the same fashion.

Although blacks in the United States may resemble the Yaquis in the area of racial and cultural diversity (Spicer 1976), they appear more like the Catalans in the limited number of symbols (Spicer 1971) which structure their collective identity. Blacks differ from both the Yaquis and the Catalans in the sense that there is no cultural persistence resulting from a former state of peoplehood. All blacks are not descendents of Yorubas or Ashantis or any other single ethnic or tribal entity. Spicer stated that "the continuity of a people consists in the growth and development of a picture of themselves which arises out of their unique historical experience ... It is an ideal image ... The system of symbols with their meanings becomes a vehicle for the cumulation of experience as each people of this sort has known and felt that experience" (1976:11).

There is, however, the continuity discussed above, not in terms of pre-mystical or mystical experience, but in terms of the actual experience of blacks in the United States. Consequently, it seems that an enduring people has been created. In short, it appears that racism and the trinity of prejudice, discrimination, and segregation, by their persistence, have in essence given birth to the black ethnic group in the United States.

| 5 |

Mormon "Peculiarity"

Recapitulation of Subordination

Mark P. Leone

The Mormons are a group with a strong sense of enclavement and a persistent identity maintained by forceful opposition to the world around them. Mormons have been and remain easily identified by all other Americans. During the nineteenth century when they were cast as pariahs who insisted on polygyny, called plural marriage, they created a church-run territorial government, which was called an organized rebellion by the United States Supreme Court. They were vilified publicly for decades; their church was disestablished; they were denied the vote for a while; carpetbag government was imposed on Utah Territory; and they and their land were occupied much as the South was after the Civil War (Arrington 1958). When this reservation of sorts was created in Utah, it was easy for Mormons to create a heritage of persecution, resistance, and persist-ence. With their heritage of opposition and persecution Mormons in the 1980s see themselves, and are seen in turn, as a people with a separate culture. Such a list of events makes it easy to epitomize Mormons as a persistent people.

A persistent people, which survives while pressured to assimilate, must possess "well-defined symbols of identity differentiating it from other peoples" (Spicer 1971:797). Such groups exist within nations where the members of the pressured group experience the interactions of daily life in a way that places them in opposition to the mainstream. Such interaction keeps a people separate and solid, and in this way enclaves persist.

There are two parts to Spicer's process of enclavement and persistence which can be specified to expand his model. Spicer writes: "What becomes meaningful [to the persistent group] is probably a function of the oppositional process. Where the pressures are focused in the cultural repertoire of the people, there the symbols and their meanings are brought into the identity system, and these pressures change as the interests of dominant peoples change" (1971:798). Thus the dominant group can control some of the identity of the subordinate group, and, as the interests of the dominant group change, so will the identity of the subordinate group. The dynamic which forms the identity of a persistent people is composed of (1) the changing pressures brought by those dominating through (2) the interactions of daily life on (3) the symbols composing the identity of the dominated. Identity formation is a continual process and is controlled not mainly by those wearing labels but by those imposing them.

Mormons in the Southwestern United States can be distinguished on economic grounds from Mormons in the rest of the country as well as from those abroad. When their forebears left Illinois and entered the basin of the Great Salt Lake in 1847, they and their church were a group and a religion but not a culture. They maintained some practices which made them like many other American utopian movements (Kanter 1972), but, once in the Great Basin, Mormons became a people and a nation, and, in fact, between 1847 and 1890 they were nearly an autonomous kingdom. In Utah Territory the Mormons lived alone more or less independently for forty years, and in that context a culture developed. Mormons shaped every aspect of their everyday life; they invented a way of life and did so because isolation allowed it and demanded it.

Beginning in the 1880s the federal government suppressed the economic and political arms of Mormondom, turning the kingdom into a church. The process was well underway when Utah became a state in 1896 but was not complete until the Great Depression, when the economic power of the church was so reduced that it could not keep Utah from being, after Oklahoma, the most economically devastated state in the union. Personal income fell from $270 million in 1929 to $143 million in 1932. Thirty-six percent of the work force was unemployed in 1932: Utah was no longer a self-sufficient entity but a broken, dependent satellite (Arrington 1961:17).

In terms of daily life, within the rural Southwest as a whole, Mormons became and remain a subordinate minority, an exploited class, an internal colony (Leone 1974, 1979). They may appear to be members of a wealthy, powerful, fast-growing church, but they are actually an owned and controlled group, like every other persistent people around the world. Some Mormons, like the Marriotts, Romneys, Jack Anderson, and Ezra Taft Benson, have become wealthy or powerful, and individual Mormons and church institutions play an important role in Utah, Idaho, Nevada, and Arizona. Although Mormons are believed by other Americans to be prosperous middle-class citizens and are indeed well-to-do compared with some other groups in the Southwest, they are not truly part of the American middle class.

The last hundred years of Utah's history, as some historians and others involved see it, has been a time of exploitation by the dominant society: they believe that through the late twentieth century Utah has been controlled by railroad, mining, and other large companies, and the federal government (acting through the departments of agriculture, interior, and defense). Together, these own or control land and its rights, water and its rights and the machinery for managing them, minerals, forests, and the scenic resources, that is, the tourist industry. The resources of the state are no longer controlled by the church or by individual Mormons. Because Utah has several Indian reservations, one should not miss the similarity between who controls them and who controls Utah: the federal government and large corporations. Such economic subordination for Mormons in Utah and the rest of the Southwest was consciously created by the federal government, acting just as it did when it intentionally created Indian reservations. While Indians were and to some degree remain wards, who in their "childlike state" were "unproductive" because they had yet to grow to "adulthood" and "productive" status, such a characterization was also true for Mormons, who were not seen as children but as pariahs, a structurally similar status. In the Southwest both Mormons and Indians have more in common with each other in economic matters than either has with the surrounding nation; neither group owns its means of earning a living, and both have had their former means forcefully taken away and knowingly kept away.

Knowledge of the conditions of everyday life among persistent peoples, including how they make a living, what happens to the fruits of their labor, and who owns their land, machines, crops, and cattle, is an important key to understanding their nature. Ownership and control of productive capacity in turn has a bearing on local politics, the school system, the communication system, the courts, and so on. The groups Spicer himself worked with and used to illustrate his idea are so well described that anthropologists tend to think that analyses of the conditions of everyday life among the Yaquis or Navajos would be superfluous. They are not. Tracing ownership, control, markets, and sources of supply show an enclave's ties to the world beyond, ties which, it is quickly seen, are not under the enclave's control. Jorgensen (1972) drew all these links carefully in *The Sun Dance Religion* and established as fact the colonized, exploited condition of everyday life among the Utes in Utah. Bennett did the same in *Northern Plainsmen* (1969), describing the ties between the Plains Indians of west-central Canada, Hutterites, Anglo ranchers, and farmers. Reference to the conditions of everyday life is an essential prelude to examining how a persistent group sees itself and its relations to the dominant group.

Once the possibility for a common classification of Southwestern Indians and Mormons on economic grounds is seen, it is much easier to examine how Spicer's notion of opposition operates, because it is the ground for the dynamic interaction between the dominant and subordinate groups. Among Indians there is the Hopi "way," Navajo "indifference," Apache "rejection," Yaqui "evanescence," or a dozen other characteristics which people use to keep themselves different. Mormons call themselves "peculiar." Indians and Mormons insist that they are not the national culture but are separate. All negate parts of American society and go out of their way to refuse some of it. Each has habits of avoidance, unique rituals, celebrations of special lore, and secret knowledge. Each carefully husbands its own history, sometimes even forbidding outsiders access to its documents, members, and important localities. These restrictions are understood by the persistent group and often by anthropologists to be ways of maintaining the integrity of the group's history, the image of its present imposed on its past. Such habits are seen as preserving the group's integrity by maintaining its differences, including the history of its opposition to the dominant group.

Mormons say they stand in "opposition in all things." Opposition expressed this way has two qualities. First, it is so constructed as to face the emotions arising from subordination and the impossibility of escaping from it. Second, such opposition actually duplicates and reproduces the subordinating conditions. This is the stance of a group in which symbolic opposition precludes violent conflict or war. Once, of course, all persistent peoples were at war with their respective dominating powers, but, when that became impossible, some other form of opposition took its place. This form may be called symbolic opposition and is more complex than war because it seeks to resolve the conflicts created by subordination but must do so without hope of actual liberation. In the expression of the first quality, opposition invites believers to witness, face-to-face, the worst and most humiliating facts and feelings of being a powerless people. This is normally done in the context of religious ritual. The catharsis accompanying an emotional encounter with the worst parts of daily life alleviates the emotional conflicts stemming from the contrast between hopes and everyday conditions. This concept is the basis for Jorgensen's analysis of the Sun Dance among the Utes. Gager (1975) and Leone (1977) use an analysis based on Levi-Strauss (1963) to describe how participation in ritual drama relieves the emotional conflicts arising from having to endure inescapable persecution.

The second and more complex part of symbolic opposition has the unintended effect of perpetuating subordination. Such opposition involves the celebration of the persistent group's integrity. Integrity is often composed of a separate, noble, and different past, a past when the group was free, a state hoped for in the future and actively detailed as a millennial setting free of the evils of the surrounding society. With these visions the group is different, opposed, and free.

Spicer has described separate groups who have kept some sense of wholeness despite severe intrusions, and he sees them as persistent. But such opposition is not mere differentiation; it has two aspects to it which perpetuate domination. The first is that integrity achieved through opposition is an image, and like all images it is structured, and like all structures it contains principles its believers are unaware of (Bloch 1977). Recitations of integrity should be seen as myth, as a product of the here and now, and, like all myth, as fixing the believer more firmly in the place he may prefer to stand above. Statements of integrity, like telling of history, contain material about subordination and domination, captivity and freedom, passivity and action, exploitation and exploiting. Such structuring of the story of integrity is drawn from the present and thus reproduces present reality; it does not free people from it.

The celebrations of integrity involving heroes, history, parades, and pilgrimages all have some facts in them which refer to how present subordination came to be or how it may be overcome in the future. However, such celebrations, regardless of the factual truth of the historical material they relate, do occur in the present and inevitably model both present social structure and present ideology. Use of material from the past inevitably molds it to needs from the present, imposes projections on it, and makes it relevant where it might not have been. The material is thus structured to reflect the relationship between the group and its adversaries. Beyond the replication of social structure, such celebrations involve ideology, in the sense of categories of thought people are not usually aware of. A celebration of integrity in the service of opposition involves implicit ideas of cause, the unempirical, time, objectivity, self, and relation of parts to the whole, all of which will stem, not from the past time of freedom, but from the present and probably from the dominant culture. These ideas, when imposed on materials from the aboriginal past or from a time of freedom, automatically rob those materials of any wholeness they may have had. In the projection of these ideas onto another time and place, they are made to seem objectively valid because the projection is not usually noticeable, and they are thus reabsorbed by the watchers and/or listeners. With reabsorption the persistent group recapitulates the very circumstances it is trying to avoid.

The second characteristic about the celebration of symbols of opposition is that as the interests of the dominant people changes, so does the identity of the subordinate group. The dominant group has an active role in changing the subordinate group's identity. Persistent peoples consciously value their differences from surrounding society, but, for Mormons at least, the symbols of identity which are meant to differentiate are really a single symbol of differentiation, empty of content. It is easy to demonstrate for Mormons that the items of difference within the symbol of differentiation change. The question is: where does the content of differentiation come from? It comes from the surrounding society, whose major trait in relation to the dominated is exploitation. Since the vast majority of persistent groups persist against industrial capitalism, persistence is not only against exploitation but also against the rapid change that characterizes capitalism itself. So, the dominant society changes continually, although the act of domination itself does not. Since specific cases of domination will change, opposition or differentiation must also change if opposition is to be effective. Thus, opposition is not the means to integrity but a means for promoting continual change.

Standing in opposition today means standing ready to change as fast as the surroundings. If Mormons fixed on a series of unchangeable items as their identity, these would become meaningless if they were not continually reflected against the dominating group. Since that group is changing, the meaning of "peculiarity" for Mormons changes too; if it did not, "peculiarity" would lose its salience. This means that persistent cultures are not in control of who they think they are nor of what they stand for, since a part of their identity is possessed by an ideology which operates to keep them in their place. One implication of this fact is that a description of Indian or Mormon integrity, when not examined in the context of subordination, is a anthropological fiction as well as an active element in native mythology.

The Mormon stand on admitting blacks into the ranks of the church's priesthood can illustrate some of these points. Until the summer of 1978 the Mormon church had excluded blacks from the priesthood. During the civil rights era, the church reiterated its stand on exclusion and created for itself and its members a unique and peculiar reputation. Mormons appeared to be the only organized, law-abiding group running counter to federal law and most of national opinion. The church's highlighting of its traditionally opposed stance came just after the nationally publicized raids on polygynous communities along the Utah-Arizona border; the national sympathy the raids evoked for people who seemed like hard-working, honest farmers called forth horror from an embarrassed church. Plural marriage, the most obvious symbol of Mormon peculiarity in the nineteenth and early twentieth centuries, generated no longer hatred but sympathy. The key symbol of opposition had suddenly produced affection. Then from the church a few years later came loud proclamations reaffirming the exclusion of blacks, and once more Mormons were truly peculiar in their own and other's eyes.

It is obvious enough that the symbol of opposition can change and indeed must, as opinions, practices, and conditions in the dominant society change. But not so obvious is the fact that the more prominent a single-faceted program of opposition becomes, the more readily assimilation can take place and the less noticeable is exploitation in all its forms. Excluding blacks was doctrinally insignificant in Mormonism but very powerful as a social and political statement. And as a lightning rod for peculiarity it hid all the similarities and pro-American attitudes developed among Mormons. It also hid, on the one hand, and rationalized, on the other, Mormons' subordinate status; for, after all, Mormons could say to each other, "There is a price for being willing to be different." The difference is subordination, and the price is blindness to it.

The illustration shows two aspects of symbolic opposition. First, control over shifts in the definition of peculiarity is not exclusively in the hands of the subordinate group. And, second, the content of peculiarity may recapitulate subordination. By excluding blacks, Mormons recapitulated and internalized their own subordinate, inferior position. They did unto others what was being done to them, and, when they did it to others, they masked the locus of reality, namely, their own true condition. Further, the doing was the becoming; by making others inferior, unacceptable, and unworthy, they acted out on others what they themselves were and so modeled their own condition. By denigrating blacks they perpetuated the structure of inferiority and so reproduced ongoing economic and social reality.

With the disappearance of the opprobrium attached to plural marriage, Mormons focused on blacks; when blacks became full members of the church because their exclusion was no longer credible among the church's leaders, Mormons faced a new set of possibilities. They organized strong opposition to the Equal Rights Amendment, birth control, abortion, and gay rights, making statements about traditional family structure. But by the early 1980s no obvious item of peculiarity has been settled on; the category through which opposition is expressed is diffused and defined by each Mormon in his or her own way. With this trend two events are possible. First, without a strong sense of peculiarity, subordination can neither be masked nor recapitulated. But should subordination become a visible fact, which will happen in the absence of a strong model of peculiarity, violence could reappear in Mormon-U.S. relations. For Mormonism continues to grow fast internationally, bringing so much tithing money to its Great Basin poor that economic subordination could be overcome by buying economic control of the area. Mormon prosperity could create a conflict with the rest of the nation, since church-generated wealth — coupled with a well-articulated sense of oppression — was the factor which originally moved the federal government to create a colony out of Mormondom at the turn of the century. Second, with the content of the symbol of peculiarity gone and thus the means for teaching themselves subordination gone, they could leave peculiarity behind and struggle for freedom.

| 6 |

Cherokee Curing and Conjuring, Identity, and the Southeastern Co-Tradition

Willard Walker

The Cherokees are among the peoples described by Spicer (1971:797) as exhibiting "persistent cultural systems." "Cherokees" may be defined as the set of individuals who participate regularly in one or another of the Cherokee-speaking communities, each of which is associated with one of the named Christian or Nighthawk Ketoowah ceremonial centers in northeastern Oklahoma and western North Carolina (Wahrhaftig 1968; Wahrhaftig and Lukens-Wahrhaftig 1979). The Cherokees, as so defined, seem to fit, roughly at least, Spicer's (1971) definition of an "enclave" population with a persistent identity system. There are, however, certain features of this postulated enclave which Spicer's model seems not to anticipate.

Cherokees do not under all conditions identify as members of a Cherokee enclave. There are contexts in which they identify as members of some smaller segment of the enclave, such as the Cherokee Indian Baptist Association, or of some still smaller segment such as the Fourteen Mile Creek Cherokee Baptist Church. On the other hand, there are contexts in which Cherokees identify as members of an enclave which extends beyond the limits of Cherokee society to include Creeks and Choctaws and members of a number of other ethnically and linguistically discrete populations. Rather than comprising a single enclave with fixed boundaries, Cherokee society seems to have mechanisms which organize and reorganize its members into an endless series of transitory enclaves. Whether these embrace large or small groups of people, they are in conformity with certain fixed premises which give the participants a sense of continuity and a feeling that the transitory enclave is but a current manifestation of an enduring, timeless enclave that persists out of the past and into the future.

THE CHEROKEES AS AN ENCLAVED POPULATION

Cherokees, as defined above, conform to Spicer's enclave model insofar as they constitute a subsociety with distinctive cultural traits integrated in a distinctive way and in that they have, quite obviously, placed a positive value on the maintenance of their cultural distinctiveness throughout their history. Also in conformity with the model, they possess a distinctive language and once claimed and defended a common territory, a fact of which they are well aware. And when allotment and the consequent loss of their commonly held land made it impossible for the Western Cherokees to maintain their geographical isolation, they continued to make consistent and effective efforts to resist assimilation and maintain a degree of social isolation which have permitted the Cherokee enclave, or, more accurately, most of the local communities which together constitute the Cherokee enclave, to persist. Wahrhaftig (1968) has provided conclusive evidence that most of the nineteenth-century Cherokee communities remain very much intact and, indeed, that new Cherokee communities are continuing to emerge. On the other hand, of course, he has also shown that some of the nineteenth-century communities have broken up. Significantly, these tend to be those which were located on prairies, that is, high-quality agricultural land which was attractive to white farmers. In many of these areas rural whites settled among the Cherokees; the social isolation of the local Cherokees broke down, mixed marriages occurred, and ultimately the native communities dissolved into rural white society.

Throughout its history, insofar as can be determined, the Cherokee enclave has consisted of a set of some fifty to sixty loosely connected communities or "towns" which are themselves small enclaves, except that, of course, there are manifold linkages between them. A given individual is likely to have kinsmen and in-laws in several communities other than his own and clansmen, friends, and acquaintances in many more or even in all of them.

The long-term importance of the local community as the basic unit in Cherokee society is attested to by the fact that, when the Cherokees were forced to "remove" to Indian Territory in the nineteenth century, they did so whenever possible as communities and then re-created their original, local communities on their arrival. Again, as Jordan makes clear (1974:131), the Cherokees converted to Christianity later in the nineteenth century, not individually, but as whole communities, and the Nighthawk movement, early in the present century, also enlisted the support of whole communities, rather than individual converts.

The Cherokee enclave, then, is best described as a set of interrelated local enclaves, local in the sense that their members are oriented toward a specific ceremonial center (Christian church or Nighthawk "fire") regardless of where they may happen to reside. The several local enclaves are known to vary with respect to their degree of geographical isolation, the degree to which the English language is used, and the nature and intensity of their contacts with other local enclaves and with various government agencies. To the best of our knowledge, however, each of the local communities conforms to the model in that it has "vigorous and exclusive forms of social organization" (Spicer 1966: 276) and a collective self-image which precludes identification with white American society.

THE CHEROKEE ENCLAVE AND THE ENCLAVE THEORY

The fact that the Cherokee enclave consists of a number of local enclaved communities does not conflict with the model. Indeed, Spicer has suggested that the identity systems of enclaves typically manifest "high positive valuation of the local community in some form" (1971:799). There are, however, certain features of the Cherokee enclave, or of its constituent subenclaves, which Spicer's model seems not to anticipate. First, the local subenclaves are all currently organized either as Christian or as Nighthawk communities; while some individuals maintain contacts with members of both types of communities, it is quite unusual for Christian Cherokees to attend Nighthawk gatherings or for Nighthawks to attend church meetings. How then does the Cherokee enclave as a whole maintain the "sentiments of solidarity" (1966:276) which we would expect to find in an enclave population? And how, under such circumstances, can the Cherokees be said to maintain "internal solidarity and the regulation of outside contacts" (1966:276)?

A second feature of the Cherokee case which seems not to be anticipated by the model is that certain local Cherokee communities have a long and continuing history of frequent and intensive contacts with Creeks and/or certain other types of non-Cherokee, and non-Cherokee-speaking, Indians. Some Cherokee individuals and local communities appear to have been influenced as much by their intense and enduring ties with non-Cherokee communities as by their links with other participants in the Cherokee enclave population. This feature, too, raises the question of how internal solidarity, desire for separation, and the regulation of outside contacts can be maintained.

Third, the process of enclavement which the Cherokees have undergone differs markedly from that reported by Spicer (1966) for the Yaquis, Tzotziles, and Quintana Roo Mayas. To be sure, the Cherokee Nighthawks early in this century turned away from Christianity, rekindled the "fire," revived the clans, and reestablished a political organization based on a council composed of representatives of each of the seven clans. But after a period of flowering the Nighthawk movement declined (Jordan 1974:149–217), and since about 1930 the great majority of Cherokees and Cherokee communities have been organized as Baptist congregations. On the whole, and certainly for the last half-century or more, Cherokee social change seems to have been gradual, superficial, nonmilitant, and nonmillenarian. In general it seems fair to say that the Cherokee enclave has not so much emerged through some historical process as it has endured — with considerable modification, of course — from prehistoric times. But even if one admits that the Cherokee enclave is the result of a historic process, one might still argue that it has not differentiated itself from the surrounding white society so much as the surrounding white society has differentiated itself from the Cherokee enclave. In both northeastern Oklahoma and western North Carolina, white society, in the last few decades, has been transformed by the growth of urban centers, tourism, the welfare economy, and the exodus of rural whites and their replacement by middle-class suburbanites (Wahrhaftig 1968). The enclave has, in many respects, remained remarkably stable in contrast to the greater society which surrounds it. To the extent that this is true, the process of enclavement has been not so much the result of a conscious and determined effort on the part of the Cherokees as it has been the consequence of rapid and far-reaching changes in the rest of American society.

Finally, I am struck by the fact that in any given instance Cherokees are not likely to behave as members of "the Cherokee enclave," but as members of some smaller or even some larger entity. The Kilpatricks have described a Cherokee national ritual, called the "Foundation of Life," which they say is "reserved for the gravest of national emergencies" and is performed in Oklahoma when hostilities directly involving the Cherokee people impend or exist; in the event of dissension anywhere in the world that is likely to affect Cherokees; in the face of severe pressure from white official-dom; when a schism has occurred in the Cherokee body politic itself. It is a symbolic "taking them to water" of the entire Cherokee nation, so that unified and spiritually reassured, it may stand before some force that menaces its life (1964*a*:1386–87).

The existence of this ritual attests to the validity of a Cherokee enclave and an associated collective identity system. This particular ritual, how-ever, is performed only in extraordinary circumstances. Other rituals are performed much more frequently and these define much more constricted social groups. One might think of a curer and his patient "going to water" as constituting a nonpersistent enclave made up of two individuals. If the therapy continues, more individuals are likely to be drawn into this enclave, often from the patient's household, matrilineage, or local com-munity. If the therapy continues without success, another curer may be called in, perhaps from a remote district, thus expanding the boundaries of the microenclave established for the cure. Such a nonpersistent micro-enclave is often defined in opposition to a second; the social boundary drawn by the curer and his ritual not only unites the curer, the patient, and their human and supernatural allies, but also pits them against an opposing force, typically consisting of a conjuror, his client, and their human and supernatural allies, all of whom, of course, constitute a sec-ond, nonpersistent enclave. As the patient's symptoms wax or wane, as practitioners, diagnoses, and therapeutic techniques are added or dis-carded, the nonpersistent enclave expands, contracts, and reorganizes it-self. Theoretically, it may expand to include the entire Cherokee enclave. It may also expand beyond those bounds if, for example, a Creek doctor is retained. Seen in this way, the Cherokee enclave is a transitory phe-nomenon, but one which, like an infinite number of similar transitory phenomena, is the product of a persistent process of enclavement.

CHEROKEES, "REAL PEOPLE," AND THE SOUTHEASTERN CO-TRADITION

Perhaps the enduring Cherokee communities can be more satisfacto-rily aligned with Spicer's model if we discard some conventional ethno-graphic categories and redefine the population, which may be said to be undergoing a persistent process of enclavement. The scholarship con-cerned with Cherokee culture and society has almost invariably been based on the assumption that the Cherokees constitute a unique and discrete social and cultural entity. Most of those who have studied the Cherokees have tended to investigate Cherokee communities exclusively and thus have emphasized the distinctiveness of these communities rather than the parallels and linkages between them and the very similar "towns" of the other "Five Civilized Tribes." Here and there in the literature, however, one does find descriptions of close and long-continued contact and consequent cultural borrowing involving Cherokees and other groups, which also, of course, have traditionally been treated as discrete ethnographic categories. The Kilpatricks, for example, whose research interests and publications were oriented exclusively toward the Cherokees, were led, nonetheless, to publish one report on Muskogean charm songs among the Oklahoma Cherokees (1967*a*). Gilbert, another student of Cherokee culture, has written that "in the main, the elements of the aboriginal material culture of the Cherokee were typically southeastern . . . . In the matter of ceremonies and beliefs the Cherokees differed but little from the rest of the Southeast" (1943:198—99). In support of these statements he offers a list of aboriginal Cherokee traits which are characteristically southeastern: some crops (maize, beans, tobacco), articles of clothing (the skin breechclout and shirt, the feather cloak), various types of tools and equipment (the dugout canoe; the blowgun; the square, gabled house constructed of poles), certain ceremonial items and complexes (the green corn feast, the sacred ark, the new fire rite, religious regard for the sun, use of divining crystals), some features of social organization (priesthoods, matrilineal clans, matrilocal residence, division of government into red and white organizations), and a random assortment of beliefs and practices (emphasis on rank and military titles, intertown rivalry in ball games, "many features of the sexual division of labor," and "animal spirit theory of disease and certain medical practices") (1943:198—99). Swanton also interprets precontact and early historic Cherokee culture as a variant of the general southeastern pattern (1946:801—5). More recently Howard (1968) has contributed an entire monograph on the "Southeastern ceremonial complex," which he describes as an enduring and pervasive cultural complex long associated with the ethnic groups native to the Southeast.

Cherokee social and cultural developments in postcontact times are also typical of the "Five Civilized Tribes," all of whom adjusted to European exploration and militarism, epidemics, the deerskin trade, missionaries, pressure to form centralized constitutional governments, "removal," civil war, reconstruction, allotment, "termination," and impoverishment in much the same way and at roughly the same times.

It is also clear that, at various times and places during the historic period, a number of southeastern groups have settled among the Cherokees. James Mooney, the classic Cherokee scholar, mentions, for example, a small town on the Tennessee River near Tuscumbia, Alabama, which, before it was destroyed by Americans in 1787, was occupied by a mixed population of Cherokees and Creeks (1975:57). Again, he describes the five "Chicamauga towns" on the Tennessee as being occupied by a mixed Cherokee, Creek, Shawnee, and white Tory population until they were finally destroyed in 1794 (1975:44, 62). Elsewhere (1975:138–40), Mooney mentions that, when the Cherokees first settled in Indian Territory, "by tacit agreement some of the Creeks who had settled within the Cherokee bounds were permitted to remain. Among these were several families of Uchee—an incorporated tribe of the Creek confederacy...." Swanton, in *The Indians of the Southeastern United States* (1946), mentions a number of southeastern ethnic groups which established communities among the Cherokees at various times and places, such as the Koasatis, Yuchis, Catawbas, Shawnees, "Creeks," Natchez, Nattaways, and Tuskegees.

To be sure, the Cherokees speak a distinctive language, and they have traditionally, and quite correctly, been viewed as a discrete social and cultural entity. But it is obvious that in their long contact with a variety of other southeastern groups they have long had cultural traits and complexes that are characteristic of what might be called a greater southeastern co-tradition.

The Nighthawk Ketoowah movement, which emerged in the 1890s under the threat of allotment and the dissolution of the Cherokee Nation, and which succeeded in revitalizing Cherokee society in the first two decades of this century, might at first glance be interpreted as a uniquely Cherokee response to external pressure. Even this, however, was rooted as much in Creek, Natchez, and even Seminole tradition as in Cherokee tradition. The movement originated on Vian Creek, a section of the Illinois District of the Cherokee Nation which had been settled by a composite band tracing its ancestry to Cherokees, Creeks, and Natchez. Its members spoke both Creek (Muskogee) and Cherokee, and had "lived in the Cherokee tribe and retained their [Creek] language since before the Removal." Indeed, many of the bilingual "Creeks" in this community were actually "descendants of a band of Seminoles led by Wildcat and Alligator—Seminole chiefs who refused to go into the country allotted to them, as they would have been under the jurisdiction of the Creeks" (Thomas 1953:136).

According to John Smith, who was a prominent Nighthawk in the second decade of this century, the "fire"—that is, the ancient Creek institution from which the Ketoowah religion and social organization evolved—was brought into the Cherokee Nation after the Civil War by (Natchez-Creek) followers of the Creek leader Opothle Yahola, when they settled on Green Leaf Creek, near the border between the Creek and

Cherokee nations (Thomas 1953:137). This particular fire, which has been moved a number of times, seems always to have been associated with a community made up of descendants of eighteenth century Natchez refugees who have always lived among Cherokees and Creeks but have retained their own community organization in one form or another. Swanton described their ceremonial ground as being "resorted to by Natchez, Creeks and Cherokee" (1928:602–3). When he first visited this fire (probably in 1908), it had "the four cabins typical of Creek practice"; on a subsequent visit, however, he found that it had been moved and had seven cabins in accordance with Cherokee Nighthawk practice. This fire was allowed to lapse for some forty years, during which time the community was organized as a Christian church, but Howard (1970) reports that it was in the process of being reestablished when he visited the community in 1969. At this time it once again had the four cabins of Creek tradition and a slate of Cherokee-speaking officers, one of whom was Creek, another Creek-Seminole, but most of whom were of mixed Cherokee and Natchez descent. Howard was told by Archie Sam, the "chairman or speaker" of this reemerging fire, that, before it could be formally reactiviated, a "medicine man" would have to be appointed and that a properly qualified man for this position could be obtained at the time "only among the Creek or Seminole." Archie Sam also stated that the Bear Clan, which is nonexistent in more orthodox Cherokee communities, occupied the south cabin and furnished the "chief," and that the east cabin was occupied by the Alligator clan, which also has no parallel in Cherokee social organization. The west cabin, or arbor, was occupied by the Bird Clan; however, while Cherokees have a Bird Clan, no Cherokee ceremonial ground has an arbor on the west side of the fire. There are other discrepancies with Cherokee Nighthawk practice, any one of which would serve to explain why only a Creek or Seminole might qualify as a medicine man for this fire, since the expertise of a Nighthawk medicine man would clearly be inapplicable.

Thus we are forced to deal with the fact that one local Cherokee-speaking community, which must assuredly be counted a part of the Cherokee enclave, is organized in terms of a clan system which is decidedly alien to Cherokee social organization, has a ceremonial ground that violates Nighthawk custom, and has a "speaker" who proclaims that it cannot formally constitute itself without the services of a properly qualified Creek or Seminole. If anything like a persistent, static Cherokee enclave can be said to exist, then we must conclude that it is not only divided, but that it overlaps with other enclaves to such an extent that the notion of a Cherokee enclave would seem to illuminate some aspects of Cherokee society only at the expense of obscuring others. It would seem that we must be prepared to deal with enclaves that expand and contract and (under certain conditions) merge and (under others) divide again.

Even in the formative years of the Nighthawk movement its most prominent figure, Redbird Smith, had as his constant companion and adviser a man named Creek Sam, who spoke Cherokee, Creek, and Natchez, since he himself had been raised in the Natchez-Creek-Cherokee community alluded to above and was, in fact, a grandfather of Howard's informant, Archie Sam. Redbird Smith and all the other leaders of the Nighthawk movement in its early years were in direct contact with the Natchez fire on Green Leaf Creek, for it was there that Redbird Smith was accustomed to meet with his committee (those appointed to "get back what the Ketoowahs had lost") and with the head District captains of the Nighthawk Ketoowah Society (Thomas 1953:142). Nor was this their only channel of communication with the rest of the "Five Civilized Tribes." Redbird Smith represented the Cherokees at meetings of the Four Mothers Society, an anti-allotment, anti-statehood group of "conserva-tive" Creeks, Cherokees, Choctaws, and Chickasas, from perhaps as early as 1896–97 until 1902, when the Cherokee Ketoowahs broke with this organization (Thomas 1953:135, 142, 148, 157). During much of this period Redbird Smith presided over Four Mothers meetings and Creek Sam served as his interpreter. Spicer's model would scarcely lead us to predict that during this period, when the Cherokees were driven to des-peration by the imminent prospect of allotment, the loss of their land, and the dissolution of their political organization, the central figure in the movement to solidify the Cherokee enclave, revitalize its institutions, and "get back what the Ketoowahs had lost" was regularly presiding over meetings at which four different "tribes" were represented. It would seem that the Cherokee Nighthawks, the Cherokee group which in many re-spects most closely approximates Spicer's model of an enclave, may never have attempted, even at the inception of their movement, to differentiate all Cherokees from all others, but rather have been resolutely bent upon differentiating themselves, together with other like-minded people, from the white society which has posed so grave a threat to their survival. The Nighthawks have not always behaved as though they identified them-selves as *anijalagi* ("Cherokees"). Not infrequently they have acted as though they identified themselves as *aniyvwiya'i*, a term often translated as "Indians," but which is rendered more literally, and in this context more accurately, I believe, as "real people."

In the following passage, quoted by Jordan from a Nighthawk leader, notice how being *Cherokee* is important only insofar as it is associated with (Nighthawk) *Ketoowahs* who provide medicine and meaningful ritual to *all Indian chiefs* and to *many tribes*.

The Spirit told them what to do. Use shells for beads, beads over the shoulder (wampums). Take the peace pipe to all Indian chiefs. The

Cherokee gathered up chiefs as he went along and went to the next chief. Many tribes made peace. They were going to all drink medicine on a bluff close to a good-sized creek. What we call Cherokee started right there. An herb called Cherokee, that is what he brought. They all drank that medicine. They were there for seven days and seven nights. They set the pot of medicine and water on the bluff. At seven in the morning, that medicine was boiled. That is when they used it. That was why they called him Cherokee, because he brought that herb named Cherokee. The right name is Keetoowah (Jordan 1974:125).

I would suggest that the Cherokee data may fit Spicer's model more neatly if we discard the notion of a Cherokee enclave and substitute that of an enclavement process which produces transitory enclaves of varying size, the theoretical maximum enclave being a group for which the term "real people" may serve as a convenient label. This is a group which speaks no single language, a fact which would violate the model if the maximal enclave were to persist, and it is not identified with any particular "tribe," either by popular or by ethnographic standards. Nevertheless, this group may conform very closely to Spicer's profile of an enclave population if it can be shown to share a common identity system, mechanisms for communication and socialization, and institutions which function to define the social boundaries of the maximal enclave and of various smaller enclaves and to enforce the adherence (or acquiescence) of its members to the crucial elements of the identity system.

The maximal enclave which I should like to postulate consists of an unknown number of local communities (probably many more than one hundred) which speak one or more of at least six distinct languages (Cherokee, Muskogee, Yuchi, Hitchiti, Alabama-Koasati, and Choctaw-Chickasas) and vary widely with regard to social and political organization, cultural tradition, and ethnic affiliation. Few of these local communities have ever been investigated, but it may well be that all or virtually all of them share a set of symbols and associated meanings and participate in a common institution which provides the "real people" with an internal organization, regulates contacts with outsiders, provides links between the constituent communities, maintains a consensus, and exercises a degree of social control through mechanisms which seldom come to the attention of outsiders and thus are shielded from their interference.

THE CURING AND CONJURING COMPLEX

The institution which I believe may serve at once to define and to integrate the maximal enclave I have postulated and to regulate its external relationships is what I shall call the curing-conjuring complex. No serious attempt has even been made to measure the extent to which the "Five Civilized Tribes" share curing and conjuring techniques, personnel, and the premises which underlie curing and conjuring practice; but Mooney (1891; 1900), Mooney and Olbrechts (1932), Gilbert (1943), Speck and Broom (1951), Fogelson (1961), and the Kilpatricks (1964*a,b;* 1965; 1967*a, b*) have made Cherokee curing and conjuring one of the best-reported institutions of its kind in North America. Close parallels have been reported for the less-studied groups: the Choctaws (Bushnell 1909; Swanton 1931), the Seminoles (Sturtevant 1955), the various ethnic groups associated with the Creek Confederacy (Speck 1911; Swanton 1928), and a wide assortment of southeastern ethnic groups (Swanton 1946:782–99). Enough information is available to suggest that curing and conjuring practices vary but little among the "Five Tribes"; this inference is supported by the fact that curer-conjurers sometimes, as in the case history to be reported below, practice across linguistic and ethnic boundaries on individuals from differernt groups.

Not surprisingly, the literature on this topic tends to be concerned with a specific ethnic group and hence seldom indicates that the "Five Tribes" have long exchanged native curing and conjuring personnel as well as techniques for curing and conjuring. Moreover, the rich body of information on Cherokee curing and conjuring, based as it is primarily on native manuscripts detailing specific curing and conjuring formulas (*idi·gawé·sdi*) and herbal remedies, has focused attention on the techniques of curing and conjuring to such an extent that little consideration has been given to the social consequences of these practices. Concern with the programmatic details of specific formulas and techniques has drawn attention away from such potentially significant phenomena as the relationships of curers to patients, conjurors to victims, and curers to conjurors. More importantly in the present context, it has drawn attention away from the curing-conjuring complex as a social institution and its implications for relationships between different communities within a given "tribe," between communities of different "tribes," and between the "real people" and such Euro-American institutions as the U. S. Public Health Service Indian Hospitals, the public schools, the Bureau of Indian Affairs, and various law enforcement agencies.

Still another consequence of the importance attached to nineteenth-century manuscripts and to elderly, traditionalist curers as primary sources of data on curing and conjuring is a lack of adequate recognition for the enduring vitality which the complex seems to me to enjoy in a great many, if not all, of the "Five Tribes" communities. Just how viable it is and to what degree it continues to engage attention and govern behavior in each of the contemporary communities is impossible to assess. Among the Oklahoma Cherokees the complex was characteristic of both Christian and Nighthawk communities as recently as the 1970s, and the literature suggests that it was no less prevalent in North Carolina in the 1950s, the same decade in which Sturtevant (1955) found the Mikasuki Seminoles in Florida engaging in similar practices. I have abundant evidence of the vitality of the complex in several Creek communities as of the late 1970s, and its prevalence in the 1930s among both church and square-ground Creek towns can be safely inferred from information scattered throughout Morris Opler's *The Creek Indian Towns of Oklahoma in 1937* (1972). Two Choctaw college students with whom I spoke on many occasions in the 1960s gave compelling evidence that the complex was alive and well in their respective communities. Thus it may well be that native curing and conjuring have retained their vitality among all the surviving Cherokee, Creek, Choctaw, and perhaps the Seminole and Chickasas communities in eastern Oklahoma and elsewhere despite the determined and long-continued opposition of white doctors, missionaries, educators, legislators, Bureau of Indian Affairs officials, and "progressive" Indians. In the communities of the maximal enclave, curing and conjuring may be as tenacious as are the local communities themselves and as characteristic a part of life as are the native languages, the scattered rural households, the social isolation from white society, and the concomitant intensity of interpersonal relationships within the several communities. Curing and conjuring are seldom referred to in the presence of outsiders and less often defended in the face of the rigid incredulity and open scorn of whites. But they persist, nonetheless, and their persistence implies that they have one or more functions, both for the individuals involved in curing and conjuring and for the communities which have for so long supported these activities.

I would argue that there are a large number of socially, culturally, and even linguistically disparate communities which together constitute a very large and diverse enclave, or, more properly, a population addicted to an enclavement process which, sometimes at least, takes the form of practices associated with what I have referred to as the curing and conjuring complex. The case history to follow suggests the possibility that this polyethnic enclave comes into being from time to time, that its potential for existence has persisted over a long time, and that the reality and persistence of the enclavement process among the "Five Tribes" may well be related to the curing and conjuring practices which seem so characteristic of the local communities that constitute this so diverse and dispersed population.

LUCILLE'S ACCOUNT

I obtained the following case history in the mid-1960s from the patient in the case, a girl whom I will call Lucille, who was the oldest child in a large Choctaw family. Her case is of particular interest in the present context because she was treated by both a Choctaw and a Creek (as well as by white doctors), because many of their several diagnoses and therapeutic treatments conform very closely to those associated with Cherokee medical practice in comparable cases, and because the therapy was so obviously well calculated, not simply to cure the physical symptoms of the patient, but to resocialize her, isolate her from the dominant society and its institutions, and reintegrate her into the local Choctaw community. Finally, and most importantly perhaps, this case is of interest precisely because, even though the therapy failed either to cure the patient or to resocialize her, it resulted, nonetheless, in solidifying the local community, clarifying its social boundaries, and dramatizing the value and effectiveness of the community's traditions, standards, and procedures to all but the patient herself.

Lucille developed pains in her side at about the age of thirteen and, although the pains grew gradually worse, she told no one in her family until some years later. By April of 1961, when she was eighteen and had a job in town, she had still said nothing of the pains to her parents, and she had never dated. In this same month, however, she began to go with a Choctaw boy from a distant community who had often sung with her father in quartets at certain Choctaw churches. At about this same time, Lucille's parents noticed that she was "acting strangely." She began going out after dark with the boy, for example, and once stayed overnight in town at the home of an unmarried sister of her father. By July she was living with this aunt in town and returning home only on weekends. During this time the pains in her side became unbearable, and she went to a white doctor who had previously treated her father. She said nothing of this, however, to her parents. Shortly thereafter she stayed with her aunt over a weekend, an act which her parents later mentioned as another instance of her odd behavior. Her mother was so distressed by Lucille's weekend in town that she came for her at work the following Monday. It was then that Lucille told her mother of her illness. Her mother took her to the white doctor who had previously examined her; he told Lucille to go home and rest but made no specific diagnosis. She went home with her mother, where she became increasingly apathetic and generally ill. She was treated by the white doctor, receiving a penicillin shot every day, but failed to respond to this treatment. She wrote letters to her boyfriend but was not permitted to see him, being allowed out of the house only to attend church on Sundays. It became evident that her parents were implacably opposed to her dating the boyfriend. His aunt was a fortune-teller and was thought to be a witch; his father had been disliked and distrusted also before his death some time before; the boyfriend's whole family and the boyfriend himself were "no good," although Lucille's family would never give her a satisfactory reason for this judgment.

At about this time her parents began to consider the use of native medicine. Her father was particularly hopeful that an Indian doctor could cure Lucille, and an appropriate curer was suggested by her mother's mother's brother (i.e., a closely related, elder male member of Lucille's clan and matrilineage, traditionally responsible for the well-being and proper conduct of the younger members of his matrilineage in all or most of the "Five Tribes"). They visited the house of this particular doctor at about nine o'clock one evening. The doctor was not at home, but his wife knew some medicine and asked a number of questions that seemed to indicate that she thought Lucille's symptoms were the effects of pregnancy. Finally, she mixed some medicine for Lucille and told her to stay home for four days. School had reopened by this time, and Lucille felt that school was the only place where she could be herself and avoid what she considered the overprotective watchfulness of her parents. She fussed and cried, behavior which her parents viewed once again as strange, but she stayed home for the four days, after which time she came home from school every night weak, tired, and dejected.

Her father decided that she was getting too much medicine and should quit one of the doctors. She quit the white doctor and the daily shots of penicillin but continued to be treated by the Choctaw doctor, who was paid in cash on each visit. His treatments were no more effective than the penicillin, however. Lucille's father would occasionally ask whether she still thought of her ex-boyfriend, apparently expecting her to have forgotten him completely. She always answered, truthfully, that she did think of him.

Before long, Lucille's parents switched to a Creek doctor who had a nine-year-old grandson who was reported to be a fortune-teller. Lucille went to this doctor's house on only one occasion; but she was left in the car while her parents went inside. The nine-year-old grandson was playing football with another boy in the yard and was called to the house by his grandmother. He had glanced only casually at Lucille while she was in the car, but, when he entered the house, he evidently diagnosed her case as pains in the side induced by someone's having made a doll and used a knife on it. The conjuror was believed to be the ex-boyfriend. When this diagnosis was reported to Lucille, however, she lost all confidence in the medical ability of the Creek doctor and his grandson, for, unlike her parents, she knew that the pains in her side had begun long before she met the boyfriend. All this, however, Lucille kept to herself. She did not tell her parents that the pains had begun before she met the boy, that she consequently had no confidence in the grandson's diagnosis, or that she took no stock in an additional theory, propounded by the Creek doctor, that the boyfriend had put conjuring medicine in her food to induce her to marry him.

Being unable or unwilling to confide in her parents, she had no choice but to go through the motions of the therapeutic ritual prescribed by the Creek doctor. The curing ceremony was normally performed at the patient's home, but there were so many children in Lucille's parents' household that it was decided to have the ceremony at the home of her maternal grandmother's brother. The patient was given something to drink to induce vomiting, but this failed. She bathed outdoors at midnight in a mixture of clay and water, then rubbed herself with a salve. A second attempt to induce vomiting failed. All those present — the doctor, his wife, Lucille's mother, and her maternal grandmother's brother's wife — stood around waiting for her to vomit, but she never did. Finally, the doctor told her to lie down on her stomach and immerse her head in the pond four times. This she failed to do also, being afraid to put her head completely under water, but she put her face under four times. Just as she finished, she heard her grandmother's brother's wife say, "Oh!", and Lucille "raised up and saw those lights." They were like Fourth of July sparklers away in the eastern sky, in the direction of the boyfriend's house.

The party then returned to the house, where Lucille's father and her grandmother's brother had remained during the therapy. Lucille stayed up for perhaps an hour while her parents consulted with the doctor, after which they went home. The doctor had given her parents some cigarettes to smoke around the outside of the house to keep the boyfriend from entering.

For the next three days Lucille had to stay home from school and take some new medicine with which she washed her face and arms every day at noon. The doctor's wife had given Lucille's mother a perfume bottle, the contents of which she sprinkled in each doorway while Lucille was washing. More was sprinkled on the patient herself when she had finished washing, after which Lucille would pour the wash-water outside and in the direction of the boy's house. She then stood outside until her body dried in the air, it being forbidden to dry herself. During this whole period several other doctors were consulted by Lucille's parents, and a number of medicines were procured, no doubt at considerable expense, which she was required to drink. Lucille never met these other doctors herself, but on one occasion she overhead a conversation between her parents indicating that one of the doctors had said that the therapy would be only partially successful in combating the boy's love magic. The boy no longer had any direct power over the patient, it was said; but, on the other hand, Lucille would never stay married to any other man for long, either. She would always have to go from one man to another. In short, she would have a life much like that of her father's sister, with whom she had lived in town.

Although Lucille never believed in the efficacy of the curing techniques to which she was subjected, she felt by this time that her parents had gone to so much trouble and had spent so much money to separate her from her boyfriend that she would comply with their wishes. She wrote a final letter to the boy telling him that their affair was over and to "just forget all about it." Meanwhile, however, she had developed a close relationship with her home economics teacher. This teacher had questioned her about her many absences from school resulting from the curing rituals. Finally, Lucille told her the whole story and asked her advice. The teacher advised compliance with her parents' desires, in general, although on one occasion she suggested marrying the boyfriend as a means of escaping her difficulties at home. In time, the home economics teacher arranged a Bureau of Indian Affairs scholarship for Lucille to get her into college and, hence, away from home. She accepted the scholarship over the objections of her father, who advised her to keep the job in a clothing factory which she had obtained soon after graduation from high school. Her father drove her to an Oklahoma state college, deposited her and her luggage, and left without a word having been exchanged between them.

As an undergraduate in college, Lucille became a home economics major, returned home infrequently, and ultimately married a white man. Her father apparently became reconciled to the fact that Lucille had gone away to college, but his relationship with her remained strained. Since the mid-1960s, when Lucille told me her story, I have lost contact with her, but a Cherokee friend told me in 1978 that he had heard that she had married a Creek some years previously.

THE CURING-CONJURING COMPLEX IN THE ENCLAVEMENT PROCESS

I have recounted Lucille's case history in some detail and at considerable length, because I think it has several important implications bearing on Spicer's enclave theory. First, it suggests the persistence of a curing and conjuring complex shared by at least some Choctaws and some Creeks in the mid-twentieth century that has obvious parallels elsewhere among the "Five Civilized Tribes." Parallel beliefs and practices are recorded for the nineteenth-century Cherokees which almost certainly derive from a pan-southeastern tradition that originated in precontact times. Thus Mooney and Olbrechts describe nineteenth-century Cherokee formulas used "to kindle discord and to sow ill feeling between a married couple, or between sweethearts" (1932:155). They also describe such practices as immersion in water, the use of emetics, vomiting into water while facing east, and sprinkling the body of a patient. The smoking of tobacco to protect a house from witches is also described and closely follows the procedure in Lucille's case except that the doctor himself smoked the house with a pipe instead of preparing cigarettes to be smoked by his clients. We seem to be dealing here with a complex that is very ancient and which crosses several social and linguistic boundaries.

Lucille's case also illustrates a common pattern among "Five Tribes" curers: the interpretation of physical symptoms and deviant social behavior as the result of conjuring. This diagnosis, of course, triggers the mobilization of an intricate and sometimes very extensive social network which may cross social, cultural, and linguistic boundaries and which, in any event, brings massive and continued social pressure to bear on individuals and forces them to sever certain social relationships, to strengthen others, to break all ties with the dominant society, and to conform to the behavioral and ideological norms of the enclave. From the point of view of her family and doctors, the essential difficulty in Lucille's case was probably not the pain in her side, but rather the fact that she was drifting away from her family and out of her community. She did not confide her problems to her parents; she formed an attachment with a boy whose family was suspect; she spent more and more time with an aunt who had never achieved a stable marital relationship; by her senior year in high school she was not only withholding information from her own parents, but was disclosing her most personal problems to the home economics teacher, a representative of a powerful and alien institution. Little by little, and as quickly as she could, Lucille was leaving Choctaw society; her parents and maternal great-uncle understandably responded by calling in native specialists to combat this intolerable threat to the solidarity of the family and community and to the very worth and viability of the reigning identity system.

The case is revealing in yet a third way, for, while it is easy to understand how successful or even partially successful cures would tend to solidify a society by resocializing and reintegrating deviant patients, Lucille's case is illuminating because it shows how the curing-conjuring complex can integrate a society even when it fails to cure the patient. Lucille's therapy failed to resolve either her physical symptoms or her social conflicts. It did, however, succeed in identifying her as an incurable social deviant and driving her inexorably out of the community, thus reuniting the community at the expense of its deviant member.

Had they acted a year or two earlier, Lucille's parents might have reintegrated her into the community. Their timing being as it was, however, perhaps no amount of therapy could have prevailed, particularly in view of the fact that she was going to school, at least intermittently, and thus was exposed to external influences while under the care of the Indian doctors. It may be that Lucille's alienation had progressed too far for any cure to be effective. She had withheld pertinent information from her parents. Likewise, the parents and doctors excluded Lucille from their discussions. The result was a diagnosis which was not only inaccurate but one which was transparently inaccurate to the patient, and hence reinforced her intransigence, eroded her faith in native institutions, and compelled her to seek support from outside, that is, from the school.

The diagnoses (pregnancy, pains induced by sympathetic magic involving a doll, and love magic involving tampering with the victim's food) all ascribed the patient's malady to causes with which native medical practice is well equipped to deal. All three diagnoses were well calculated to relieve the patient of both blame and shame, since her supposed pregnancy, pains, and strange behavior were attributed explicitly or implicitly to the activities of the boyfriend (perhaps in collusion with a conjuror). Since the boyfriend was held responsible, rather than, for example, the home economics teacher or a white high-school student, and since the boyfriend was Choctaw, it was reasonable to suppose that Choctaw (or Creek) curing techniques would be effective. It might be said that such techniques would be equally effective if the aunt in town were singled out as the conjuror. This interpretation, however, would jeopardize the unity of the family. It would also fail to capitalize on the opportunity to heap all the blame on the individual whose relationship to the patient it was thought imperative to sever.

When it became apparent that Lucille was not responding well to the therapy, by failing to vomit, for example, and was cooperating only minimally, as when she failed to immerse her head, this unhappy circumstance was acknowledged with the (probably) accurate prediction that she would break off her relationship with the boyfriend but would never achieve a stable marriage with an acceptable Choctaw husband. This prediction is interesting in that it may be to a considerable degree self-fulfilling: once again it transfers all blame from the patient not only to the conjuror, but to the particular individual whose relationship to the patient the therapy was designed to destroy. The prediction also explains the partial failure of native curing in terms of the strength of native conjuring, the opposite side of the same coin. The prestige of the curing-conjuring complex was thus reinforced, in the minds of all save the patient, even under the most adverse conditions and when prolonged therapy had failed to achieve the desired result — the cure and social reintegration of the patient.

With regard to the persistence, isolation, and homogeneity of the enclave, however, Lucille's cure was a complete success, for it identified Lucille as an incorrigible deviant and a threat to the basic values of the community, and it proceeded to drive her from the fold. It would appear that the curing-conjuring complex, whether it dramatically resolves or dramatically fails to resolve social conflict and physical distress, has the effect of sealing off the enclave from non-Indian society and preserving traditional values and institutions, traditional wisdom, and the integrity of the group, however large or small, which in any given instance constitutes the enclave.

The curing-conjuring complex is probably only one of a number of institutions which serve to define and to integrate the "real people" in their manifold and transitory enclaves within enclaves. It may be among the most important of these institutions, however, since it appears to be old, persistent, and pervasive. Moreover, it may be among the most revealing for the social sciences, since curers (and conjurors) define social boundaries around their patients (and victims) by creating, maintaining, restoring, or destroying social relationships, and thus tailoring the enclave to the size and proportions most appropriate to the objectives of the moment. In any given curing or conjuring episode, the practitioner attempts to mobilize a set of human and supernatural beings to oppose those human and supernatural beings who are working against him. Thus any attempt to cure or to conjure involves the creation of a temporary enclave, large or small, and a temporary identity system to oppose some other transitory enclave. Thus, like Spicer's persistent identity systems, the transitory identity systems created by curers and conjurors are "intimately bound up with the conditions of opposition," and "it appears that the oppositional process is the essential factor in [their] formation and development" (1971:797). Curers and conjurors in the "Five Tribes," however, tend to direct hostility not against the dominant society, but, as in Lucille's case, against some other segment of their own maximal enclave. Thus the curing and conjuring complex divides as it unifies and unifies as it divides, continually creating short-lived but clearly defined enclaves with collective identity systems out of the unstructured totality of the "Five Tribes" population.

A persistent enclave composed of all the members of all the local communities of all the "real people" has never developed. There may be good reason for this. Such a persistent enclave would imply an opposing persistent enclave toward which the "real people" would direct all of their hostility. The opposing enclave, however, could be only the dominant society, and to channel aggression against so powerful an opponent would be to court disaster. It is far wiser to direct the pent-up wrath of smaller enclaves toward some luckless boy (as in Lucille's case) or some old man or woman and their nefarious colleagues.

The maximal enclave, embracing not only the members of a single ethnic or linguistic group but all the "real people," could occur as a temporary phenomenon, of course, and may actually have existed from time to time. We know that such an eventuality has been conceived of, but perhaps only in the visions of holy men who have fasted and gone without sleep and drunk the herb named Cherokee, the "right name" for which is "Keetoowah."

Part Three

Ritual and Persistence

| 7 |

The Ritual of the Cultural Enclave Process

The Dramatization of Oppositions Among the Mayo Indians of Northwest Mexico

N. Ross Crumrine

Within the symbolic realm — the culture — the ethnicity of the Mayos of northwest Mexico is characterized by fusion or syncretism and by messianic beliefs and movements. However, in regard to technological or economic behavior, Mayos reveal very little in the way of separate identity, being better characterized as rural peasants and small-scale farmers (Crumrine 1981). Thus culture change in the Mayo area is neither simple assimilation nor complete rejection of new ideas and methods. Rather, it exhibits assimilation in the techno-economic sphere and ritual and mythic elaboration in the ideological sphere, producing a Mayo "persistent cultural system" which also functions as an "identity system" (Spicer 1971). Since organized behavior is necessary for both technology and ideology, the opposition between technological assimilation and ideological persistence is mediated through a fluid, adaptable social organization, in part structured by traditional principles of Mayo social structure and in part modernized through an intensive history of contact between Mayos and Spaniards or mestizos, depending upon the time period in question.

Spicer (1970) shows how conditions of contact contributed to the contrasting developments of Mayos versus Yaquis. He argues that accelerating nineteenth-century disruption of Mayo community organization shifted Mayo goals from local autonomy to complete supernatural destruction of the mestizos or of non-Mayos. Undergoing considerably less disruption, Yaqui communities remained intact until their defeat in the 1880s. Later, re-established Yaqui community members demanded local political autonomy instead of creating ideological, messianic movements. In the Mayo case a ritual of cultural enclavement, a symbolic ceremonial system, dramatizes and mediates oppositions and sets Mayos as believers and actors apart from non-believers and non-participants, be they mestizos or even other Mayos or Yaquis. The system of Mayo identity can be seen as a community of believers and of actors working out sets of oppositions.

TRADITIONAL MAYO IDEOLOGICAL SYSTEMS

In contrast to their technological and economic assimilation, Mayos have experienced little direct outside influence on their religious and symbolic systems since the removal of the Jesuits from the New World in 1767. For the patron saint's day ceremonial, a priest says mass in the large Mayo ceremonial centers, but otherwise Mayos control their own church organization and ritual. The few local priests have neither time nor interest to visit the smaller Mayo churches. Between 1611 (the time of the first intensive missionization in the Mayo area) and 1767 the Jesuit missionaries successfully converted and reorganized the Mayo religious and political life. Since that time Mayos have worked toward autonomy and consistency in their system of belief and ritual, which represents their unique fusion of precontact belief and symbolism, seventeenth- and eighteenth-century Catholicism, and modern Christianity. Yaqui and Huichol ritual symbolism, studied by Spicer (1964*a*), shares elements of the Mayo system.

Superficially, considerable differences exist between Yaqui and Mayo beliefs and specific rituals, but much of the underlying structure reveals close parallels. The Mayo system proves more difficult to classify than the Yaqui one: "[The Yaqui ceremonial system] is an example of a religious system which is not Catholic in its foundation because it does not have an individualistic orientation toward salvation, nor does it have an emphasis on the punishments and rewards after death" (Spicer 1964*a*:28).* In

---

*[El sistema ceremonial yaqui] es un ejemplo de un sistema religioso que no es católico en su fundamento porque no tiene orientación individualística hacia la salvación, ni tiene énfasis sobre los castigos y las recompensas después de la muerte." English translation by the author.

contrast to the Yaqui one, the Mayo system appears to involve a broader pattern of fusion, including the level of structure as well as that of surface form. However, certain underlying structural elements must have been shared in the aboriginal and the Christian systems. For these reasons it is more difficult to classify the Mayo religion as non-Catholic than the Yaqui. Although Mayos resist committing themselves on the subject of the life after death, some believe that good people go directly to live with God. Very evil people are taken by the Devil, and persons who have been somewhat bad may be reborn as birds or animals as a form of punishment. Thus elements of the concept of reward or punishment in the afterlife exist, although this belief appears to be rather unimportant. As in the Yaqui system the concept of individual salvation is not developed in Mayo belief, although it does exist. Besides latent functions, such as maintenance of Mayo group unity, the major orientations of Mayo ceremonialism pivot around (1) sickness and death and (2) respect and love for God and the supernaturals. One makes a contract, a promise *(manda)*, with a supernatural for a cure; if cured, the recipient must pay by sustaining the supernatural. Ceremonials and prayers, like food for humans, provide sustenance for the supernaturals. The visitors attending the ceremonial act as human verification that the manda was completed. If the cure is unsuccessful and death results, an elaborate set of Mayo rituals for dealing with the dead and purifying the living takes place. These are more restricted in attendance than the ceremonial center rituals but are characterized by much of the same ceremonialism, such as ritual eating, prayers, and dancing. Mayos also make smaller and more localized ceremonials out of respect and love for the supernaturals. Modern Mayo cult ceremonials based upon messianic experiences are freely supported by healthy individuals who fear the wrath of God and wish to compensate for earlier bad behavior or for the lack of respect regarding the supernaturals. Certainly supernatural curing and fear of God's punishment and of the destruction of the human world are crucial parts of evangelical Christianity. But these also are themes which have deep roots in precontact Mesoamerica and Andean South America.

Duality in Huichol and Yaqui Ceremonialism

Huichol and Yaqui ceremonialism is characterized by a dual division (Spicer 1964*a*). This duality focuses upon wet season and female divinity versus dry season and male divinity. The Mayo ceremonial cycle may be incorporated into this model. However, in the Mayo case the model is abstract and analytical rather than apparent in everyday conversation and behavior. It represents a structure which Mayos would likely recognize but

is not the folk model which they openly present in discussing their ceremonial cycle. Their folk model focuses upon the birth, life, death, and
resurrection of Christ, the saint's day ceremonies, and the rituals for the
flags of the saints. The Mayo data fit the dual pattern of proto-central
Uto-Aztecan ceremonialism in the following manner. Briefly, in the Mayo
area there tend to be winter-spring crops and summer-fall crops, although
there may be considerable overlapping depending upon the specific crop.
Cold winter and dry, windy spring weather is followed by humid, hot
summer and drier but stormy fall weather. The return of the dead and the
ritual of the life, death, and resurrection of Jesus take place during the
colder winter-spring period, and the patron saint's day ceremonies during
the summer period. The ceremonies of the Holy Cross in May and September provide a transition from one period to the next, although the fit is
not as clear or abrupt as in the Huichol case. Modern Huichols, Yaquis,
and Mayos have each adapted both the natural year as well as their ceremonialism to form integrated yet differing systems.

The break between the Huichol dry winter-spring and wet summer-
fall is striking. The dry period becomes progressively drier until the
summer rains begin in late May or June. With the coming of the rains the
agricultural cycle begins, and corn, among other crops, is planted. Corn,
the ritual symbol of the wet season, is replaced by deer and deer-hunting
symbolism during the dry season. The rituals of each season are closely
integrated with these activities. Coupled with this dramatic seasonal and
ritual change is a shift of supernaturals and rituals: *Padre Sol* (Father Sun),
Abuelo Lumbre (Grandfather Fire), *Bisabuelo Cola de Venado* (Great-
grandfather Deer Tail), and the ritual deer hunt, deer dance, and peyote
pilgrimage all pertain to the dry season; *Abuela Nakawé* (Grandmother
Growth); *las madres del maíz* (the mothers of the corn); *Madre Tierra* (Earth
Mother); *los espíritus del agua y de la lluvia* (the spirits of the water and the
rain); and dances in which are used an image of the corn goddess, a ritual
stick of Abuela Nakawé, and offerings which are placed in sacred pits in
their small temples all pertain to the wet season. In the dry season the
appropriate symbolism and ritual focus upon the deer hunt, and in the wet
season the ritual and symbolism complement the corn cycle with rites for
the preparation of the soil, the seed, the first fruits, and the harvest.

The integration between the Yaqui agricultural and ritual cycles is
not as directly correlated as in the Huichol case, and no clearly agricultural ritual exists. Nevertheless, there is an underlying duality quite
similar to that of the Huichols (Spicer 1964*a*). The year is divided into a
short, dry period during Lent and extending up to May 3rd, the day of the
Holy Cross, and a more extensive wet period incorporating the remainder
of the year. As in the Huichol case, Yaqui ritual, sacred symbolism, and

supernaturals change abruptly with these two seasons, although the modern agricultural cycle is not integrated with the ceremonialism. Even though one might argue that the Yaqui ritual cycle reveals acceptance of the Catholic calendar, Spicer believes these are superficial adaptations and that the underlying structure is similar to the Huichol pattern. Dramatic seasonal shifts in ritual actors, types of sacred dances, feeling, and the sacred environment in general provide evidence for dualism in Yaqui ceremonialism. Jesus, or *El Señor,* holds the position of major supernatural during the dry period (all of Lent to May 3rd) and acts as the patron of the dominant dry-period ceremonial sodalities, the *Kabayum* (Horsemen) and the *Jurasim* (Pharisees). On Easter Saturday the Jurasim are defeated in a ritual battle and are gradually replaced by another ceremonial sodality, the *Matachinim,* a male, church-based dancing society. Dedicated to *María Santísima* (Holy Mary), they prepare to give the ceremony for the Holy Cross which culminates on the third of May. Their rituals intensify until July, when they all merge for the ceremony in honor of the *Virgen del Camino* (Virgin of the Road) in the town of Bataconsica. This ceremonial takes place around the time of the beginning of the summer rains. The Matachin groups appear for the remainder of the village ceremonials until Ash Wednesday. During Lent they do not dance because their symbols, especially flowers, are prohibited. In summary, a dual principle exists in Yaqui ceremonialism, shifting from the dry season (Lent) and Jesus and the Jurasim, to the wet season and la Virgen del Camino and the Matachini groups.

Ecological, Ideological, and Structural Limitations

The Mayo data not only support Spicer's (1964*a*) dual model but add interesting complications. The data validate his contention that Yaqui and Mayo ceremonials form a variant type of the proto-central Uto-Aztecan ceremonial, but they also suggest that the ecology of the specific region plays a significant role in determining local variations of the underlying proto-structure. Historical contingencies have also affected culture change differently in the various regions and thus provide another parameter which must be taken into account. For example, in the Yaqui and Mayo cases the Catholic calendar provides a framework and certain ultimate limitations and restrictions which may not be broken, although whether they are recognized and how they are modified provide crucial data for inference regarding the proto-structure. Of course, the Huichols have also undergone some Catholic acculturation; however, they also are bounded by certain rather restrictive ecological conditions which color their adaptation and modification of the underlying proto-structure. In

Myerhoff's (1970, 1974) analysis the Huichols seem to have been a rather marginal group of hunters who were pushed into their present mountainous country and forced to accept farming. They never have completely absorbed the ideology and values of the peasant farmer. Their ceremonialism ritualizes and attempts to integrate this opposition between hunting and farming. These ecological, ideological, and structural limitations suggest that modern Huichol ceremonialism is an extreme attempt to modify the proto-structure to fit the local situation. On the other hand, Weigand (1978*a, b*) prefers to conceive of the Huichols as long-time inhabitants of their present area. However, in either case the Huichol regional ecology is more marginal than that of the Yaqui-Mayo river valleys. The more adaptable, limiting ecological parameters coupled with a deep identification as peasant farmers may have permitted the Yaquis and Mayos to retain many of the principles of the proto-structure which the Huichols were forced to modify. Of course, the Yaquis and Mayos accommodated the proto-structure to the Catholic structure and to the values of colonial and modern Mexico. Thus modern Huichol ceremonialism has modified the proto-structure in terms of a different set of parameters than has modern Yaqui-Mayo ceremonialism. Therefore I am not in full agreement with Spicer's accommodation of the Yaqui data to modern Huichol ceremonialism. This point will become clearer as we examine the Mayo rituals and symbolism and discover certain deep structural resemblances to Aztecan ceremonialism from further south.

The modern technological and economic systems of the Mayo area are essentially isolated from what might be called "Mayo culture." It is likely that the separation of these systems has been gradually taking place for a long period of time, perhaps even extending back into pre-contact periods. Although Spicer (1961*c*) has indicated that, for pre-contact Yaquis, hunting and gathering was of great economic importance, surely farming must have been somewhat more important for Mayos and the groups living just to the south of Mayo country. Certainly after the arrival of the Spanish, farming became the way of life with hunting and gathering and fishing also playing important roles. With seasonal rains and flooding to dampen the fields and river water for irrigation, rainfall often came to be associated with unpleasant, cold, damp weather in the winter which rotted crops and violent storms in the summer which destroyed crops. In the Mayo area two crops a year are possible: wheat, *alinasa* (linseed), *cartamo* (safflower), or cotton planted around December or January and harvested from mid-April through the summer months, and corn and sesame planted in the summer and harvested from November into the winter months.

Although Mayos recognize winter rains and summer rains with drier periods in between, they do not seem willing to deny rain at any time of the year. Even during the Lenten processions a little cloud will lead people to comment, "It's going to rain." This always surprised me because I had believed that rainfall was unheard of during the dry Lenten period and that the *equipatas* (slow winter rains) occurred during December and January. However, in 1976–77 the equipatas did not appear, but a single general rainfall occurred the weekend before Palm Sunday extending from Mazatlán north to Tucson. Thus rainfall is possible during Lent, although it is quite rare.

Duality in Mayo Ceremonialism

Although they do not speak of a wet-dry seasonal shift, Mayos do discuss at length the cold/hot seasonal shift. The first of November is spoken of as the first of the cold season just as the first of May is the beginning of really hot weather. The ceremony for the flag of Banari, the ceremonial center of the *Santísima Tinirán* (Holy Trinity), combined with that for the Virgin of Guadalupe on December 12th, is seen as difficult and uncomfortable due to cold weather, whereas the ceremonies for the Santísima, Tinirán, *Espíritu Santo* (Holy Spirit), and *San Juan* (Saint John) in late May and/or June are characterized as very hot. Lent is conceived of as a cold, extremely windy, dusty ceremonial period. As in Spicer's model, the ceremony for the *Santa Cruz* (Holy Cross) on May 3rd represents a transition from cold to warm weather, and the ceremony for the flag of the Santa Cruz early in September punctuates the end of the extremely hot summer weather. In October the dead visit Mayo homes, an occasion culminating in the ceremonialism for All Saints and All Souls the first and second days of November. Mayos associate the appearance of cold winter winds and cooler winter weather with the dead, and by the first of November cold winter weather has appeared. The first harvest of the corn crop takes place about this time. Pork and green-corn tamales are eaten and offered to the dead. The major corn harvest takes place in December around the time of the ceremony for the *Bantera* (the flag) and for Guadalupe. On the other hand, the first fruits of the spring wheat crop appear around the time of Holy Week, and the harvest takes place a month later, about the time of the Holy Cross ceremony. On Thursday and Good Friday the only decorations on the altar of the Banari church are sprigs of wheat flowers or tassels and palm fronds. During very dry spells San Isidro, known among Mayos as the special saint of farmers, may be petitioned or a procession may go into the fields to pray for rain, although the latter is essentially a custom of the past. Watermelon may be placed on the altar for the ceremonial of San Juan toward the end of June which coincides with the first summer rains. Thus a dual model for Mayo ritual reveals hot/cold, corn/wheat, and life/death parameters. The agricultural cycle is minimally integrated with the ceremonialism: wheat flowers in Easter week, corn tamales with pork for the dead, the first watermelon for San Juan, and the occasional procession for rain. Perhaps an indication of the lack of intensive integration between agriculture and ceremonialism, no pueblo ceremonialism exists in honor of San Isidro. Nevertheless, ceremonialism and the crop cycle both suggest duality, with Holy Week and the Santa Cruz ceremonialism paralleling first fruit and wheat harvest and symbolizing the coming of hot summer weather, and the Bantera of the Santa Cruz and All Souls ceremonialism paralleling first fruit and corn harvest and symbolizing the arrival of cold winter weather.

As in the Huichol and Yaqui cases, Mayo deities and ceremonial sodalities also reflect this dualism. In the lower Mayo River valley, from the September Santa Cruz Bantera ceremony to the May Santa Cruz ceremony, the major ceremonialism focuses upon male supernaturals and upon the dead. The major exception is the December 12th ceremony for Guadalupe. Since Guadalupe is the national symbol and the Virgin of Mexico, the date of the ceremonial cannot be assimilated to the dual pattern. But in the Banari case the ritual is in honor of both Guadalupe and the Bantera of the Santísima Tinirán. Since the Santísima Tinirán is an extremely powerful male image, the ceremonial plays down the out-of-season female saint and ritualizes the arrival of the new flag, the Bantera, of a male image. Thus Mayos assimilated Guadalupe as best they could to the dual ritual pattern. On the other hand, the May–September ritual period does not fit the dual Huichol pattern, as huge pueblo ceremonials take place in honor of both male and female saints. But this is the period for large pueblo ceremonialism, with pilgrimage groups arriving from distant points, as opposed to the winter ceremonial period of local cemetery and local church ritual. Shifts in ceremonial sodalities also take place. Like the Yaqui Jurasim, the Mayo *Parisero* sodality, which acts as the army and pursues, captures, and crucifies Jesus, organizes and carries out much of the Lenten ritual. They are not alone, however, as the *Paskome* (*fiesteros*, ritual hosts of the local church) assist them in making the ceremonial. The masked members of the sodality burlesque the Friday processions and ultimately the *Pilatom* (Pilate) crucify Jesus. As in the Yaqui case, the Matachini dancers do not appear during Lent until Easter Sunday, when they dance in the church. The Parisero masks are burned on Holy Saturday, and their power is finally destroyed on Easter Sunday. The Matachini society grows until hundreds of young dancers, both young men and young women, take part in the gigantic ceremonies for the Espíritu Santo and Santísima Tinirán in late May or early June. These ceremonials parallel the Yaqui one in honor of La Virgen del Camino. It is intended that they also dance for the ceremonies of San Juan in late June and the Santa Cruz Bantera in September, but, after the huge Santísima Tinirán ceremony, many lose interest and few if any turn out for these later ceremonies. The more professional dance sodalities, the Deer and *Paskola* dancers, costumed ritual dance specialists, do not appear during Holy Week until Christ has arisen from the dead early on Holy Saturday morning, nor do they appear for the All Souls ritual in honor of the dead. Thus their pattern is more complex than the dual one that we have developed to this point.

Division Between Male and Female Deities

Examination of specific symbolic entities and patterns illustrates some of the underlying structural uniformities among the Huichols, Yaquis, and Mayos. Perhaps the most pervasive ritual symbol cutting across all three groups is the division between male and female deities. The shift from one set of deities to the other parallels the shift in the cycle of the seasons. For the Huichols the dry season is associated with the Sun, Fire, Peyote, and Deer Tail gods, all male. Only one female deity, representing the moon, appears during the dry season. On the other hand, the wet season is associated with La Abuela Nakawé (Grandmother Growth) and her assistants, called *Nuestras Madres* (Our Mothers), and only one unimportant male deity appears. Sun, Fire, Peyote, and Deer Tail are considered very powerful and extremely dangerous. Peyote and Deer, especially, are sources of medicine and curing power. Thus, male divinity symbolism is associated with dryness and curing, and well-being depends upon these gods and the dry-season rituals. These rituals aim to limit and control the dangerous powers of the male deities. In contrast, La Abuela Nakawé and her assistants, Nuestras Madres, provide benevolent influences and stimulate the growth of the crops. They are associated with water and rain, many being rain spirits or serpents of the differing directions, conceived of as good by the Huichols. Heavy rains and flooding, which destroy crops, provide the only exception to this positive view of water. Rather than controlling and restricting, the wet-season rituals aim to animate and augment the deities' fertile, benevolent powers.

The Yaqui set of deities also is divided into two groups, one male and the other female. The male images tend to be identified with Jesus and with Lenten ritual: El Señor, or Jesus; *El Nazareno; El Ecce Homo; El Jesús Niño,* the patron of the Lenten Kabayum group, and *Jesús crucificado,* the patron of the Jurasim group. They tend to be located on the right side of the church apart from the female images located on the left side of the church. La Virgen, Nuestra Madre (Our Mother), has several manifestations: La Virgen del Rosario, La Virgen Loreta (who acts as the *patrona* of the Matachini dancers and travels with them), and the Santa Cruz (Holy Cross). El Señor acts as a powerful curer, as El Nazareno cured as he travelled around Yaqui country years ago. The Lenten ritual is enacted as a remembrance of the suffering of El Señor and is conceived of as a period of intense discipline and stringent taboos during the dry, uncomfortable Lenten season. Since the Virgin stimulates well-being and happiness, her rituals lack the tension, austerity, and danger associated with Yaqui male supernaturals. She does not impose taboos: the all-night dancing in her honor reflects solace and relaxation rather than the severity associated with Lent and the service of the male deities. Thus the structure of Huichol and Yaqui ritual symbols suggests numerous parallels: dry/wet, male/female, curing/fertility, danger/benevolence, control/augmentation, and suffering-taboos/happiness-relaxation.

The Mayo data reveal one more crucial opposition: death (the dead)/life (the living); however, generally the parallels between the three groups of ritual symbols prove to be amazingly close. Beyond any doubt, the major and most crucial division among Mayo ritual symbols or supernaturals is that between *Itom Achai* (Our Father) and *Itom Aye* (Our Mother), with all the male deities being classified as Itom Achai and all the female ones grouped as Itom Aye. This can be very confusing because specific images are often referred to as Itom Aye or Itom Achai, terms which leave the listener uncertain as to which specific image is being discussed. When requested to clarify, Mayos often simply add a name to the category: for example, *Itom Achai O'ola* (God the Father), *Itom Achai Usi* (Jesus), *Itom Achai Adan* (Adam), *Itom Aye Eva, Itom Aye María Dolorosa,* or *Itom Aye Guadalupe.* The Holy Family, a crucial ritual symbol for Mayos (see Crumrine 1977), incorporates and integrates these groups into a fertile, productive family with Jesus filling the position of child. As at Yaqui altars, with male images on the right side of the church and female on the left (see Spicer 1964*a*:31), Mayo images also are positioned in terms of their sex, with female images on the worshipper's right and male ones on the worshipper's left as he or she stands facing the main altar. This pattern carries over into ritual participation; during Lent the *Bai Mariam* (Three Marys, the women and girls) position themselves on the female side of the church and the *Bai Reyesim* (Three Kings, men and boys) on the male side. At a more general level, males participate as *maestros* (lay ministers) and as members of the Parisero sodality and the Matachini, Paskola, and Deer dancing societies, and women participate as *cantoras* (church singers) and altar attendants.

The Mayo wet/dry or hot/cold seasonal, cyclical symbolism suggests a more subtle configuration than that of the Yaquis. In Mayo ritual no clear correlation exists between male supernaturals and the cold winter season and female supernaturals and the hot summer season, although many lines of evidence point in this direction. Mayo ritual and belief focus upon oppositions which, when mediated, produce new emergent levels of ceremonialism, yet within the parameters of the underlying structure, itself a synthesis of oppositions.

Mayo Seasonal Symbolism

The ceremonial for the flag of the Holy Cross in September, and the return of the dead in October and their leave-taking the first of November, initiates the winter cycle. The small, local ceremony in honor of Guadalupe in Banari also celebrates the arrival of the new Holy Trinity flag, the flag of a male image. In fact, most of the ritual focuses upon the flag, although the image of Guadalupe is placed in the center of the altar. The Santa Cruz Paskome (ritual hosts) from a nearby church assist, but no saint visits and the major encounter and climax of the ceremonial occurs at the bank of the Mayo River when the new flag is unveiled and carried back to the church. The image of Guadalupe is not a part of this procession to the river and return to the church accompanying the new flag. Ceremonialism for the visiting dead takes place in individual homes and local cemeteries. Lenten ceremonialism is also local in organization; that is, it does not involve visiting saints. Focusing upon questions of death and resurrection, its major roles are played by male supernaturals and the male sodality, the Pariserom. The dead are said to bring the cold, windy winter weather of November, and the extremely unpleasant, cool dusty winds of Lent are explained as the footsteps of Itom Achai as he travels around Mayo country. The Pariserom who are dedicated to God also have his permission to crucify Jesus, although their masked "soldiers" are also linked to the Devil by some Mayos. Ultimately the power of God, in the form of the sun, symbolically burns up the Pariserom at noon on Easter Saturday, and later the masks are destroyed on a real bonfire. At the same time several masked Pariserom, Paskolam, *Alawasim* (ritual hosts), and the Deer Dancer run three times from the altar out to the church cross and bells directly in front of the church, where they whip the earth with long mesquite branches. As they run, the bells ring and people throw flowers and shout, "Loria" (Gloria).

Both Jesus' return from the dead on Easter Sunday and the ceremony for the Holy Cross on May 3rd symbolize the shift to the hot summer season. Yet a synthesis of the male/female and seasonal oppositions appears in the Mayo data. Mary plays a crucial role in Lenten ceremonialism, and the Parisero sodality, which I had earlier thought was an exclusively male group, includes female members called *Verónicas*. One family, whose daughter was promised as a member of the sodality and participated during many of the seven weeks of Lent, called her their "little Parisero" and conceived of her as a Parisero. During Lent both Christ (a crucifix) and Mary are carried in the Friday processions, and Mary is carried in most of the Easter week processions. After Jesus is crucified on Good Friday a split procession, with Mary carried in one direction and the cross with the image of Jesus removed borne in the other, is described as "Mary looking for Jesus." On Easter Sunday the encounter takes place with Mary, San Juan, and Jesus playing the major roles. Jesus, accompanied by San Juan and the Santa Cruz Paskome, is carried out from the Paskola dance ramada. The image of Mary escorted by the Santísima Tinirán Paskome moves out from the church. The processions do not meet but stop several hundred feet apart, and, while everyone throws flowers and confetti, San Juan "runs" (is carried by a boy) three times between Jesus and Mary announcing to her that her son is returning. She does not believe him, but after the third run the processions move together and the encounter between mother and son takes place amidst much flower-throwing and cracking of confetti-filled eggs over the heads of the former Pariserom. The summer ceremonials after the Santa Cruz ceremonial on May 3rd involve equally dramatic encounters between a visiting saint and the local host saint, usually one male and the other female, and are spoken of as the "embrace between Our Father and Our Mother" (for these descriptions see Crumrine 1977).

In summary, a dual seasonal cycle exists in Mayo ceremonialism, but it is coded somewhat differently than among the Huichols or Yaquis as a result of differing ecological and contact conditions. The cold, windy, rather dry winter season is strongly associated with male deities, the dead, and death. Danger, suffering, and taboos characterize this ritual period. Both male deities and the dead are extremely strict and demand attention and respect. Sickness, a punishment of the dead, is associated with the cold fall weather and the arrival of the dead. Certain curers lose ritual power during this season. God, as the sun, will burn up those persons who do not respect him, as he destroys the Pariserom. God also grants curing power, and Jesus was a great curer when he lived in this world. Therefore, as in the cases of the Huichols and the Yaquis, Mayo winter ritual provides a means to control the powerful, strict, demanding male supernaturals; to serve the dead and ritualize death; and to obtain the curing powers of God. Deer and tobacco also are linked to this complex. An ancient Mayo curer too busy to heal God was dismembered and transformed into a deer. Thus modern deer are slightly satanical and strongly associated with curing powers. Taking pity on an ugly woman, God transformed her into Mayo tobacco, which is used today in curing and communicating with God. Thus danger, control, curing, deer, and tobacco are linked with the dead, male supernaturals, and the cold, windy winter season as one half of the Mayo manifestation of the central Uto-Aztecan, dual ceremonial structure.

For Mayos the warmer, damp summer season is strongly associated with female deities or male-female encounters, fertility, benevolence, and the living. Like Yaquis, Mayos feel relaxed and happy with Itom Aye (Our Mother) because she is forgiving, loving, and not dangerous *(ka hue'ena)*. She will not punish her children and does not demand respect as does Itom Achai, who is characterized as *hue'ena* (dangerous). The summer ceremonialism, which focuses upon augmentation and glorification of the powers of Itom Achai and Itom Aye, contrasts with the winter ceremonialism, which symbolically controls death and the dead. The encounter of visiting and hosting saints in summer ceremonialism symbolizes the productive union of Itom Achai and Itom Aye. Colorful fireworks, nourishing meat stews and ritual foods, many pilgrims, and Matachini and Deer and Paskola dancing provide an exciting and happy atmosphere for the mass in honor of the host saint and for the encounter and visit of the entertained saint and members of the visiting community. In contrast to winter ceremonials, in which local people sit around the graves of their dead and masked Pariserom enforce proper kneeling ritual in Lenten processions obscured by clouds of choking, biting, wind-driven dust, the summer ceremonials bring huge crowds of people together in colorful, exciting interaction. Nevertheless, the symbolism here is more complex, and certain parallels with Huichol and Yaqui patterns are even more explicit. As in Huichol belief, the Mayo Itom Achai controls and in fact is the sun, and the Mayo Itom Aye, identified as the moon and "nature," controls the fertile power of growth which permits plants to sprout and mature. In contrast to Huichol belief, the Mayo Itom Achai also controls the rain, although the productive powers of water, of the earth, and of life are controlled by Itom Aye. Oppositions are established only to be mediated through myth and ritual such as the encounter of Jesus and Mary or of Itom Achai and Itom Aye in the summer ceremonials. In summary, the following oppositions characterize the structure of the proto-central Uto-Aztecan belief and ritual system: male/female, winter (dry, cold, windy)/summer (wet, warm, damp), curing/fertility, danger/benevolence, control/augmentation, suffering-taboos/happiness-relaxed, dead/living. Thus the underlying ritual structure proves surprisingly uniform and the surface symbolism considerably divergent. Much of this surface symbolism reflects contact conditions and what might be called a Catholic systemic pattern, especially in the Yaqui and Mayo cases, and precontact and ecological conditions in the Huichol case.

Ritual Symbols

As for specific ritual symbols, Spicer (1964*a*), elaborating the Yaqui ritual symbol flower, discusses the "battle" between the church organizations, including the Matachini group, the Deer and Paskola, and the congregation versus the Jurasim (Pariserom), which takes place on Easter Saturday. It symbolizes the defeat of the male gods of the dry season by the female deities and their supporters aided by the power of the flowers, which are thrown during the "battle." As described above, a similar ritual takes place in the Mayo ceremonial center of Banari but does not seem to represent a "battle." While God, the sun, is burning up (destroying) the Pariserom, a special group of some ten persons runs three times out of the church and whips the earth directly in front of the bells and church cross. It seems strange that this group consists of several Alawasim (ritual hosts) representing the Holy Trinity patron of the church; several Paskolas and the Deer Dancer, representing the world of the forest; and several masked Pariserom, representing the Parisero sodality. These three groups cooperate and "have God's permission" to make the Lenten ceremonial. The only explanation Mayos give for this ritual is, *"Es la costumbre"* ("It is the custom."), even though I have supplied them with suggestions: for example, the whipping awakens Itom Aye and her fertile powers, or they are punishing the earth for eating us when we die. Although one still suspects that at one time the Mayo ritual must have symbolized the change in ritual cycle from male-dead-winter to female-living-summer, today it does not clearly represent a "battle" as does the Yaqui ritual. The Mayo Deer and Paskola dancers are active both during Lent and during the summer ceremonial cycle, and they dance in honor of both male and female saints. They present themselves as in the service of God; however, their world, the *huya ania* (the forest world), is controlled by a little old man, the *huya o'ola*. He parallels the Huichol male-dominated world of the deer. For Mayos the world of the ocean is controlled by the *hawe hamyo'ola* (the old woman of the sea), which parallels the Huichol use of fish blood for female deities. The orientations mentioned by Spicer (1964*a*), including emphasis on intense arduous ceremonial labor, and power in ritual dance, songs, and the areas where these take place, also hold for Mayo ritual. Yet in Mayo belief I do not find the linked blood-flower ritual symbol which Spicer reports in Yaqui belief. Although Mayos do claim that Jesus saved the world through one drop of his blood, they do not know the Yaqui

story that flowers grew from the drops of Christ's blood or that Mary
turned herself into the cross and Jesus died in her arms (see Spicer
1940:254, 1954a:116; 1964a). For Mayos the Santa Cruz is Itom Achai,
male, and not Itom Aye, as is the belief among Yaquis. After the crucifixion the masked Pariserom paint red rings around their arms and legs
representing the blood of Jesus; these resemble the rings decorating the
Easter *Judios* (Judases, Pharisees) of the Cora Indians. Rather, for Mayos
this ritual symbol appears to consist of deer-flower-tobacco. Flowers,
representing an offering or a contract, are presented to both male and
female supernaturals. Tobacco, the sacrifice of the ugly woman, also is
smoked as a contract, as an offering to and communication with supernaturals, and as a medicine in itself. The Deer Dancer is decorated with
flowers, just as the real deer "eats flowers in the forest," and has supernatural senses since he represents the sacrificed, transformed curer. In
summary, although some of the specific ritual symbols are modified, the
underlying structures of Mayo, Yaqui, and Huichol religion represent
variations on the proto-central Uto-Aztecan pattern. The seven characteristics suggested by Spicer for Yaqui and Huichol ceremonialism also
typify the Mayo data: a dual ritual calendar; sex division in supernaturals;
kinship organization extended to the supernaturals; strict, difficult ceremonial labor; ceremonial labor which harmonizes social relations; sacred
dance, song, and patio; and (with the addition of tobacco in the Mayo
case) the blood-flower symbol, which provides important links between
man and deity.

MODERN TECHNOLOGY
VERSUS TRADITIONAL IDEOLOGY

Mayo technology and economy reflect a highly integrated relation
with modern Mexican agriculture, except that Mayos are at one extreme of
the continuum as rural agriculturalists who rely upon irrigation water,
modern seed, fertilizer, fungicide and insecticide, modern machinery, and
worldwide markets. Yet their ideology and ceremonialism reflect a precontact structure fused with a Catholic systemic pattern of surface symbolism and ritual. Out of necessity, modern Mayo social organization is
adapted and even generated to mediate this opposition. When the opposition becomes greater than the mediating ability of the social organization,
Mayos generate revitalization movements in an attempt to maintain their
ideological structure and explain the contingencies of the modern world
within the terms of their traditional symbolic and ritual system. Thus
modern Mayo social organization represents an artifact of the opposition

and necessary integration of the modern techno-economic conditions with a fused symbolic system acting as a mechanism of Mayo boundary maintenance.

Although the traditional Mayo social organization focused upon the extended household, in the late twentieth century the nuclear family acts as the basic socio-economic unit, with ritual kinship, ejido, and neighbor relations replacing the extended kinship system. As an extension of the ideological system, the Holy Family (Itom Aye, Our Mother; Itom Achai, God; Itom Achai Usi, Jesus) provides the explanatory model and design for these developments in the social organization (see Crumrine 1977). The nuclear family is well adapted to the modern techno-economic conditions and thus mediates the two opposing levels. A value for extended households still exists, but modern ecological and economic conditions are crucial variables, since a young family, receiving a grant of land as a member of a newly formed ejido, may have to live alone near their fields. If the young husband works as a fisherman, the couple will live in one of the fishing villages.

Mayo ceremonialism stands opposed to the modern pattern of nuclear family households because the traditional rituals require large cooperative groups. Ritual kin bonds supply the modern Mayo nuclear family with the assistance formerly provided by *Wawari* members (the extended kindred) or distant real kin (see also Spicer's discussion of ritual kinship among Yaquis, 1940:91–116). With inflation, gradually increasing expenses, and more commercial cash-cropping, ceremonies have become more expensive and hosts require more cooperation in the form of cash than in the form of foodstuffs or labor. Rituals are crucial if Mayos are to maintain their separate identity, and, with more cash but less buying power, it is unclear whether the modern social organization can meet the heavy mediating demands being placed upon it. The Mayo interpretation of unusual social and natural events, however, reveals that the underlying symbolic structure is still very powerful. In complete acceptance and belief a Mayo friend related the following account:

> Juan, a former Paskoma (ritual host) in Banari, saw Itom Achai and Itom Aye Guadalupe during the hurricane Liza. The wind was terrific and there were many clouds and much lightning but very little rain. Juan looked up in the sky and in the clouds he saw Itom Achai and Itom Aye. Itom Achai was trying to burn up the world and was throwing down lightning rays to ignite the world. Itom Aye was carrying a bucket of water. She was dumping the water on the fire and keeping the world from burning up.

Numerous other Mayos volunteered that "Liza" was a punishment of God directed against the people of the Mayo area. This supernatural experience relies directly upon the structure and symbolism of the proto-central Uto-Aztecan model; the angry, dangerous male deity using fire tries to destroy the world, and the helpful, forgiving female deity using water tries to save the world. Thus this structure and symbolism is capable of generating new surface manifestations in response to ongoing ecological situations.

Mayo and Yaqui Adaptations to Contact

The differences between Mayo and Yaqui responses to modern conditions in Sonora are based on differences in conditions of culture contact (Spicer 1970). During the 1800s a larger number of Mexicans colonized down the Mayo River valley than in the Yaqui River area. The city of Alamos, in the upper Mayo area, was the colonial capital of the entire area and a rich mining region. Gradually Mayos lost autonomy to colonists during the nineteenth century and were subdued in the 1880s. Before and even after this period Mayos attacked and often burned newly established mestizo towns. Even after subdual, Mayo opposition continued to exist, especially during the revolution years of 1910 into the mid-1920s. Mayo war leaders such as Bachomo in the Fuerte area and Totoriwoki, who was finally executed near Huatabampo, continued to harass and attack mestizo communities. But sheer numbers and intensity of contact, as mentioned by Spicer, (and, I would add, the natural ecology of the areas) proved interesting variables in differential selective adaptation on the part of Mayos versus Yaquis. Evidence presented by Spicer (1970) and collected by myself suggests that proto-militaristic and proto-ideological structures existed and that Mayos and Yaquis adapted both structures to real contact situations. Modern differences are rooted in the specific historical events and successes in structural adaptation, which stimulated further elaboration and application of symbols and behavior drawn from the more aggressive or more symbolic aspects of the proto-structure. Thus, as Spicer (1970:113) suggests regarding Yaqui supernatural experiences, such as the appearance of the Archangel Michael during the signing of the peace treaty of 1897, we are dealing with the selective elaboration and the variables associated with success or failure in structural adaptation rather than the absence or presence of one pattern or another.

Without a doubt the structure of contact directly affects the social organization, which mediates the techno-economic and ideological structures and therefore may effect changes throughout the system. Spicer (1970) deals at length with this variable, although he neglects to mention that there was minimal but continuing guerrilla resistance on the part of Mayos. Certain ecological differences also prove interesting. Obvious differences exist between the Huichol and Yaqui-Mayo areas, which we have already discussed. Although the Yaqui and Mayo live in the same ecological zone and only fifty miles apart, some important micro-ecological differences exist. A brief trip through Yaqui and Mayo country and a glance at a map suggest rather different locations of mountain areas, areas of guerrilla refuge, and different coastal-plain and river-flow patterns. Large broken mountainous areas stand only a few miles above much of Yaqui country, while in Mayo country they exist only in the Alamos area, traditionally an area of light Mayo population but heavy Spanish and later mestizo colonization. It must have been relatively easy for Yaquis to escape to mountain refuge, to visit villages at night, and to be supported by "subdued" villagers, but Mayo escape into the mountains was blocked by the Spanish and later mestizo stronghold. Today most of the Mayo River valley is cleared and cropped, especially around and below Navojoa. This pattern has considerable time depth. With the exception of several peripheral small mountains the entire area is quite flat and low, the river flowing directly southwest across the coastal plain. It would be difficult for very many Mayos to hide successfully in this area for any lengthy period of time. Escape might have been accomplished to the southeast or northwest along the coastal plain and then up into the mountains to the northeast. In this context it is interesting to note that between 1880 and 1890 two of the Mayo prophetic centers and points of ritual concentration were located in or near the foothills, one to the south near Maciaca and the other, Cabora, to the north. These prophetic centers were to act as refuge points from the floods being predicted by the Mayo prophets.

Flowing directly across the low coastal plain, the Mayo River contrasts with the Yaqui, which bends to the west and flows up the coastal plain through Yaqui country. The Yaqui River somewhat parallels the mountain ranges, and the villages tend to be located on higher ground to the north of the river itself. The upper Yaqui River and its tributaries spread over a huge area, thus assuring a more constant supply of water than the much smaller Mayo River. This also suggests that flooding would be more dramatic along the Mayo, especially since there is little high refuge in the entire lower Mayo River valley. Acosta (1949:9) notes that in aboriginal times Mayos, and apparently also Yaquis, constructed platforms in large trees where they could cook and find refuge during periods of flooding. The loss of this custom after the arrival of the Spanish left the Mayos in a more precarious and anxiety-producing situation than before. Being the larger of the two rivers, the Yaqui had a more secure water supply, although during the late twentieth century both Yaquis and Mayos have been short of water. Thus a difference in river conditions suggests a more intense pattern of both flood and burning-sun symbolism among Mayos than among Yaquis. Numerous disastrous floods have been reported from the Mayo area. Spicer (1970:119–20) mentions 1868 as the worst flood year in Mayo history and suggests that it may have stimulated the prophetic movements of the 1880s. Heavy flooding also occurred in the first half of this century. Mature Mayos clearly remember and can graphically describe these floods. Even though a dam now controls flooding, Mayos live in fear that it may break and wipe out the communities in the river valley. The Mayo religious movement of the late 1950s and 1960s, initiated by Antonio Bacasewa (see Erasmus 1961; 1967; Spicer 1970:109–11), whom I named Damian in my earlier publications (Crumrine 1975, 1977; Crumrine and Macklin 1974; Macklin and Crumrine 1973), was characterized by intense fear of flooding and destruction. "Everyone around here was really frightened when they heard Damian speak or heard about the coming flood." In August 1972, after a heavy, three-day tropical rain, the Mayo valley stood devastated and flooded (see Crumrine 1975). Many Mayos were sure the world was ending, and a Mayo woman saw God, Itom Achai, in a small Mayo church during the rains. By October a second Mayo woman was experiencing visits from Itom Achai, although these were not specifically connected with the rains. She and her husband organized a group which ultimately founded and constructed a new Mayo church. Thus natural disaster, especially flooding, has a long history of association with the appearance of new Mayo religious movements. Neither the tropical rains nor hurricane Liza hit Yaqui country. Thus different micro-ecological conditions of the two river systems appear to have a bearing on the Mayo selection of indigenous flood symbolism for current symbolic and ritual elaboration and the Yaqui rejection of such symbolism.

Floods and Revitalization Cults

In the 1957–60 and 1972 movements the major driving symbolism involved the anger of Itom Achai (God) and his threats to punish man by destroying humanity either by flood or by fire. Thus the primary, overt purpose of the ritual of the cults was control of a powerful, dangerous male deity. Disease and curing also quickly became associated with the cults, especially with the 1957–60 movement. Certain "traditional" innovations appeared in the 1972 movement. Women participated separately from men and stood on the worshipper's right side of the altar. God was particularly angry with long hair in men and short skirts in women. The former represented a symbolic blending of male and female : "long hair in a man is like a woman." Worshippers learned the prayers in Mayo and spoke only Mayo at the new Center, drank and ate fiesta foods from traditional pottery containers, and sat on mats on the ground while eating because tables are not "traditional" and Itom Achai did not want them. Due to the ritual labor associated with the new cult, Itom Achai has not yet chosen to end the world but he will do so in the near future. Water, in the form of a flood, will come from one direction and fire from the other. The church at the Center will be surrounded by destruction but will be saved by the power of Itom Achai. Without going into further detail, it is clear that this entire set of ritual symbols and ideological structure has been lifted directly from the proto-structure with very little accommodation. At first this cult was very strong and enthusiastically supported by nearly all the Mayos I knew. Everyone either visited the Center or tried to send contributions to the Center or to the many home ceremonies taking place. But, not having a great deal of spare time or money, most Mayos rather quickly lost interest, although a core of devout followers persisted. Thus the symbolism and ideology of the cult was readily accepted by most Mayos as being Mayo and as basically true, demonstrating that the ideological structure and system of ritual symbols still played a powerful role in Mayo perception of and reaction to the modern world.

Although the revitalization movements of 1957–60 and 1972 failed as innovative political movements, they nevertheless generated new ceremonial centers. This phenomenon suggests a general historical pattern of generation and migration of Mayo ceremonial centers. Thus the revitalization cults contain adaptive, survival, and productive aspects even though the original founder and messianic fervor quickly disappear. The traditional ceremonial center of Banari grew directly out of Santa Cruz, the original mission pueblo, through Huatabampo, the late nineteenth-century and early twentieth-century ceremonial center. In the nineteenth century Santa Cruz was burned, and, perhaps due to warfare or flooding, the saints were moved to the growing center of Huatabampo. As Huatabampo gradually became more mestizo, the Mayos were pushed out and the saints were re-established in Banari early in the twentieth century. After some factionalism and during a flood, a group split away and established a second Santísima Tinirán church a few miles away on a sandhill, an area which some Mayos claimed was safe from flooding. Another ceremonial center in honor of the Santa Cruz was established only several miles from Huatabampo and, as a direct result of home fiestas given in support of the cult of Damian, a second Santa Cruz church was established in the 1960s somewhat farther away from Huatabampo. The church of a later religious movement also in honor of the Santa Cruz was built in 1973 near Etchojoa. Thus the creation and migration of ceremonial centers has some historical depth in the Mayo area. Flooding seems to have been one of the contributing factors coupled with the more recent growth of mestizo population in the area. In contrast, the Yaqui ceremonial centers appear to have been relatively stable (see Spicer 1970:115–17), perhaps owing to higher locations and lesser flooding and to differential experiences regarding pressure of the mestizo population within the pueblo ceremonial centers themselves. However, the entire missionary-generated process of concentration appears to have been somewhat different and more successful in the Yaqui area than among the Mayos, many of whom continued to live in small household clusters at the edges of their fields. Perhaps micro-ecological factors play some role here as well. Destruction in the Mayo area due to flooding versus the higher location of at least some of the Yaqui mission pueblos, coupled with a longer, more dispersed river valley in the Yaqui case, may have encouraged more successful and enduring settlement of the Yaquis' Jesuit-established "Eight Pueblos." Mayos still maintain an "Eight Pueblo" ideology, although there is not much general agreement regarding the specific eight pueblos and the same person may even mention different villages at different times. Although Mayos no longer control the village political organization, which probably broke down because of micro-ecological and contact conditions and the resulting migration of ceremonial centers, they do accept the concept of "Eight Pueblos" as a sacred symbol. Unlike the mestizo-controlled political organization, Mayo ceremonial centers are controlled by Mayo church officials, leaders of ceremonial sodalities, and maestrom (lay ministers). Thus, not all Mayo power and control has been lost; it is maintained through migration and creation of new ceremonial centers, a somewhat different mechanism than that used by the Yaquis. Nevertheless, this mechanism has developed as a successful means of maintaining control over the Mayo ideological and ritual symbol system.

Mediation of Oppositions

In summary, modern Mayo life mediates a dual set of interrelated oppositions: (1) mestizo culture and society versus Mayo social organization as mediated by the contact social structure and (2) the techno-economic system versus the Mayo ideological system as mediated by the Mayo social organization (see Fig. 7.1). One set of oppositions exists within the Mayo system and the other between the Mayo and the mestizo systems. The integration of these systems of the dual opposition generates the contact social organization and the Mayo social organization. Although the contact social structure provides a range of possibilities for integration between the groups (see Crumrine 1977), unresolved opposition and tension still exist, especially regarding land ownership. Most Mayos have been deprived of the aboriginal lands, and even those who hold some lands, either as members of an ejido or as small property

Figure 7.1 The set of dual oppositions in modern Mayo life

owners, usually have no more than eight or ten hectares. In 1976 a pattern of invasions of both private and ejido lands developed, and even the state governor, Alejandro Carillo Marcor (1976:1, 7), recognized that a settlement had been made with the Yaquis but that Mayo land had simply been taken over by others. This he considered one of the "greatest injustices of the Revolution" and close to Mayo "genocide." Since the inauguration of President José López Portillo in 1977 the situation has stabilized; however, Mayo-mestizo relations and, in general, peasant-farmer relations have remained rather volatile and unpredictable in the 1980s.

When the social organization no longer smoothly mediates the opposition between the techno-economic system and the ideological system, alternative responses appear. In the Mayo case the new religious movements reinforce the underlying ideological system through overt manifestation and dramatization of the ritual symbols rooted in the underlying ideological structure; the new cults thus restate the opposition in slightly differing forms and create new, deeply Mayo, ceremonial centers more isolated from mestizo control than the older, more established centers. In many ways the Mayo case resembles that of the Coras as developed in the interesting paper by Hinton (1981), just as the Yaqui case resembles that of the Huichols; that is to say, Huichol:Yaqui::Cora:Mayo. Thus the crucial role of opposition, so important in the creation and maintenance of an opposition culture and social group and a persistent cultural system, provides a major impetus to the dynamics of the modern Mayo identity system in northwest Mexico:

. . . certain kinds of identifiable conditions give rise to this type of cultural system. These may best be summarized as an oppositional process involving the interactions of individuals in the environment of a state or similar large-scale organization. The oppositional process frequently produces intense collective consciousness and a high degree of internal solidarity. This is accomplished by a motivation for individuals to continue the kind of experience that is "stored" in the identity system in symbolic form. [Spicer 1971:799]

Among the Mayos of northwest Mexico, opposition is dramatized and mediated by means of rituals and symbols drawn from their traditional dualistic belief and ceremonial structure and modified to fit their unique historico-geographical experiences and techno-economic limitations within modern Mexico.

| 8 |

Ritual as Interethnic Competition

Indito Versus Blanco in Mountain Pima Easter Ceremonies

Timothy Dunnigan

The importance of ritual in resolving social conflict has received considerable attention since Gluckman's (1954) seminal lecture of "rites of rebellion" in African societies. The cathartic effects of openly expressing social
group antagonisms in prescribed ways, such as engaging in limited types
of role reversals, may result in a significant reduction of potentially destructive tensions. However, it can also be argued (Norbeck 1961:211–12;
1967) that the dramatization of conflicts, particularly when they involve
members of different cultures and contain elements of competition and/or
derision, can intensify hostile attitudes. Crumrine (1970) has compared
the results of his research on the Mexican Mayo with other studies to show
how ritual drama is an important element in the adjustment between
social groups that are unequal in power. Rites that promote identification
with the subordinate society are contrasted with those that provide the
means for individuals to become incorporated into the dominant social
structure. Ritual can either promote cultural maintenance or accelerate
assimilation.

The assumption that ritual reduces conflict by reinforcing traditional values or by facilitating assimilation does not seem justified in the case of Mountain Pima Easter ceremonies as conducted in the village of Oijig. These rites provoke as much conflict as they resolve. At one level of analysis, the Easter ceremonies of the Mountain Pima and the way they articulate with blanco celebrations can be viewed as a dramatic enactment of interethnic relations that shape everyday social interaction. They are also an occasion for mobilizing powerful symbols in support of Pima identity and separation from white society. The most significant aspect of the Pima ceremonies, however, is the intense competition involving fundamental issues of political control over economic resources. These rites are not merely symbolic of something that has transpired in another arena. They are the substance of both inter- and intraethnic conflict, a striving for enhanced power in a very dynamic situation.

THE PERSISTENT CULTURE

Data on Mountain Pima Easter ceremonies was collected during three periods of observation between 1965 and 1970 at a Mexican town in eastern Sonora which I will call Oijig, a Pima pseudonym meaning 'a place that is cultivated.' My first impression of Pima ritual life in Oijig was that it had declined to a point where it could not be sustained much longer. Faubert (1975) has noted the survival in another Mountain Pima community of native dances and medieval Christian rituals that were no longer practiced in Oijig. The disparity between accounts provided by Oijig residents concerning Easter celebrations held in the 1950s and the practices of 1965–70 seemed to indicate that the more numerous but politically weaker indigenous population was rapidly disappearing as a distinct culture group.

By the end of my field research, I realized that such assumptions about the survival of Pima culture were not supported by the data. The Oijig Pimas possess what Spicer (1971) calls a "persistent identity system." An examination of their history and contemporary culture patterns show that they continue to participate in the three areas of common understanding considered by Spicer (1971:799) to be necessary for the maintenance of ethnic identity. The Oijig Pimas communicate among themselves in a language comprehended by few outsiders, they share the same moral values, and they are politically organized for achieving the objectives of group policy.

These areas of common understanding have become more strongly expressed since the 1940s in response to the threat posed by aggressive whites. The competition between Pimas *('o'ob)* and non-Indians *(dudkam)* and the resulting rise in Indian militancy exemplify Spicer's (1971:797–98) concept of the "oppositional process." The opposition between *indito* and *blanco,* the commonly used Spanish terms for Oijig's two ethnic groups, has become one of the most salient features of the Pima Easter ceremonies. The Pimas have a strong political interest in seeing that these rituals continue in some form as a way of exercising self-government. The blancos have become hostile to these celebrations because of the political implications and would like to see them absorbed into blanco-sponsored religious observances, if not discontinued entirely.

Because they cannot rely on legal remedies or wait for a vigorous defense of Indian claims by governmental institutions at the state or federal levels, the Pimas must take every opportunity to assert their rights, which are constantly under attack. Easter provides such an occasion, and the Pimas cannot afford to have their rituals die out completely. Considerable change and compromise has been forced by circumstances but, in view of the modern function of these ceremonies, they are likely to continue for some time. The oppositional process is, to some extent, self-perpetuating.

The Town

The Mountain Branch of the Lower Pimas, including both Sonora and Chihuahua settlements, probably numbers no more than 1,500 persons, most of whom practice subsistence agriculture. Due to the patchy distribution of cultivable land in the Sierra Madre Occidental, the dominant settlement pattern is one of many small and widely separated *ranchos.* Typically, a rancho consists of a few loosely clustered farms occupied by related nuclear families. Mountain Pimas also reside in small numbers on the periphery of ranching towns and sawmills where they stay as long as work is available and the seasonal demands of rancho farming do not arise. Occasionally, individuals labor in the agricultural industries of the Sonoran lowland for a short period, and more rarely an entire family moves to a lowland city or town for an extended stay.

The in-town residents of Oijig are mostly blanco, that is, white ranch owners and their overseers (about twenty-five families), while the approximately five hundred Pimas live for the most part on satellite ranchos which are ten minutes' to five hours' walk away. Oijig proper serves as a ceremonial center for the Indian population. Here are located the old mission chapel and a newer church erected by the blancos. The chief civil official of the Pimas, the gobernador, has a residence in town, and it is to Oijig that the rancho dwellers must come in order to participate in community-wide religious fiestas and to conduct their political affairs.

Pimas also visit Oijig out of a need to patronize blanco stores and look for wage work.

As is the case with other Sierra Indians, such as the neighboring Tarahumaras and Warihios, the Mountain Pimas have a political organization which is highly atomistic. A sense of common tribal identity is shared by Pimas living in a number of settlements on both sides of the Sonora-Chihuahua line, but each village is completely autonomous and without a tradition of inter-community alliances beyond its satellite ranchos. Even the rancho enjoys considerable independence, since it can dispose of local lands free of effective interference from other sectors of the community. The lack of intervillage political linkages has seriously hampered the Pimas in taking concerted action against blanco incursion.

Historical Background

Because of its isolation, Oijig did not experience strong acculturative pressures from non-Indians until late in the nineteenth century when ranchers began reestablishing themselves in the Sierra subsequent to the pacification of the Apaches.* Oijig was given *ejido* status in 1905 with an area in excess of 1,700 hectares. Only a small percentage of the land was allotted, some to several blanco families, and the remainder was unassigned. Large tracts were claimed by blancos to the east and west of the ejido lands which the Pimas traditionally considered their own. In this way many Pima holdings were completely surrounded and eventually engulfed by the blanco ranches. Notwithstanding their exclusion from the official ejido, the traditional sociopolitical links between the outlying Pima ranchos and Oijig proper continued to be observed by the Indians.

Before the Mexican Revolution of 1910, the invasion of blancos remained sufficiently limited so that open conflict with the indigenous population was avoided. There was still enough reserve land so that internal migration on the part of the Pimas could temporarily solve the problem of increasing territorial pressures from the blancos. The indigenous civil and religious institutions remained intact, and the Pimas governed their own affairs while tolerating the blanco presence. After the Revolution, blanco settlement rapidly increased to the point that land shortage became critical for the Indians. Some of the dispossessed Pimas obtained new lands from close relatives, while others formed economic patnerships with kinsmen by agreeing to contribute their labor and income to a

---

*The history of early European contacts with the Mountain Pimas is detailed in Spicer (1962) and Dunnigan (1969).

common agricultural venture. This kind of cooperation was not something new for the Mountain Pimas, but the pooling of resources became more important as Indian holdings shrank in size.

The mines, and later the sawmills, provided an occupational alternative for some Pimas. Working for wages was not, however, an entirely satisfactory answer to the economic undercutting by aggressive ranchers. When the mines closed down or men were laid off at the mills, the ensuing depression was difficult to endure. Livestock-herding, fence-building, and other short-term jobs offered by the ranchers could support only a few, and any Pima who did accept a blanco as his *patrón* was usually required to plant on shares. This meant that the patrón supplied seed and plow beasts in return for half the crop and pasture rights to the land of the Pima. Credit in the form of high-priced store goods might also be extended by the blanco. In order to avoid further dependence on the local blancos and at the same time support rising standards of consumption, increasing numbers of Pimas came to rely on seasonal agricultural jobs in the Sonoran lowland.

Political Structures

The Pima gobernador is the modern counterpart of the traditional *mo'otkar* or headman. As moral leader of the Indian community and chief arbiter of its disputes, he holds the most influential position among the Pimas. The role of assistant gobernador is without any real significance. The creation of six ejidal offices followed the decision of a federal commission in the 1940s to expand the communal lands of Oijig to almost 4,000 hectares. Like the position of gobernador, these are elective offices. Their functions are somewhat unclear, and only the president of the ejido appears to command even slight authority. His job is to investigate Pima complaints of land encroachment, cattle theft, crop damage by roving livestock, and so forth. When only Pimas are involved, the president may be able to successfully mediate a settlement, sometimes with the help of the gobernador.

The authority of the Pima officials is severely constrained by the blanco power structure. Oijig is a dependency of the *cabecera* or administrative center of the county-like regional unit called a *minicipio*. The representatives of state government in Oijig are the blanco comisario and his assistant, both important ranchers. The comisario is directly answerable to the president of the cabecera, but Oijig's isolation gives the local blancos an added measure of discretionary power. Also, several wealthy ranching families living in the cabecera have holdings in the Oijig area and can be expected to support the decisions of the comisario against the

Pimas. The ability to exercise strong controls became even more important for the blancos when the ejido was again enlarged in the 1960s, this time to more than 17,000 hectares. Only persons listed in a 1943 census of Oijig have legal rights in the ejido along with their heirs, and the vast majority are Pimas. Unfortunately for the Pimas, the boundaries of the Oijig communal lands have never been surveyed. Until this is done, the blancos can continue to exploit all disputed territory as long as they remain politically dominant.

The Setting

Most religious activity in Oijig during Holy Week centers on the ruined mission church (*capilla*) of the Pimas and the new church (*iglesia*) of the blancos. Both are located on the western side of the large town plaza with the iglesia in front. The blancos erected their church, they say, to house the various santos and other relics which were poorly protected in the partially roofed capilla. As the result of this transfer, the blancos gained control over the community's most significant religious symbols and became the custodians of the alms box, which often receives donations from persons traveling long distances either to ask a favor of Oijig's patron San Francisco or to repay some benefit already bestowed by the saint. The church keys are held by the *guardiana,* the widow of a blanco rancher, and her permission must be obtained if the Pimas wish access to their own *santos.*

THE CHRONOLOGY OF HOLY WEEK

There is often a marked difference between what is reported by Pimas to be appropriate conduct during Easter at Oijig and what actually occurs. As already indicated, it would be a mistake to interpret such differences as merely symptoms of deterioration in Pima ritual life leadng to imminent extinction. The apparent deviations from behavioral norms described in oral traditions that pertain primarily to the mission period reflect a more recent set of strategies for dealing with blancos. Both Indians and blancos use the occasion to demonstrate their political power and test the prerogatives of their opponents. Factions within the Indian community also maneuver against one another during the observance of Easter. The situation necessarily will remain dynamic while the contending ethnic groups struggle for advantages that are both symbolic and real.

On the Saturday preceding Palm Sunday the gobernador assigns several Pima men the task of gathering bear grass and juniper boughs to be used the next day in making small crosses which are staked around the plaza to mark the Stations of the Cross. The Pimas are anxious to see that this responsibility is delegated in a timely way. According to tradition, the gobernador will have to relinquish considerable authority to ceremonial leaders during Holy Week, and it is important to obtain his full cooperation. The gobernador's direct supervision is particularly needed when many of the Pima men are forced to stay at jobs in other parts of the Sierra until after Holy Week ceremonies have begun.

At noon on Wednesday all Pima males who wish to volunteer as *fariseos* (pronounced *farisé* in Pima), or Pharisees, gather inside the capilla. The fariseos served few important governing functions in the 1960s, but they were once the sole civil authority in Oijig during Holy Week. The gobernador formerly transferred all the powers of his office to this group by formal declaration and, except for a few brief appearances, was expected to remain in the background until these powers were returned to him or his successor on Easter Sunday.

The modern gobernador may not want to cooperate in a process that diminishes his authority, even for a short period. As the primary link between the Indian community and various segments of blanco society, he enjoys many opportunities to enhance his power and economic status. The gobernador has also become less dependent upon a unified Pima constituency to remain in office. Disaffected Pimas can call for new elections on Easter Sunday, but any transfer of power has been difficult to accomplish since the early 1960s. Anyone serving as gobernador can be expected to extend his tenure beyond the prescribed two years. Threatened with the possibility of new elections, the gobernador has shown a reluctance to completely support Pima Easter celebrations. His frequent absences from Oijig at critical times detract from the legitimacy of political acts taken by the ceremonial leaders.

During the post-mission period when the Pimas had the only organized government in Oijig, it was customary for the gobernador to first obtain written permission from the cabecera before turning the town over to the fariseos. Assurances were given that Oijig would be properly administered and all laws strictly enforced. A symptom and further cause of an erosion in the political autonomy of the Oijig Pimas has been the expedient introduced by the gobernador of conferring with the comisario without bothering to contact the cabecera. This places the Pimas more directly under the authority of local blancos and mitigates most of the controls fariseos might wish to impose on non-Indians.

The role of the fariseo is physically demanding. Boys as young as eight or nine may join the fariseos provided they are capable of remaining awake and extremely active from Wednesday of Holy Week to the afternoon of Holy Saturday. It is expected that the majority of the fariseos will be adult males in their late teens and early twenties. Many of the older men hold back until Holy Saturday when Easter Week celebrations reach a climax.

Fariseo initiates smear their faces with a thin paste of white clay and water. The young boys sometimes plaster their hair with this mixture, while the men wear caps made from bandanas or scarves. At least part of the face-painting takes place before the statue of San Francisco, but initial applications may occur elsewhere. This is the case when Pimas are forced to become fariseos through capture.

Any Pima male not volunteering for service can be challenged to a wrestling match by a fariseo, usually one of the leaders. Each contestant ties a sturdy piece of cloth around his waist to provide a handhold for the opponent. If the challenger wins by throwing his opponent to the ground, the other fariseos quickly apply white paint to the face of the defeated Pima while he is still lying on the ground. Anyone refusing to wrestle can be run down and held by the fariseos while the leaders daub his face with the clay solution. Once marked in this way, strong social pressures compel him to stay with the group and participate fully. Only young men are challenged in this way. The boys are ignored and the older adults are allowed to enter service at their pleasure.

The fariseos elect officers when they organize on Wednesday of Holy Week and submit their selections to the gobernador for ratification the same day. The titles associated with these offices have been adopted primarily from Spanish military terminology. The position of *general (henráar)* is held by a revered older man whose only public duties are to direct activities on Holy Saturday. The full-time leader of the fariseos is the *capitán (kapc)*, an individual at least in his twenties. Standing next in order of authority are the *cabo* or 'sergeant' *(kav)*, the *mayor (maaír)*, and the *comisario ('uusigam;* literally, the 'stick-bearer' who hurries stragglers).

The fariseos perform several different roles which appear somewhat contradictory. Another Pima term for fariseo is *yaavil*, a borrowing of the Spanish *diablo* or 'devil.' As henchmen of Judas, the yaavil have the license to act like boisterous clowns in sacred places such as the capilla and iglesia. They also serve as ceremonial guards during religious processions when it is necessary to be serious and reverent. A third area of responsibility for the fariseos involves keeping the peace and enforcing certain prohibitions, such as abstaining from meat, bathing, and all work other than that involved in the preparation of food or the construction of ceremonial artifacts.

Travel into the town of Oijig after Wednesday of Holy Week was formerly restricted for both Pimas and blancos. Persons arriving on foot had to contribute a few pesos to the celebration fund of the fariseos. Movement on horseback or with pack animals was strictly forbidden. Both beasts and cargo were taken away and kept until a fine was paid. In the 1960s and 1970s a traveler could enter town on foot at any time without being fined, and mounted blancos were ignored as long as they used the roads outside the plaza. The fariseos still try to enforce the prohibition against riders and pack animals in the plaza after Wednesday of Holy Week. This has led to confrontations, which the blancos have been able to settle by offering at least a token fine such as a package of cigarettes.

Although policing Oijig during Holy Week has become chiefly the responsibility of the comisario, the fariseos have limited powers of incarceration and punishment. In one case a fourteen-year-old blanco boy was seized for pitching rocks at the fariseos and made to kneel on large pebbles before the altar of the iglesia until he apologized. The boy's loud complaints attracted the attention of several blanco adults, including the assistant comisario, but no attempt was made to interfere. Breaches of the peace involving only Pimas are normally left to the Indian community to handle. Thus, the fariseos may be called upon to intercede in Indian domestic quarrels and restrain Pimas who are fighting or exhibiting public drunkenness.

Besides the fariseos, the only other formally organized group active during Holy Week are the *judios*. These are blanco teenage boys who don dresses over jeans and shirts and cover their faces with painted masks made from cardboard. Armed with lariats and the license to deliver moderate verbal insults against all adults, they roam about town lassoing dogs and creating a general uproar. The judios even invade the iglesia when the fariseos are holding vigil with the santos. No real friction exists between the two groups because of their mutual recognition of the fariseos' dominant position. They sometimes clown together by engaging in comical dances or mock fights, but this ceases as soon as the kapc signals that the judios should withdraw and continue their games elsewhere.

Some Easters have passed without the appearance of any judios, the few eligible persons preferring to emulate the young blanco men, who are preoccupied with other diversions at the local cantina. The lack of judios may also reflect a tendency for blancos to reject any status that is subordinate to that of a Pima.

While the fariseos are preparing themselves in the capilla late Wednesday morning, some of the older men begin construction of two portable bowers used by the Pimas to transport sacred relics around the plaza as they recite the Way of the Cross. These palaquin-like structures, called both *bultos* (Spanish) and *şaşanat* (Pima), are made from materials brought to the capilla by Pima men who go into the hills a day or so earlier to collect bear grass, juniper boughs, button willows, sapling wands, and sprays of pampa grass. The blancos contribute several strong ropes and the two chairs needed for the ṣaṣanat. The finished ṣaṣanat are carried from the capilla and placed on the floor of the iglesia. This is the sign for the fariseos to embark upon the first of several food *limosnas*.

Starting with the houses of prominent blancos on the southern edge of the plaza, the fariseos make a complete circuit of the town. The younger fariseos, acting like greedy clowns on the verge of starvation, beg cooked food from each household. The joking response of those giving the food is to indiscriminately pour beans, corn gruel, noodles in broth, and sometimes coffee into buckets carried by three or four of the fariseos. Donations are also made of tortillas heaped with beans, cooked squash, and fried potatoes. These are stacked in laminated layers and wrapped in cloth bundles which ooze their liquid contents. Cups of heavily sugared coffee are passed around, and most Pima families try to have *tesgüino* (corn beer) on hand for the older fariseos. Upon completing their rounds, the fariseos return to the iglesia and consume the gifts of food.

The Pimas strongly feel that all residents of Oijig are obligated to support the food limosnas, but some blanco families have shown such hostility in the past that their houses are often avoided. A particularly aggressive kapc may insist that every household be approached and asked for a contribution. The fariseos are also expected to visit the outlying Pima ranchos in order to formally invite their residents to join the celebrations in town. The complete trip may take several hours in the case of the most distant rancho. The fact that fariseos have sometimes restricted their visits to Pimas living fairly close to Oijig has resulted in criticsm by Pimas who wish to see the entire Oijig ejido involved as a community.

The fariseos circulate through the town after dark in order to ensure that Easter is being celebrated with proper decorum. Their passage is announced by the noise of a drum or loud clappers. Several small boys are left behind to maintain lighted candles placed before the ṣaṣanat.

The routine of the fariseos is much the same from Wednesday through Friday. Food limosnas are made during the day, and the night vigils continue. Several processions are held daily in the plaza during which the ṣaṣanat are carried by Pima men and women along the route marked by the crosses made of juniper boughs. Although these processions mainly attract Indians, some white women walk in a small, tight group behind the ṣaṣanat on Good Friday afternoon while reading the liturgy. At the station representing the crucifixion of Christ, one of the older white women sings the Passion of Christ from memory.

When the Way of the Cross is performed for the last time on Good Friday around seven o'clock in the evening, most of the principals are white. An informal sodality of young, unmarried women belonging to the more powerful ranching families meets at the guardiana's house on the afternoon of Good Friday to prepare a bulto, or *urna blanca,* for carrying a crucifix at the head of the evening procession. Some of the Pimas participate in this last performance of the Way of the Cross but leave behind their bulto representing Christ. The older white women walk at the back of the procession carrying candles and reading aloud from their prayer books.

At sunrise on Holy Saturday the fariseos emerge from the capilla carrying buckets of water. Their objective is to douse every hearth in town so that the inhabitants can "begin the year with a new fire." White reaction to this custom has become quite negative, and very few non-Indians are willing to admit the fariseos into their houses. Some blancos will toss a burning brand through a partially opened door for the fariseos to extinguish. The fariseo practice of dousing fires was at one time tolerated by the blancos. None of the Pimas are exempted from the attentions of the fariseos, and anyone barring the door is likely to have water poured down the stovepipe. Rather than passively submitting to these invasions, the Pima families are expected to return the favor by throwing water back at the fariseos. A water fight ensues and lasts as long as the fariseos are shown any resistance. In the 1960s several white women in their early twenties remembered engaging in such exchanges with the Pimas as young girls. These same persons now close their houses as long as the fariseos are about with their buckets of water.

When the last Pima fire has been extinguished, the fariseos regroup in the capilla and start readying themselves for a final series of rituals in which the devil's cohorts are symbolically defeated by the Pima santos. The fariseos paint designs on their faces with black, red, yellow, green, and blue pigments over fresh applications of white clay. The henráar, who serves as parade leader of the fariseos, appears for the first time in the capilla on Saturday morning and prepares himself in the same manner, except that his forearms are also covered with white clay and multi-colored designs. The fariseo officers may choose to wear crowns constructed from cardboard or wood and decorated with brightly colored paper and cloth.

The fariseos line up single file and march out of the capilla at noon and into the plaza where they perform military-like parade maneuvers under the direction of the henráar. Anticipating the eventual arrival of the fariseos at an area just north of the iglesia, blanco males crowd the nearby porches. From these vantage points they can trade insults with the marchers and better observe the ensuing ceremonies. While several Pimas and sometimes a paid blanco or two play popular music on their guitars, the fariseos halt their marching for about fifteen minutes in order to pair off and dance in humorous imitation of boy-and-girl couples. The spectators respond with laughter mixed with a few obscene remarks. The fariseos then resume their marching for several minutes before returning to the capilla.

The Pima women, who have been watching the parade from in front of the iglesia, quickly move to the capilla and crowd against the walls of a small room that once served as the sacristy. As the adult fariseos enter, each takes from his pocket a small potsherd representing a piece of silver which he uses to play catch with a partner. The exchange of "silver" lasts for about five minutes, and then the sherds are thrown high into the air so that they rain down upon the female spectators. This rite is said to increase fertility in women and ensure good spring and summer rains. To stand under such a shower also brings luck in the form of wealth.

The fariseos now form a closed circle by lining up front to back and grabbing the next person's wrestling belt from behind. Suddenly, all begin tugging vigorously backward. After a minute or two of struggling, the fariseos collapse to the ground as the communion bell from the iglesia is rung by a white girl standing at the back of the room. With the fariseos lying still on the floor, a young Pima girl runs forward with a willow switch and lashes several of the prostrate men. This is a signal for the fariseos to jump up and run in a crowd towards the main chamber of the capilla. Blocking their way is a rope barrier tied between the two sides of a pine bough arch. The fariseos crash into the rope and carry away the arch as the gobernador and blanco comisario make pretended attempts to fend off the attack.

Once inside the main chamber, the fariseos issue a general invitation to all adult males to come forward and wrestle with them. Most of the contests are between fariseos, but a few of the blancos join in the sport. When the judios were more numerous, they provided the principal opposition, and it is still true that the interethnic conflict figures importantly in the competition. A person indicates his willingness to compete by stepping over a white line of powdered clay drawn across the front entrance to the capilla. A fariseo hands the new contestant a length of cloth to be used as a wrestling belt, and the two square off in what is supposedly friendly combat, *"luchan por amistad."* If neither contestant gains the advantage after the first five minutes or so, the match is called a draw. The informal leaders of the young blanco men pointedly accept the challenges of the fariseo leaders. In these contests the struggle is somewhat sharper and of longer duration. Should a person be dissatisfied with his performance, as is often the case when a blanco opposes a Pima, he can ask for a rematch. Besides the town officers and the young men volunteering as wrestlers, the only other blancos admitted into the capilla are the elder patrones who have attained an age and social status which prevents them from personally competing with Indians.

When the kapc and kav are not themselves engaged in matches, they circulate among the wrestlers to act as referees. These officers quickly intercede should it appear that two opponents are becoming overly aggressive. Every attempt is made to keep traditional antagonisms in check, although there is marked division of sentiment among the spectators. The blancos loudly cheer their own from the front doorway and positions along the top of the decaying walls, while most of those within the capilla, including women and children, shout encouragement to the fariseos.

A small delegation of Pima women removes the statue of San José from the iglesia during the wrestling competition and returns with it to the smaller room of the capilla. At the conclusion of the wrestling, which lasts thirty to forty minutes, the fariseos step aside to allow all the Pima women to walk with San José up the center of the church and out the front entrance. Gathered in a tight group, the women proceed towards the plaza, where they are overtaken and surrounded by the fariseos. Upon reaching the middle of the plaza, the women turn back in the direction of the iglesia. A few yards short of the iglesia, the fariseos separate their lines so that the women can "escape" by running into the church. San José is replaced on the altar, and women emerge to find the fariseos standing in a half circle around the front door. The women greet each fariseo with an embrace and handshake along with a wish for the other's safe return next year. The fariseos respond in like fashion and then move off in a body to visit the houses of the comisario and his assistant, where they exchange the same greeting with the blanco officials and invite them for a cup of tesgüino at the house of the gobernador. At this point the authority of the fariseos comes to an end, and the gobernador reassumes his position as leader of the Indian community. The blancos soon leave the company of the Pimas, but everyone else stays as long as there is a supply of tesgüino to support friendly conversation. The tired ex-fariseos afterwards disperse to visit the homes of friends or take short naps before the execution of Judas later that evening.

The procedure for disposing of Judas has slipped from Pima control. Prior to blanco involvement, the Judas figure was ridden out of town, shot by a Pima firing squad and finally burned, sometimes with an exploding powder charge inside. According to a later informal agreement, the fariseos would deliver the effigy to the blancos on the morning of Holy Saturday. The señoritas dressed Judas in men's clothing and turned him over to the young men, who placed a beer can or liquor bottle in Judas's hip pocket before mounting him on a burro in front of a human rider and leading him to a hillside north of town for execution around five o'clock in the afternoon. The local civil authorities strongly discouraged the use of firearms by the Pimas, so that the blancos were eventually doing all the shooting. In fact, the event became an intimidating show of power on the part of the blancos, who attacked the effigy with an impressive array of weapons after first packing it with several sticks of dynamite that detonated when struck by a bullet. The Pimas no longer accept this arrangement. On Easter Saturday they claim that someone stole Judas the previous night. The excuse is not meant to be believed but only to express the Pimas' dissatisfaction with a one-sided relationship.

The final activity of Easter Week takes place on Sunday evening when the young, unmarried Pima men and women gather together for the purpose of visiting the houses of the town, particularly those of the blancos, and begging provisions for a party. San José is brought along by the women, who present the santo to the families that receive them. The señora takes San José into her house in order to obtain the saint's blessing. She then places small gifts of food in sacks carried by the Pima men. Those who run the small stores where many Pimas buy supplies are expected to give the most. The response of the blancos fluctuates from year to year depending upon the climate of interethnic relations in the community. The general trend is one of decreasing generosity toward the Pimas.

DEVELOPMENT OF THE OPPOSITIONAL PROCESS

The history of Indian-white relations in Oijig is reflected in the changes that have occurred in local religious celebrations. The Pimas continued to be the dominant force in community government as long as there were few resident blancos. This political control was expressed and reaffirmed through such community activities as the observance of Easter and the feast day of the town's patron saint. The blancos acquiesced for a time but eventually were able to organize parallel rituals just as they managed to establish a separate system of government. Questions arose over who would have priority in the use of the community's religious symbols. This use presupposed timely access to space within the town and the right to direct the behavior of persons within that space. The celebration of Easter evoked the issues of territorial control, authority over local residents, and consumption of foodstuffs produced on land legally belonging to the Pimas. Although the erosion of the Pima position has been great, we should not assume that there is an irreversible trend towards the derogation of the Oijig Pimas to the status of landless peasants who are culturally little different from other rural poor. The Pimas of Oijig have demonstrated considerable tenacity in continuing a distinctive set of rituals. The content has changed as these rituals have come to serve an additional function, that of expressing and implementing Pima concepts of interethnic relations.

Easter is a time when the indigenous community must struggle to resolve internal political differences while trying to establish a favorable balance in its exchanges with the blancos. The two objectives are closely related. The blancos are capable of seriously undermining the influence of the Pima gobernador through the imposition of economic sanctions, such as denying certain Pimas employment or refusing to sell them supplies. Any nominee for the position of gobernador must enjoy some degree of acceptance by the blancos, and this acceptance can cause him to lose the support of at least part of his Pima constituency. Difficulties arising from this predicament are to some extent offset by the fact that many of the benefits and all of the meager protections extended by non-Indian society are channeled through this person. Thus, the gobernador does not have to fulfill the traditional concept of his office because of his indispensable position as liaison between the two ethnic groups. His bureaucratic function has become more important than his moral leadership.

Prior to the establishment of a separately governed non-Indian society in Oijig, the Pima gobernador was an esteemed elder selected by the male heads of all families living within the ejido, including Oijig's many satellite ranchos. His tenure seldom lasted longer than a few years, although particularly able and popular leaders were sometimes reelected. The choosing of new officers took place on Easter Sunday. Instead of disbanding on Easter Saturday, as is the modern custom, the fariseos stayed at their posts and did not relinquish authority until the Pima men had gathered at the capilla and indicated a consensus candidate.

The emergence of Indian factions under the divisive influence of the blancos has greatly confused procedures for replacing a Pima gobernador. An incumbent is now likely to try to extend his tenure indefinitely. This is possible provided he has the backing of a significant Pima faction, usually favored relatives who constitute less than half the total population. The gobernador may even attempt to impede the work of those organizing Pima Easter celebrations. There is always the chance that influential persons will be able to instigate the long-delayed elections that would remove him from office.

The validity of new elections can be called into question if the transition of power lacks certain legitimizing features. Some gobernadors have tried to redefine the role of Pima fariseos as that of judios found in rural mestizo towns, a prankish group of carousers who have few religious functions and who must operate within limits set by the fulltime village officials. To this end, the gobernador is careful not to confer absolute authority upon the fariseos at the inauguration. If strong sentiments for new elections are known, he can be absent "on business" at the commencement of Holy Week to avoid any declaration regarding the surrender of power. Not until disaffection becomes very widespread and the conduct of Easter rituals is accepted by forceful personalities is it possible to effect a change in leadership.

The responses of blancos to the Easter ceremonies of the Pimas ranges from enthusiastic participation to hostile rejection. The determining factor is the nature of the reciprocity involved and its implications for hierarchical relationships between ethnic groups. Some blanco children enjoy helping in the preparations and, in some instances, entering into the performance of rituals. Their presence is fully accepted by the Pimas, who feel that the Indian-sponsored ceremonies should represent the whole community. The small sodality of white women who are organized to perpetuate "orthodox" Catholic liturgy in Oijig depend upon the Pimas to share the use of certain ceremonial artifacts and provide some of the personnel needed to conduct certain rites. The non-Indians reciprocate by opening their church to the Pimas and presiding with official prayers at several predominantly Indian affairs on Good Friday.

Although most of the town's sacred symbols are in the custodial care of the blancos during the rest of the year, the Indians claim unhindered access to them. They resent having to ask permission from the guardiana and are apprehensive that the blancos will someday try to refuse Pimas the use of these objects. Thus far, the blancos have not denied their requests, nor have they seriously encroached on the space used by the Pimas for their most important rituals. The capilla, iglesia, and town plaza are placed at the disposal of the Pimas from Wednesday through late afternoon on Saturday of Holy Week. Non-Indians will occasionally test the resolve of the Pimas to maintain their position, but the Indian community continues to resist these pressures.

Outside these areas it is difficult for the fariseos to exercise any control over non-Indians. The adult blancos are more often bemused spectators who dislike any suggestion of obligation to contribute to Pima activities. Some of the blanco men readily accept the challenge of wrestling with fariseos, but gifts from blancos in the form of food and drink have been reduced to token amounts. The contributors are likely to be patrones who feel some responsibility to the Indian workers. Formal requests for assistance, such as the loan of tools and materials, may be accepted at the doorway by the head of a blanco household, but the fariseos are not allowed admittance, particularly for the purpose of involving the occupants directly in the celebration, such as in extinguishing the hearth fire. The role of the Pimas in the ritual killing of Judas has been reduced by stages as the blancos, who are better equipped and strongly attracted to such diversions, have asserted ever greater responsibility for the actual execution. With the Pimas supplying the victim and then being excluded from its disposal, the balance of reciprocity was shifted in favor of the blancos to such an extent that interethnic cooperation completely failed.

Almost all Pima families make some investment of time and goods in Easter Week celebrations. There are no alternatives to the social and religious activities sponsored by the Indian community. Pimas have little chance of being accepted by the blancos of Oijig as non-Indians. Transculturation from Indian to blanco is rare in small Sierra communities where interethnic relationships are based on hostile competition. Unlike the urbanized areas of the lowland, the local ranching economy cannot support a large, heterogeneous *clase humilde* that lives solely on wages. The Pimas would find it very difficult to survive as individuals without the help of close kin (Dunnigan 1969). The few Pimas who have disassociated themselves completely from other Indians have left the area.

The Pima Easter rituals obviously do not encourage Indian assimilation. Rather, they are performed with the tacit goal of involving all members of the community in political structures controlled by the Pimas. The blancos will not accept these arrangements and have countered with a general strategy of gradually decreasing cooperation. The closely regulated competition of the ceremonial wrestling matches undoubtedly does relieve some of the tension inherent in contacts between the two ethnic groups. However, the celebration of Easter in Oijig has an overall effect of heightening such tensions by giving expression to basic conflicts for which there is no universally satisfactory set of solutions. Since the handling of issues changes from year to year in response to shifting power relations, both sides are to some degree anxious about the outcome. The results will be found unacceptable by one or both parties, as is the case when Pima and blanco struggle to throw each other to the ground.

The maneuvering for political gain within the Indian community that sometimes occurs at Easter can cause considerable discord, but it still is true that most Pima families support the continuation of the rituals. The most popular governador cannot afford to be absent during the entire week of Easter. His presence is particularly necessary on Holy Saturday, and any failure to perform as expected would be regarded as an abandonment of the Indian community.

A better understanding of how Easter rituals positively reinforce Pima social organization can be gained by a closer examination of role-switching by the fariseos and the types of interaction they have with other members of the community, matters beyond the scope of this discussion. The ritualized confrontations between the men acting as cohorts of Judas and the Indian women are particularly important in providing an opportunity for the Pimas to both participate in and aggressively reject certain kinds of behavior in favor of more highly valued roles.

RITUALS, POLITICS, AND ECONOMICS: SOME CONCLUSIONS

The vitality of Pima ritual life in Oijig is difficult to assess. If we apply such measures as continuity of form, ritual elaboration, or organization of performance, the conclusions will be negative unless the specific economic and political situation of the Pimas is also considered. The lack of economic opportunities in the Oijig area forces many families to reside for most of the year at distant settlements where employment in the form of temporary, low-paying jobs can be found. It is often difficult to arrange a week's stay in Oijig without running the risk of being permanently displaced by other working poor. Attendance for even a few days at the Easter celebrations in Oijig may require some sacrifice. Yet Pima families continue to make the pilgrimage to Oijig in order to be present for at least a part of the ceremonies.

Internal factionalism may be giving new impetus to traditions of rancho autonomy. There are fears that the timber, land, and water resources of some ranchos will be alienated to blancos with the tacit consent, if not complicity, of certain Pima officials. It is when they feel threatened that the rancho dwellers become increasingly active in the ceremonies of Easter. One of the significant features of these rituals, as viewed over several years, is that participation seems to be stimulated by political conflict. The basic steps in the performance of Pima Easter rituals are well known, but there may be delays, false starts, and an initial appearance of disorganization until the overall political strategy of celebration is decided by senior fariseos. Should the intention be to make a strong statement about the political rights of Pimas, it is sometimes necessary to find stand-in officers until the most effective leaders become available.

An upturn in the Sierra economy enables Pima families to be less dependent upon blanco patrones. Reciprocity arrangements between several families makes it unneceseary for them to share the use of land with non-Indians for the purpose of obtaining work or the capital to plant. Interethnic friction is further exacerbated by Pima petitions to higher government authorities for a redress of injustices. Constant apprehension over possible government moves to return Oijig lands to the control of the Pimas causes the blancos to exert unremitting pressure on the Indians to leave the area. A condition of hostile symbiosis devolves at times into open conflict. Indian rights can be guaranteed only through federal intervention, since the Pimas do not appear to have sufficient political resources to regain their former ascendency. While waiting for outside assistance, they must wage an aggressive campaign to retain the few prerogatives left to them by the blancos. The continued performance of their Easter rituals is a means to that end.

ACKNOWLEDGMENTS

I wish to thank Frank and Susan Lobo for their valuable assistance in carrying out a part of the research upon which this discussion is based. Financial aid was provided in part by the Comins Fund, Department of Anthropology, University of Arizona.

A NOTE ON PIMA ORTHOGRAPHY

The vowels /i, a, o, u/ are pronounced as in Spanish. Greater vowel length is represented by a doubling of the symbol. Major stress (') is usually on the initial syllable of a word. This general rule does not aply to many recent borrowings from Spanish which have two or more syllables. These are pronounced with major stress on the final syllable. Only borrowed forms contain the Spanish /e/. Most of the Pima consonants used in the text are similar to those of Spanish. Exceptions are lamino-alveolar voiced stop /j/, laryngeal stop /'/, and apico-domal retroflexed fricative /ş/. The symbol /c/ has been used in place of /ch/.

Part Four

An
Applied Perspective

| 9 |

Applied Anthropology and Cultural Persistence

John van Willigen

Anthropology as an applied discipline grew and developed in association with the increase in interest in culture-change research. This affiliation was particularly strong in the United States and came to be manifested in a conception of applied anthropology as basically a strategy of change, sometimes carried out through direct action but most frequently through the auxiliary role of researcher. This orientation is best represented by such anthropologists as George Foster, who has defined applied anthropology primarily in terms of its potential change-producing effects. To quote Foster, "'Applied anthropology' is the phrase commonly used by anthropologists to describe their professional activities in programs that have as primary goals changes in human behavior believed to ameliorate contemporary social, economic, and technological problems, rather than the development of social and cultural theory" (Foster 1969:54). Similar positions have been enunciated by other anthropologists.

It has been argued that the orientation mainfested by George Foster and others is a product of applied anthropology's origins "in the prewar

colonial epoch" (Thompson 1976:2). Thompson asserts that such significant cases in American applied anthropology as the Micronesian Trust
Territory activities, the Cornell-Vicos project, and the Fox project manifest overtones of the "colonial yoke" (1976:2). Thompson notes that the
applied anthropologists "were motivated by an intent to bring about
'introduced' or 'directed' change in the cultures of the communities under
consideration" (1976:2). This motivation is based on an implied
ethnocentric assumption about the way things should be. That is, the
anthropologists engaged in such activities are assuming that these people
are in need of change.

The idea that applied anthropology is change-focused is not inconsistent with the general theoretical stance of cultural anthropology. Since the
advent of culture-change theory (such as it is), the amount of attention
paid to issues of persistence has been limited. There is clearly a bias
toward change-producing studies. One perspective on this issue is delineated by Clemmer in his discussion of the process of resistance among
American Indians (1969:214). Clemmer charges that the cultural significance of resistance has escaped anthropologists because of the incomplete-
ness of theories of acculturation: "In losing the significance of resistance,
anthropologists have lost a major key to the revolutionary changes affecting the relationship between United States society and the societies of
native peoples. This is not the result simply of intellectual myopia or
careless research. Rather, it is the result of a subtle but significant bias
that permeates anthropology and has especially dominated research on the
native peoples of this continent" (1969:215).

The conception of applied anthropology as solely a change-provoking
discipline is unduly confining. There are anthropologists actively engaged
in kinds of application who reject the label *applied anthropologist* because it
is so closely associated with the provocation of change. This position is
clearly expressed by Weidman in a discussion of the basis of her preference
for the role-label *psychiatric anthropologist* vis-à-vis her approach to application. Her view of applied anthropology is strongly linked to a change-
focused conception of the role. To quote Weidman, "the applied anthropologist," in contrast to the psychiatric anthropologist, "earns his
livelihood through changing cultures, not by transmitting a body of
knowledge and theory within a framework outside the traditions of the
anthropological discipline itself. In my opinion, the *applied anthropologist*
label (and identity) implies a proselytizing, ethnocentric posture which
violates the basic, alienated, transcultural, species-oriented stance of our
discipline" (Weidman 1976:114). For all its polemical excesses Weidman's
characterization is operationally defensible in that most applied anthropology has been focused on change-producing activities.

Applied anthropology has not been limited to the change-producing realm, however. I will discuss a range of examples in which the applied anthropologist has engaged in change-limiting behavior. The science of anthropology can be applied with equal facility in strategies which limit, resist, or reverse change. Thus, applied anthropology can be defined as a complex of related, research-based, instrumental activities expressed through a variety of occupational roles which produce socially desired change or stasis in specific cultural systems through the provision of data, the formulation of policy, and/or the initiation of direct action. While applied anthropology is purposive, its purpose need not be change. Applied anthropology can therefore be conceived of as a set of strategies which can either produce change or maintain stability. Since anthropology can be used equally well to produce effects of either change or stability, it is clear that applied anthropology can contribute to situations in which the goal is persistence. A review of the field in historical perspective reveals a rather consistent although limited commitment to the goal of cultural persistence. The cases discussed in this chapter reflect a range of significant — though not exhaustive — subtypes: resistance, revival, and accommodation.

RESISTANCE

As Clemmer (1969) points out, the study of resistance as a "creative" phenomenon is rare in anthropology. It is, however, becoming increasingly frequent in the realm of applied anthropology (Dozier 1951; Gerlach 1979; Schweri and van Willigen 1978). Resistance can be defined as a complex of actions which either persuades or forces a dominant, change-inducing group to desist or fail.

The resistance process can be illustrated by the work of John Hostetler with American Amish communities. An Amishman himself, Hostetler has been engaged in studying Amish communities all of his professional life. From his research experiences with Old Order Amish communities in Pennsylvania, Ohio, Indiana, Iowa, and Ontario, he has provided balanced accounts of various aspects of Amish life. In processual terms the essence of Old Order Amish culture is stability (Hostetler 1963:vvi):

> Changes in technology are taken for granted in modern society. The determination to improve, modify, or create, gives birth to a constant flow of new inventions. The effect of machines and inventions on the social life of people in modern life is also taken as a matter of course. If a school is too small or does not meet new ideas

of fire prevention, Americans build a new one. If the demand for a new consumer product is evident, a business corporation is brought into being.

But there are small groups on the modern scene that are reluctant to change with the great society. They have refused to go along with civilization. The Amish people are one example in the modern industrialized and highly mobile world of a closely integrated small society. They are a slow-changing, distinctive cultural group who place a premium on cultural stability rather than change.

The Amish are historically derived from a group of Swiss Anabaptists who became divided in the 1690s. Their separation led them to migrate to various places in Europe and the New World. Amish people appeared in Pennsylvania in 1727. The persons left behind have become merged with the mainstream of Mennonite sect. Thus the groups in North America represent the main expression of Amish culture, a distinctive cultural system. Its distinctiveness is seemingly assured by its ideological commitment to separation from the world at large and to the proscriptions of Amish life. The Amish communities of America are threatened enclaves in what is from their viewpoint a sea of irreligious, blasphemous individuals. In order to show proper respect for God they must follow the proper life. The worst threat to this life is the potential loss of the children to the outside world. One part of the Amish strategy of preventing this loss is to limit the participation of their children in the formal education system of the community at large. Usually this means that Amish students only attend school through the eighth grade. This practice has led to conflicts between Amish families and local school ordinances concerning compulsory education. Amish people have been fined and arrested, although they "took the position that compulsory attendance beyond the elementary grades interferes with the exercise of their religious liberty" (Hostetler 1963:144). They feel that it is necessary to withdraw from the world in order to escape its effects on their community.

There have been many incidents between the Amish and the law over these issues. One of the most significant events was the arrest of three Amish parents in 1971 in Green County, Wisconsin (Pullman 1972:539):

Jonas Yoder, Adin Yutzy and Wallace Miller were parents of school children and members of the Amish religion, the former two belonging to the Old Order Amish sect. A Wisconsin trial court labeled them criminals for their violation of a Wisconsin compulsory school attendance law: the offense was not sending their children to school beyond the eighth grade and until age 16. Their refusal to comply was in consonance with firm Amish beliefs that such action would cause the eternal damnation of their offspring.

The Yoder conviction was affirmed by the Wisconsin Circuit Court. In an appeal to the Wisconsin Supreme Court the convictions were reversed. These findings were reviewed by the United States Supreme Court and upheld. The Supreme Court held that religious freedom was to have overriding importance. The Court recognized that the fabric of Amish society was inseparable from their religion, and that the impact of compulsory high school attendance would be negative and severe.

To a very significant extent the Amish case was built around the testimony of anthropologist John A. Hostetler, who clearly predicted the negative impact of compulsory education. As he noted in testimony, "I think that if the Amish youth are required to attend the value system of the high school as we know it today, the church-community cannot last long; it will be destroyed" (Hostetler 1970:51). The impact of Hostetler's testimony is clearly apparent in the majority opinion which supported the Amish communities' right to maintain a stable community (United States Supreme Court 1972:235–36):

> It cannot be overemphasized that we are not dealing with a way of life and mode of education by a group claiming to have recently discovered some "progressive" or more enlightened process for rearing children for modern life. Aided by a history of three centuries as an identifiable religious sect and a long history as a successful and self-sufficient segment of American society, the Amish in this case have convincingly demonstrated the sincerity of their religious beliefs, the interrelationship of belief with their mode of life, the vital role that belief and daily conduct play in the continued survival of Old Order Amish communities and their religious organization, and the hazards presented by the State's enforcement of a statute generally valid to others. Beyond this, they have carried the even more difficult burden of demonstrating the adequacy of their alternative mode of continuing informal vocational education in terms of precisely those overall interests that the State advances in support of its program of compulsory high school education.

In this case anthropologically derived knowledge was used to resist legally induced acculturation pressures on a highly bounded ethnic community. Hostetler provided a certain number of ethnographic facts and a theoretical framework within which these facts could be interpreted. The framework is a more or less pristine structural-functionalism. Interestingly enough, a review of Hostetler's published works does not explicitly reveal the same theoretical orientation. It should also be noted that Hostetler's response did not grow out of a deep-seated commitment to applied anthropology; instead, his feelings of responsibility to the community seem to have been the most important motivating factor.

REVIVAL

In contrast to resistance, the concept of revival in various guises has been rather thoroughly studied by anthropologists in the sense of revitalization, nativistic movements, and other such ideas. By revival is meant the return to or the reemphasis of an aspect of traditional culture. The term *revitalization* is not used because of its rather clear association with the concept of "revitalization movement" (Wallace 1961), encompassing a step-wise progression which is not part of the conception of revival offered here.

An account of one such activity is provided by Karl H. Schlesier's discussion of his work with the Southern Cheyenne between 1971 and 1973 (Schlesier 1974). Schlesier labels his efforts as *action anthropology* after the work of Sol Tax among the Fox in Iowa (Gearing et al. 1960). An examination of that mode of application suggests that Schlesier's approach is different from Tax's.

Schlesier was an anthropologist with an interest in native American ethnohistory. In 1968 he began work with the Southern Cheyenne, engaging in ethnohistoric research. As he noted, while the research efforts "added useful data to the Cheyenne literature, they did nothing for the Cheyenne themselves" (1974:278). Yet Schlesier became concerned for the welfare of the Cheyenne: "I saw a small people caught by poverty and economic exploitation; by discrimination and unequal treatment in the courts, law enforcement agencies, and schools; by unemployment, underemployment, and public-welfare dependency; by intragroup stresses leading to extreme alcoholism, high suicide rates, and violence; by general apathy; by poor health and poor housing conditions, etc." (1974:278). Schlesier came to be struck with the irony of engaging in reconstructive ethnohistory and ethnography among a highly stressed group. In response to these problems, he "decided that Plains ethnohistory could wait, that action anthropology was needed" (1974:279). To begin with, he became involved in the Cheyenne literature, and from this study he developed a deep commitment to traditional Cheyenne culture: "I learned a great deal about the Cheyenne from anthropological sources describing them. The general picture of the Cheyenne that emerged from the literature, partly confirmed by my own brief field experience, suggested to me that I should do everything the Cheyenne traditional way. This I set out to do" (Schlesier 1974:279).

The first direct step in the process of following Cheyenne tradition was to visit the most sacred place in the Cheyenne cosmology: Bear Butte, near Sturgis, North Dakota. This place was regarded by Plains people as an important source of political power. For the Cheyenne, Bear Butte was especially important because it was the site "where the last and most influential of their culture heroes, Mutsoyef (Sweet Medicine), went on a vision quest" (Schlesier 1974:279). During this time the culture hero learned from various spirits and upon his return was able to provide his people with the Cheyenne cultural message. This message included the patterns for the basic social organization of the Cheyenne, the ceremonial system, and certain key symbols.

While at Bear Butte Schlesier attempted to enjoin the spirit world of the Cheyenne to assist him in his "action quest": "We camped at the base of the mountain; I went halfway up its slope and, after making the traditional gift, offered my help for the benefit of the Cheyenne in much the same way as Cheyenne vision seekers have offered themselves over the centuries to this day" (1974:279). Through this action Schlesier's relationship with Cheyenne traditional leaders was greatly strengthened. His relationship with the people intensified as did his commitment to the goals of the people (Schlesier 1974:279):

> Looking back, I know that my interest in the past had taught me something important: a deep respect for many things of the past, for the quality of cultural traditions and for people gone. Behind the squalor of contemporary Cheyenne life I saw the hidden face of the wholeness and the splendor and the different despairs of another time. Perhaps I dreamed that hidden face; I helped the Cheyenne to dream it. Perhaps it had always been dreamed and I had only become one of the dreamers.

Although Schlesier began his process with a mystical act, he soon turned to a traditional anthropological activity, that is, research. He attempted to document the conditions which existed in Cheyenne communities. Out of consultations with Cheyenne leaders, Schlesier developed a National Science Foundation proposal which called for a series of research teams consisting of anthropologists and traditional tribal leaders. The project was rejected by the National Science Foundation. Prior to this failure Schlesier had experienced a traditional Cheyenne dream in which he saw himself sitting with the traditional Cheyenne leaders dressed in leather and feathers. Though he thought that the failure of his grant proposal had ended his encounter with the Cheyenne, he informed them of his dream. The Cheyenne seemed to take this as an important sign. They visited him and through a tape recording presented him with sacred knowledge concerning the origin of the Cheyenne (Schlesier 1974:280):

> The presentation was as logical as it was extraordinary. Since I was to join the traditional leaders in working for the Cheyenne future, I had

to be taught about Cheyenne beginnings and the immense course of their journey through time. I also had to be taught that, however well-intentioned and honest my goals as a person and an anthropologist, I had to accept for myself, as the traditional leaders present had accepted before me, no less than a sacred role, because I stood to affect the affairs of a people created and still guided by the supernatural.

Schlesier and his Cheyenne colleagues decided to undertake a vision quest at Bear Butte. The traditional leadership was also committed to submitting another National Science Foundation proposal. The vision quest was necessary in order to consecrate these important activities. Prior to the quest Schlesier underwent extensive training in the sacred knowledge of the Cheyenne. He testifies that the leaders revealed knowledge concerning the "hidden Cheyenne world," the world of values, religious life, and epistemology retained "after 100 years of oppression.... It is a world permanent and dynamic, since new elements are constantly being added to it upon recommendation by the tradition. It is a world closed to outsiders, because it is threatened; but it has been threatened throughout its existence in the Plains, even before the white wars, and was probably threatened before the tribe's entrance into the Plains. It is a system marginal to the dominant society and protected by this marginality" (Schlesier 1974:280).

The group took the position that Cheyenne suffering and poverty was part of an adaptive strategy of cultural survival. In order to survive, it was felt that the Cheyenne had to withdraw from or avoid participation in the white world around them. Poverty was a means of cultural survival. Survival was contingent on the continued existence of the traditional leadership of the Cheyenne. Further, it was reasoned that the only meaningful sources of a new Cheyenne adaptive strategy were the holders of the sacred knowledge and symbols, the keepers of the arrow, the traditional leadership of the Cheyenne. Schlesier became intensely committed to the goals of these leaders.

In July of 1972 the small group undertook the vision quest planned earlier. Schlesier camped with the Cheyenne at the foot of Bear Butte and began the fast so necessary to the achievement of the vision: "On the basis of dreams and other experiences, our quest was interpreted as successful. The Arrow Keeper's search for new methods of Cheyenne survival had been blessed; my presence near him had been sanctioned" (1974:280). The goal became the "reorganization and revitalization" of the Southern Cheyenne's institutions. The Arrow Keeper traveled through the Cheyenne area consulting with the people. The Arrow Keeper, according to Schlesier, held the most powerful supernatural sanctions and thus had the ultimate leadership role. The others, traditional chiefs and headmen, were secondary to him. In the traditional context, the power and responsibility of this man was awesome, though it had not been used in historic times. Finally, "in the fall of 1972 he called on the traditional leaders to come forward and take tribal affairs into their hands once again" (Schlesier 1974:281).

A meeting was held in which Schlesier and the traditional leaders developed an idea for a new organization which would assist the development and preservation of the Cheyenne way of life. This organization represented the first recognition in the historic period of the traditional Cheyenne leadership in the world at large. As Schlesier notes, "After 100 years of suppression and exclusion by government agencies from decision making in tribal affairs, now, at last, the genuine Cheyenne leadership had stepped forward and claimed its inherited position. From now on, the guardians of the sacred symbols and old institutions will lead the Cheyenne into the future as a people" (1974:281). It was in this way that anthropologist Schlesier reported his work to revive the traditional leadership of the Southern Cheyenne.

ACCOMMODATION

Perhaps one of the most significant types of persistence-producing applied anthropology is accommodation. Accommodation can occur when the anthropologist serves as an interface between two cultural systems such as the community and the service-providing or development-stimulating organization.

An example of this type of activity is represented by the Health Ecology Project developed in Miami, Florida, by Hazel M. Weidman and others (Weidman 1976). The Health Ecology approach was designed to serve the multicultural clientele of a large, county-owned general hospital. Work on the project began in 1971. Initial activities were focused upon describing the health beliefs and practices of the area. This description was matched with an attempt to define the dominant ethnic groups of the hospital's service area. These groups were American blacks, Bahamians, Cubans, Haitians, and Puerto Ricans. In addition, the rather large Anglo elderly population was noted. The project's research activities revealed certain of the distinctive features of this population (Weidman 1975:313):

Our research concentrated on the ethnic groups, and preliminary findings led us to accept the fact of culturally patterned differences in health behavior among five sample populations. The differences we observed had to do with which symptoms were considered "worrisome," the way these symptoms were clustered into syndromes that often went unrecognized by the orthodox health care system, and perceptions of bodily functioning that defined the pattern of symptoms and syndromes within each group.

Research into community characteristics is of course a rather typical way for such a project to begin. From this base the project team developed an action-guiding conceptual framework which included the concepts of culture, health culture, coculture, culture broker, and culture mediation. The last three of these concepts are especially crucial to an understanding of the Miami Health Ecology project and the accommodation process. The term *coculture* labels the culturally distinctive ethnic groups within the environment and was used in place of *subculture* to imply "parity or coordinate status" (Weidman 1975:313). In other words the group attempted to deemphasize the notion that the ethnic groups were subordinate to the dominant group. This perspective, although subtle, is very important in terms of the key issue of cultural persistence. The goal implied here is not cultural change. That is, the Health Ecology Project was not conceived of as a representative of a dominant, superior cultural system. The goal was not to transform but to mediate between two systems which are functionally equivalent although different in content and to provide a means of synthesis rather than a means of change. The focal concept in this strategy is the role of the culture broker.

Derived from the literature of social change (Wolf 1956), the concept of the culture broker is appropriate to a conception of cultural pluralism which stresses parity (Weidman 1975:314):

> The label seems applicable whenever there is need to recognize the existence of separate cultural or subcultural systems and to acknowledge a particular person's role in establishing useful links between them. In Miami we have assigned responsibility for such links. Multifaceted brokerage responsibilities are inherent in the position of culture broker as we have structured it. His role includes research and training components in addition to those of service; it is designed to elicit constructive change in the orthodox health care system, as well as in various communities by reciprocal processes.

The concept of the culture broker's role was brought into the program design explicitly. Therefore the primary focus of change was between the health-care establishment of the community and the health culture of the ethnic communities. The culture broker was idealized as an individual who held sophisticated knowledge concerning "the structure and func-

tioning of both systems involved in respective sets of negotiations, such as the traditional health culture of the community vis-à-vis the orthodox health culture of the psychiatric facility, and the community vis-à-vis key structures within a larger social system" (Weidman 1975:314). It was also expected that the individual culture brokers would be familiar with the literature on social change and community organization as well as that on medical and psychiatric anthropology and transcultural psychiatry.

The culture brokers headed up teams, each of which was specific to one of the cocultures of the service area. The teams consisted of personnel "indigenous to the area and of the same ethnic background and cultural extraction as those whom they serve" (Lefley 1975:318). Each team was given a certain amount of guidance from a community-based advisory body. The culture brokers, trained at the Ph.D. level in one of the social sciences, operated in two sectors. In the clinical setting their activities included teaching the health-care professionals and community members about each other. In the Miami project the culture brokers had teaching assignments in the local medical school. Culture brokers were also involved in consultation with therapists such as physicians. In these cases they provided a culturally informed interpretation of a particular disease manifestation, such as explaining the meaning of illness behavior specific to a culture or defining behavior as "culturally normal" which standard psychiatric classification might have labeled as pathological. Brokerage may also mean attempting to change the health-care providers's role expectations vis-à-vis the ethnic identity of the patient population. On the other side, the culture broker attempted to provide data concerning the health-care establishment to the community so that users could better exploit facilities and get more effective health care. Brokerage activities also extended to community organization work within the community.

When anthropologists are involved in persistence-producing applied anthropology, they most frequently engage in accommodation. In the accommodation process the anthropologist serves as a bridge between two cultural systems, usually a community and some type of development or service organization. The primary activity in accommodation is the use of anthropological knowledge to increase the appropriateness of a program. In many cases this means working to limit the deleterious effects of a specific program of change, perhaps by giving it a more appropriate cultural focus. Accommodation relates to persistence somewhat indirectly, usually in the sense that the changes are designed to fit into a community's existing framework of values and beliefs. That is, the anthropologist may be placed in the role of supplying information on a particular group so that the "package of changes" can be fine-tuned. Through these procedures the cultural transformations produced by the development or service activity are controlled in some way. In these cases the agency obtains data about the community in order to adjust program design to limit trivial or negative results and/or to enhance utilization rates. The Miami case described above did not have this specific goal.

CULTURAL PERSISTENCE AND APPLIED ANTHROPOLOGY IN HISTORICAL PERSPECTIVE

A review of the historic literature indicates that persistence-focused applied anthropology has been part of the field for a long time. Even applied anthropologists in service to colonial regimes were in some ways committed to accommodation, although usually as part of a change-producing program. It is beyond the scope of this chapter to thoroughly review the literature relevant to the relationship between applied anthropology and persistence, but a few examples of various subtypes are indicated below.

A very early example of accommodation is the so-called Golden-Stool incident. Captain W. S. Rattray, a government anthropologist during the early 1920s in West Africa, investigated the cultural meaning of the Golden Stool, which had been the focus of conflict between the British and the Ashanti of West Africa. The stool was interpreted by the Ashanti as a repository of the nation's soul, whereas the British assumed the stool was a symbol of royal authority. In response to their assumption the British tried to obtain the stool to solidify their leadership. Their attempt led to armed conflict with the Ashanti. Rattray suggested that the British view was wrong and that they stop attempting to obtain the stool. His advice was followed and had the proper ameliorative effect. In this way there was an accommodation between the two cultural systems (Rattray 1923). A similar example of accommodation is the work of F. E. Williams on the Vailala Madness movement in New Guinea (Williams 1923, 1934). In both these cases the anthropologist provided to government administrators alternative interpretations of the meaning of a native behavior, thus reducing the threat of the behavior by cognitive change.

A kind of accommodation occurred in cases in which anthropologists worked to support the use of indirect rule in colonial administrations. For example, because of the Dutch scholar van Vollenhoven's (1933) research into adat law, the customary law of Indonesia, it was continued as the basis of civil law there as part of the Dutch program of indirect rule. In this way this law based on tradition persisted.

A very interesting, somewhat more recent case of accommodation-producing applied anthropology was carried out in the 1960s in the Navajo-Cornell Field Health Project at Many Farms, Arizona. This project represented an early, sophisticated attempt to improve the quality of

Anglo health-care delivery to a non-Anglo population through the cooperative efforts of a team of anthropologists and health-care professionals. This complex project provides a number of examples of accommodative practice in the context of what was basically a change-producing program. Anthropologists involved in the program attempted to increase the utility of Anglo medicine to the Navajo in various ways, while minimizing its disruptive impact on Navajo culture and recognizing the positive contribution of Navajo medical practice on the health of the community. This project had many facets which were accommodative in nature, including the use of Navajo paraprofessionals in health care (Adair 1960), Navajo translations of Anglo medical terms (Adair and Deuschle 1970:108–27), and the use of culturally appropriate treatment for the congenital hip disease so common among the Navajo (Burnett and Rabin 1970:128–39; Rabin et al. 1965).

As can be seen from our limited review of the literature, accommodation is a frequent anthropological activity. In contrast, revival and resistance are much less frequent. Most cases of revival tend to focus on narrower aspects of culture such as artistic expression. For example, the work of Gwyneth Harrington (personal communication), an anthropologist associated with the Technical Cooperation-Bureau of Indian Affairs in the 1930s, included attempts to revitalize Papago basketry techniques. More recently, in the 1970s, James Griffith (personal communication) has worked to revive and support the development of various kinds of ethnic music in Tucson, Arizona, through community fairs. A related activity rather frequently engaged in by educational anthropologists is the development of ethnic heritage curricula (Walter E. Precourt, personal communication).

The third type of persistence-generating anthropology, resistance, occurs with increasing frequency. For example, anthropologist Stephen Schensul (1973) worked in conjunction with certain Chicano leaders of Chicago's South Side. In a multifaceted project Schensul used anthropological research skills to assist the community in resisting zoning changes which were viewed as having adverse effects. In 1969 and 1970 I assisted Papago tribal leaders in resisting certain Department of the Interior policies relating to the Papago cattle industry (van Willigen 1971). These policies were viewed as fundamentally threatening by the Papagos. My role in the resistance activities involved doing research and writing position papers as well as forming strategy. The work of Fay G. Cohen with the American Indian movement in Minneapolis also illustrates how anthropologists can assist resistance activities (Cohen 1976).

When anthropologists use their skills in resistance or revival activities they usually are clearly involved with the community. Accommodation, however, usually takes place in conjunction with a project or agency which is organized to serve a community but is not a part of it in tradition. The primary activities of anthropologists in resistance and revival tend to supplement those of the leaders and other members of the community. Typically these anthropologists act as data providers and consultants rather than as "up-front" resisters. Often their knowledge of the culture to be resisted is of crucial importance. Papago tribal leaders found that the anthropologist's ability to write up the tribe's position on a matter was very valuable to them. This role required an understanding of the historic context of Papago culture and Papago values as well as writing skills. In other cases the anthropologist's objective, disinterested expertise is what is valued, as was apparent in Hostetler's defense of Amish schooling.

It is difficult to assess the potential significance of the various types of applied anthropology which support cultural persistence. Clearly, generalized accommodation practices have had a long-term presence in anthropology and will doubtless continue. Cultural brokerage as an explicit primary program goal will most likely remain an infrequent activity. Resistance and revival activities will probably increase in number. These changes will not be a product of the transformation of anthropology, however. What will be most important in the process will be the changing nature of anthropology's subjects, the communities of study. There will be much closer identification with the goals and interests of the subject communities. Although this development will be encouraged by the increased ethical awareness of the anthropological community, the primary influence will be the increased politicalization of the research relationship. That is, anthropologists will have to be more responsive to the needs of their subjects, and oftentimes their subjects will make clear their need for stability or persistence.

These changes have come to affect both applied and general anthropologists. However, in applied anthropology the change toward closer involvement with the community is more striking. Admittedly, much applied anthropology can be done in relative isolation from the community of study. Starting in 1950, though, there has been an increase in the number of approaches in applied anthropology which are contingent on close relations between the community and the anthropologist. Many of these approaches, such as action anthropology and research-and-development anthropology cannot operate through intervening bureaucracies. As direct relationships become more frequent, the emphasis on change-producing behavior will decrease.

Preparation for professional work in the applied anthropology of cultural persistence is not unusually complex. The most significant difference is an increased need to understand the dominant culture's characteristics. That is, the anthropologist providing assistance to a "persisting" community often best serves his client as an interpreter of the dominant culture. Interpretation of course implies research, involving what Laura Nader (1969) referred to as *studying up*. Specifically, we mean a kind of studying up in which the goal is to increase the level of control which the powerless have. Although studying up requires certain new skills, the primary obstacle which must be overcome is the anthropologist's resistance to the new political relationship with the community of study.

Part Five

Adaptive Perspectives

| 10 |

On the Tarascanness of the Tarascans and the Indianness of the Indians

George Pierre Castile

As an avowed cultural materialist I have, in fieldwork in Mexico and on Indian reservations in the United States, often been at something of a loss to cope with the apparently mentalistic issue of ethnic identity. What, I have found myself asking while studying Cherán, a Tarascan community in Michoacán, is so Tarascan about the Tarascans? While engaged in work with modern reservation cultures, I have encountered not only an insistence on individual tribal identities but (in the Pan-Indian phenomenon) a widespread insistence on a collective Indian identity such that I must ask not only, "What is so Yakima about the Yakima?" but, "What is so Indian about the Indian?" If, as many do, one means by identity the preservation of a genetic purity, a unique language, or cultural lifestyle traceable to undisturbed precontact cultures, then the answer to all of the questions is "Not much." While pointing out in this chapter that the issue raised in this way is a false issue, I also want to suggest that all of the identity systems mentioned are very real if de-mentalized and de-mystified, and relatively understandable as adaptive systems developed in certain varieties of contact conditions and surviving to confer adaptive advantage on their membership.

DEFENSIVE ENCLAVEMENT

Although the topic in this chapter is not the rise of the enclaves but their persistence, there must be some mention of their origins in the interest of defining the issues. The Tarascan villagers are best understood in the context of Wolf's (1967) concept of the "closed corporate community," and it was in that light that I undertook my study of them (Castile 1974a). In 1939, according to Beals' (1946) data, they fit that model rather closely. Spicer (1966, 1969b) has discussed the general concept of enclavement and the special situation of Meso-American communities in the context of political incorporation, while I have argued elsewhere against a mentalistic explanation of this phenomenon and in favor of an adaptive model stressing the importance of external forces and the inexorability of adaptive necessity (Castile 1975).

Cherán, once part of the complex and distinctive Tarascan nation-state in western Mexico, was shorn of its connections to that larger entity by the actions of the conquering Spanish and reduced to a single community unit, compelled by external circumstances to cope with the new developing, pluralistic society on its own and allowed by other circumstances to do so as a community. Forced to accept Spanish dominance, Cherán and other of the developing, closed corporate communities took aspects of the new cultural situation and adapted them to defensive purposes, coalescing their new adaptations around the inward-turning *carguero* system. This system of ranked religious offices (*cargos*) did much to stabilize the disrupted communities. The pre-Columbian form of the community, with its links to the wider Tarascan state, was largely destroyed within a generation or two as its structures became irrelevant or forbidden and the hybrid civil/religious hierarchy came quickly to fill the gap. Over time this defensive, isolating adaptation continued to succeed only in those areas called by Aguirre-Beltrán (1967) "regiones de refugio," where pressures for their absorption were less. In all of these developments there was little that need be explained by individual choice or other mentalistic mechanisms.

The rise of the reservation cultures of the United States is at once simpler and more complex than the development of the closed corporate communities of Meso-America. I and others have elsewhere discussed the reservations under the label of "administered communities," and in the relatively uniform imposition of this system of dominance there is considerable simplicity (Castile 1974a; Kushner 1973). The greater range of

North American pre-Columbian variation and the relative isolation of the individual tribes through most of the reservation period makes for greater complexity at some stages in outcome even under the influence of the common experience of administration.

Borrowing Spicer's felicitous phrase, which he applied to the Japanese in relocation camps, reservation Indians are "impounded peoples" intentionally confined to limited parcels of undesirable land and there subjected to conscious and purposeful programs of deculturation aimed at their dispersal and assimilation into the larger society (Spicer et al. 1969). The Spanish tolerated the continued existence of Tarascanness when it did not interfere with their interests, but the federal reservation system has actively sought through most of its existence to deal with *all* of its inmates in the intolerant spirit expressed in the educational goal once set for their children: "Kill the Indian in him and save the man" (Pratt 1964:310). The closed corporate communities are in some limited sense "voluntary" adaptations while the reservations are clearly imposed, but both are in the long run successful structural mechanisms for the preservation of distinctive peoples in the face of assimilative pressures. There is a special irony for the North American Indian peoples that the mechanism designed for their socio-cide is in fact the principal instrument of their survival.

These questions of origins, important though they may be, are not my present issue except to point out their non-mystical quality. Erasmus (1967) has pointed out the pitfalls of explaining the phenomena in terms of themselves such as when some announce that conservative communities (i.e., Indian) are conservative because they are conservative. In this context he addressed the differences between Mayo and Yaqui adaptations and examined the divergence of two originally similar groups. By considering a number of environmental variables such as relative population size, physical isolation, variable agricultural potential, access to areas of withdrawal, and the like, he shows that the adaptation of the Yaqui was not in fact a viable option for the Mayo, who did make some similar attempts. Waldemar R. Smith (1974) made a similar point in his critique of the understandings of Colby and Van de Berge in relation to the maintenance of ethnicity in southern Mexico. His comparative treatment strongly suggests that the persistence of ethnic identity has a great deal to do with the relative success of a group in coping with the problems of adaptation to outside forces. The critical factors he cites — roads, markets, and communications — are remarkably similar to my own observations about change in Cherán (Castile 1974a). Materialists have in the past sometimes begun to flounder, as I have suggested, in understanding those situations in which such enclaves, originally visibly distinctive, have gone far in losing much that sense and reason could describe as cultural differentiation. Is the persistence of ethnic identity at this point possible to understand in the same adaptive way as is the original process of enclavement?

MORE ETHNIC THAN THOU

The poverty of the "normal" approach to the question of who is an Indian was brought sharply to my attention in a three-cornered journal debate touched off by Acheson in an article entitled "Limited Good or Limited Goods? Response to Economic Opportunity in a Tarascan Pueblo" (1972). It came to involve Nolan (1974) and Foster (1974). Though the question of whose community was or was not Indian (as opposed to mestizo) was not the major subject of their debate, they belabored one another over it. Foster quoted his own earlier statement, "Tzintzuntzan is not and has not been for generations an Indian village" (1967:35), while both he and Acheson seemed to agree that Cuanajo (Acheson's study site) was indeed Tarascan. Some wrangling between Nolan and Acheson about "degree of acculturation" elicited the comment from Acheson that "to the best of my knowledge there has been no detailed study of 'acculturation' in the Tarascan area" (1974:51). In fact, an excellent study by Moone (1973), using Guttman scaling techniques to quantify degrees of national integration in twenty-two communities in the Pátzcuaro area, was available at the time, and I had used it in my own report on the village of Cherán in the Sierra Tarasca.

In following this debate I found myself in a state of confusion as to what was meant here and elsewhere by "Tarascan" or even by "Indian." Van Zantwijk, in his study of the Laku community of Ihuatzio, is misleading when he insists that "the most striking fact about Ihuatzio today is the persistence of fundamentally indigenous ideas and concepts" (1967:228) and offers up the carguero system and "dual forms of organization" as instances (1967:199). Foster (1967:35) had earlier come very close to illuminating the problem (at least partially) when he pointed out that as an aspect of the cult of Indigenismo in Mexican nationalism "many Mexicans seem anxious to maintain the fiction that Tzintzuntzan, with its ancient pyramids and its fine colonial monastery, is still an Indian community." Nelson (1974), in a paper based on her work at Erongaricuaro, was struck by this notion of fictionalization of ethnicity but stressed that it could also be applied to the sense of identity felt by the supposed Tarascans themselves. The issue, it seems, is not the reality of Tarascanness but the reality of the belief in it, and that belief, if present, cannot be called a fiction except by the historical purist.

Spicer, in dealing with the Yaqui culture as a persistent identity system, talks of "the entity that maintains continuity at the same time that it undergoes change" (1976:1). His point can be applied to the Tarascans who were Tarascan in their own eyes and in the eyes of their conquerors when Nuño de Guzmán swept down on them and who are still Tarascan in the sense of mutually recognized ethnic identity, even though there is virtually nothing in common between the Tarascans at the two points in time. They have undergone drastic, almost total restructuring, culturally and socially, yet they remain an identifiable people.

The word *mestizo* is freely used in Michoacán as if it had some degree of its original meaning of genetic admixture of Indian and non-Indian. The people of both Tzintzuntzan and of Cherán are the descendants of pre-Columbian Tarascan populations, but after many centuries of contact and movement there is no doubt that all peoples of this area are, in this physical sense, to one degree or another mestizo. Still, in a loose "popular" way there is a tendency to talk of Cherán as somehow racially Tarascan and Tzintzuntzan as not. Those called Tarascans are not possessed of racial purity, although the strength of their identity system may be greater because the *myth* of this purity persists. Ethnic persistence is in large part a dynamic interplay between the enclaves and the larger society, in which the beliefs of both are real to the extent that they are accepted and acted upon. Spicer (1976) debunked similar popular myths about the basis for Yaqui persistence in order to make plain their inaccuracy, but they cannot be ignored as part of the real cultural environment to which the enclaves must adapt.

Language, particularly monolingualism, seems to be important to many who seek to isolate the "Indian," and certainly persistence of a language in daily use indicates some degree of cultural continuity with the pre-Columbian past. In 1969–70 in the community of Cherán, which virtually all agree is Tarascan, there were few, except some of the very old, who could not cope with my own simple Spanish. Both there and on reservations in the United States I have nursed a suspicion that affecting monolingualism is an efficient way to save oneself a lot of bother with troublesome government officials and inquisitive anthropologists, so much so that official reporting may tend to exaggerate the extent of monolingualism. Whatever the case, there were those in this supposedly most Tarascan of Tarascan communities who complained of the inability of the young to speak the language, and much of the daily business of the town that I was able to observe was conducted in Spanish. Again, a "national" language may be an important element in reinforcing the belief in a separate ethnic identity for the enclave, but it is not a final requirement for defining boundaries when there are many who are certainly members of the group but who make no use of it. In the United States,

Indian delegations have insisted on making their remarks to congressional committees in their "native" tongue, although the majority of peoples they represented would probably have understood no more than did the congressmen — a rather dramatic example of a conscious reinforcement of identity through an insistent belief in mythological linguistic purity.

I did not set out to study Cherán in terms of the persistence of ethnic identity but, as noted, to test the degree to which the closed corporate community model of Wolf (1967) seemed to fit the data presented by Beals (1946) for the town in 1939. This approach, however, involved a concern with the extent of national integration as opposed to the traditional, relatively autonomous, status of the closed communities. Here I ran aground on the very considerable and obvious shift of the community away from the traditional in terms of general cultural differentiation, while there appeared to persist a very strong and seemingly almost baseless identity differentiation. The carguero system was no longer effective, differential accumulation of wealth was occurring, and patron-client relations were breaking up the egalitarian economic order. Isolation had been completely broken, and because of land/man pressures a great many of the people were intimately and necessarily involved in outside economic activities. Moone's (1973) attempt to quantify degrees of national integration for twenty-two Tarascan lake communities had used twenty-one criteria in four separate scales; applying the comparable data areas, I attempted to place Cherán — supposedly Tarascan/Indian, conservative, and closed. I found that it ranked second only to Quiroga, a large and undeniably nationalized mestizo community. It was only in terms of those factors that Moone labeled "value consistency" that Cherán failed to rank nearly at the top of the nationally integrated communities, and that scale was concerned primarily with questions of language use and identity factors. Despite such thorough national integration a persistence of a sense of separateness undeniably existed and was recognized by the larger society, most dramatically by the placement of the Instituto Nacional Indigenista (I.N.I.) regional coordinating center on the edge of Cherán.

Working with the reservation cultures of the United States and their system of administration reveals an even more emphatic lack of connection between Indianness and retention of undisturbed pre-Columbian characteristics. There are certainly peoples, like the Navajo, who retain territory they originally occupied, although that retention of a sacred homeland is not only historically anomalous but something of a longer-range fiction, since the Navajo, most scholars now agree, probably arrived almost as recently in their "homelands" as did the intruding Europeans. Still, many Navajo (not all) can and do speak their own language and observe a great many distinctive cultural patterns in kinship, religion, and the like. These characteristics, however, are not true in any but the most limited way of a great many other reservation peoples who, nonetheless, insist on their identity with as much conviction and fervor as the Navajo. They are not in their original homeland, few speak any language but English, their lifestyle is distinctive only in its poverty, and yet, persistently, they regard themselves as Indian. Many of mixed genetic background [including, as Bonney (1977) has noted, some of the members of the activist "nationalistic" movements], representing both the ancestral marriages between peoples in the forced mixing bowls of the reservations and the assimilationist policy that has dominated that system, lay more stress on being simply "Indian" than on being members of a specific tribal people.

On an individual tribal basis the genetic/linguistic/cultural purity varies widely but is nowhere great. The Navajo, who are as distinctive as any tribe, are also the basis for Vogt's (1961) model of "incorporation" which describes a kind of acculturation phenomenon stressing the controlled integration of borrowed elements. The Navajo, in line with that model, have taken and modified traits from all of the cultures with whom they have been in contact. Linton (1937) teased us all some years ago with his article "One Hundred Percent American" and dramatized our Anglo/American debt to the cultures of the world, but both we and the Navajo continue to think of our trousers as part of *our* culture, not that of the Persians of Xerxes' time. Fry bread is always described as distinctively Navajo, while also often being offered as a generalized Pan-Indian culture trait. It was, of course, simply a product of attempts to make some edible use of ration flour and grease during the early reservation period. A great deal that is "Indian" might better be thought of as "reservation," which is why I have sometimes spoken of reservation cultures — rather than native North Americans or Indians — as a distinguishable social type.

As Linton did for the non-American American, an endless list of non-Indian Indian traits could be made for the single Navajo tribe, which is usually offered as so truly culturally distinctive. Peyotism, pickup trucks, and sheep-dipping are no less Navajo (and no more) than weaving, wage labor, and silversmithing. All are additions to the totality that is the Navajo and are in the spurious purity/pre-Columbian sense ultimately non-Navajo. They are also essential features of the Navajo as they exist in the 1980s. One could add to them a list of traits that *are* undeniably Navajo, most of them in the area of world view and cosmology and the ritual which dramatizes these areas, but those are not the only areas that the Navajo, or their neighbors, regard as Navajo.

The Pan-Indian phenomena was described tellingly by one author under the title "The Search for an American Indian Identity" (Hertzberg 1971) and by Spicer (1964b) as a variety of "indigenismo." Many "enduring peoples," while persisting individually, seem also to be molded into a single people. There was, of course, never a single Indian language, culture, or sense of common identity prior to contact, but almost from the first, as Hertzberg points out, the pressures of disruptive Anglo/American contact gave rise to movements of one sort or another that had at least partial focus on the creating of a single people out of the many. Hertzberg, however, errs in my view in stressing the negative aspects of the reliance on "white stereotypes," saying that "all the Pan-Indian movements reacted strongly to this Indian image" (1971:319). In fact, the Pan-Indian movements, early and modern, are all fusional and rely heavily on concepts of Indianness ultimately and necessarily derived from the larger society. One may deplore the stereotype of the Indian based on the be-feathered horsemen of the plains, as does Hertzberg (1971:319), calling it "naiveté," but if so then such a perjorative term must be extended to the Indians themselves. The pow-wow and similar intertribal gatherings sometimes held as "tribal fairs" universally feature a generalized Indian costume and activity pattern which draws very heavily on the plains traditions: "war" dancers, buckskins, beads, horsemanship, and of course feather headdresses. Southeastern peoples (Creek, Cherokee, and others) might "authentically" adopt body tattooing and toga-like garments, while northwestern peoples could, with similar "authenticity," appear in woven conical hats and nose rings, but both groups freely and without self-consciousness in fact appear in plains-derived dress. Beads and southwestern turquoise jewelry — or, for the more dedicated, braided hair — are to be found universally displayed as an affirmation of Indianness by many whose true specific tribal traditions include nothing of the kind.

This spurious Indianness insisted upon by the Indians and the dubious Tarascanness of the Tarascans can only be understood in terms of Spicer's rather alarming observation that "the continuity of a people is a phenomenon distinct from the persistence of a particular set of culture traits" (1971:798). Although most cultural materialists would surely insist that a tribe is, as a social entity, not the same as a chiefdom or industrial nation-state, Spicer's perspective would suggest that a "people" can remain the same "people" through almost total cultural change, including such gross shifts as that from one sociocultural "level" to another, as long as the continuity of its identity system is unbroken. However, in reference to the persistence of such a system for the Yaqui, he stresses its symbolic nature and says, "The symbols themselves have replaced one another, moved in and out, as it were, of Yaqui consciousness" (1976:7). I think an examination of Tarascan and North American Indians lends weight to the observation that the symbol system need not be "real" as long as it is believed in, and in the absence of other kinds of continuity (material and structural) we can agree with Spicer's observation that "identification of the symbols by which the meanings of a people's existence become known from generation to generation is the means for describing their identity systems" (1976:7). There can be little argument that these symbols are the essential core of persistent systems, since adherence to such shifting symbols is *all* that is left when every other aspect of the people has changed. The beads, even if made in Japan, are in this symbolic sense truly Indian as long as both wearer and observer attach that significance to them.

Obviously, if it is true that some such set of identity-maintaining symbols is the essence of the persistent peoples, it is necessary to suggest how such systems persist and, more importantly, why. I hasten to add that I mean "why" in the evolutionary sense of explaining the utility of the identity system as an adaptive mechanism. The language of cultural evolution falls afoul of some circularity of expression or at least reflects a fondness for ex post facto explanations. An adaptation which stresses ethnicity can be regarded as viable only if it succeeds, a statement which, of course, could be translated to say that it is adaptive only when it is adaptive. More correctly, our emphasis stresses the necessity of determining the nature of the advantage conferred on those groups which persist in their separate identities and denies that such persistence can exist or long endure if no advantage exists. The image of a people suffering forever for their "beliefs," which is very often associated with the mystical perspective on "peoplehood," flies in the face of all logic and of the historical data. Suffering may be temporarily endured by any group over a short term, but permanent destructive stress and disadvantage is a contradiction in evolutionary terms, unless one is able to envision a society composed entirely of masochists and consistently able to violate numerous of its "functional prerequisites" (Aberle et al. 1950).

INDIOS AND INJUNS

The maintenance of ethnic identity has historically had demonstrable disadvantages for Native North American and Tarascan populations in their relations with the larger societies. "Indio" can still be taken as a perjorative word in modern Mexico, tending to carry the sense of a person foolish and crude—in fact, the opposite of "gente de razón." In the modern United States there seems no consistent special term of disparagement, but the word *Indian* itself is usually combined with colorful modifiers to describe the negative aspects of these peoples. Indians are still widely regarded as drunken and shiftless, living off the government or imaginary oil, and the like. Aside from these varieties of vilification specially focused on the Indians, they are also subject to the general range of insults typically directed at all poverty/minority populations in the United States and which have done duty for many years to describe peoples ranging from the Irish to modern Mexican Americans and blacks. Where and when one lives, of course, determines to whom one applies these terms, and they are focused on Indians in those areas where there are concentrations of Indians and at times when there are "problems" with Indians.

Paradoxically, in both dominant societies there exists, at the same time as such disadvantageous prejudice, the very positive myth that the native populations possessed a glorious and superior lifestyle in the imaginary past. Mexican nationalism leans heavily on an Aztec/Indigene identification to separate it from the degraded, conquering Spaniards and officially glorifies this past at the same time that local "Mexicans" condescend to the foolish "Indio." The Native North American became in the 1960s (as occasionally in the Rousseau-influenced past) the descendant of peoples who were "natural ecologists" and who had a harmonious relationship with "our mother the earth." It is, of course, these positive stereotypes that have formed part of the Indians' own system of identification, but all are also aware of the negative aspects. In some cases "progressive" Native Americans, seeking to separate themselves from such identification, have attributed these same negative stereotypes to "conservatives." As has already been suggested, in the face of such obvious maladaptive aspects of persistent identity systems, further explanations are needed to account for the adherence to the shifting sets of symbols by the enclaved peoples.

The case against the rationality of ethnicity becomes superficially even more convincing with a glance at any account of the current or historical economic status and life conditions of the Tarascans and the reservation peoples. Both are poverty populations ranking at the very bottom of the scale in their respective countries on virtually every index commonly used to describe undesirable conditions — education, income, health, housing, and the like. Given that both forms of enclave are (and have long been) under intense assimilative pressures, such that the absorption of the membership into the larger society appears to be an "instrumentally efficient" and probable choice, the puzzle becomes greater.

Indeed, the assimilationist orientation of virtually all of United States Indian policy and the constant consternation at its failure seems to indicate that the puzzle has never been solved at the policy level (Castile 1979).

Spicer's answer to the dilemma appears to lie in what he calls an "oppositional process," which he tentatively suggests is "the essential factor in the formation and development of the persistent identity system" (1971:797). Spicer appears to veer dangerously close to the mentalistic when he says of Yaqui enclaves and their adherence to a symbol set that the set is based on "that unique experience which only Yaquis have had" and that "to know this and feel it in the Yaqui way one has to be brought up in a Yaqui household or undergo an enculturating experience through participation with Yaquis in their community life" (1976:7). While we can certainly agree that some structure must exist to transmit and maintain the symbol system, this insistence on such a narrow choice of possible mechanisms seems inconsistent with much else that he says. The general process which he describes under the "oppositional" label stresses "a continued conflict between these peoples and the controllers of the surrounding state apparatus" as the apparent means by which boundaries are maintained (1971:797).

This emphasis on conflict also seems to be a narrow orientation toward the relation of the enclave to the larger society. Barth has reviewed a number of perspectives on ethnicity; among them is the one he labels "ecological," and about which he says, "Interdependences can partly be analyzed from the point of view of cultural ecology, and the sectors of activity where other populations with other cultures articulate may be thought of as niches to which the group is adapted" (1969:19). Barth occasionally seems to emphasize, more than is convincing, conscious choice-making by ethnic group members seeking to maximize their social advantage, but his basic ecological perspective as to the nature of boundary maintenance is usable in an adaptive analysis. It is necessary, however, to bear in mind that it is the systems which are adapting and not an aggregate of choice-making individuals. Spicer's concept of "opposition" seems more useful if expanded to include the total class of possible interrelations between the segments of a plural society — in fact, an ecological analysis — in which conflict is but one of several possible states. Since the enclaves are focused actively in some way on the preservation of separate identity, then the maintenance of boundaries might be described by some substitute word as *tension* in place of the confrontational connotations of *opposition*. Tension is used here in the sense of a dynamic balance, tenuously maintained, but which may be free of direct and open conflict at many points. While seeking a larger, more comprehensive analysis of ecological relations we must agree with Spicer that some such tension is an inevitable aspect of persistent identity systems else they would quickly merge with the larger society.

STRUCTURES AND STRICTURES

Some of the apparent irrationality of the enclavement adaptation probably springs from confusing a successful adaptation with a *perfect* adaptation. In their classic paper on the functional prerequisites of a society, Aberle and the others describe one of these as "provision for adequate relationship to the environment" (1950:104). The key word is "adequate." How much is "adequate" is ultimately highly variable, and, while the enclaves do persist, many tend to view them as anomalous out of a refusal to accept the condition of subordination to some other group as a satisfactory and workable structural relationship. Spicer, in defining his concept of "enduring peoples," says it "includes a great many peoples who have not gained control of nation-states, but have remained politically non-dominant peoples within nation-states" (1976:5). Much of the literature of pluralism, such as the landmark work of M. G. Smith (1969), has stressed this dominant-subordinate characteristic of plural societies, although neither he nor most others would deny the theoretical possibility of relatively equal power/authority relations among enclaves within a single political structure. Political subordination may be distasteful to those imbued with the egalitarian ethos of our own society, but that feeling must not be allowed to cloud the workability or "adequacy" of such structural matrixes.

The enclavement adaptation has allowed Cherán and the Tarascans to endure for more than four hundred years, through occasionally intense but always present assimilative pressures, but it has not enabled them to triumph over the dominant sector nor to prosper materially at the same level as that sector. The reservation system has left the Indian peoples Indian, but it has also left them the poorest of the poor. Though I do not argue for a necessary connection between enclavement and relative deprivation vis-á-vis the larger society, it is very often the case that political subordination is related to some degree of differential access to resources. So frequently is this so that some such as Despres (1975) have stressed resource competition as a primary factor in pluralism and suggested that ethnicity is best understood as an aspect of systems of stratification.

In pursuit of an understanding of the structures that maintain systems of persistent identity and the adaptive purposes such systems serve, we can point out that some of the boundary-maintaining structure and process lies entirely outside the enclave itself. In both the Tarascan instance and the reservation cases there have been long periods of time, particularly in the early formative phases of both plural societies, during which the larger society quite simply did not permit the option of individual assimilation or system absorption. Although not usually as extreme as the mechanisms of slavery, segregation, and formalized prejudice that have afflicted blacks in the United States, attitudes and expectations have elsewhere existed which simply would not hold open ethnic apostasy as an option, no matter how unadvantageous the momentary position of the enclave. With the blacks the complete closure of the assimilationist option has in some sense forced the *creation* of an enduring people, as Greene discusses in this volume. The situation of the reservation peoples is not dissimilar in outcome, although the starting point and the mechanisms of denying assimilation are radically different. In the instance of the blacks a people has been created out of an aggregate of atomized individuals, torn from many cultures, through persistent denial of assimilation, while in the reservation case a people (or many peoples) has been preserved by mechanisms which, designed for absorption, have in fact functioned to frustrate the very goal they seek (Castile 1974*b*). There are, of course, non-reservation Indian peoples whose persistence is the product of a process of alienation similar to that of the black experience although ironically, with some groups in the southern United States, the insistence of separate identity as Indians has in part been motivated by attempts to avoid being labeled as black (Blu 1980). The seeming madness of adherence to disadvantageous ethnicity may in all of these cases sometimes be simply the result of a lack of choice.

Still more of the appearance of irrationality can be clarified if the enclaves are viewed as macro-temporal phenomena rather than micro-temporal, particularly if this approach is combined with the perspective which views the peoples as total systems enduring over much time rather than as aggregates of individuals making personal and immediate choices. Viewed at a point in time, the insistence on separate ethnic identity may appear maladaptive, even disasterously so, as in those periods when Jews have been subjected to pogroms, Yaquis to mass deportations, and Indians to forced re-education. At such moments many individual members of the persisting people may in fact abandon, or attempt to abandon, their allegiance and identification if it is possible to do so. Those who wonder at the loyalty to "belief" that is, for example, ascribed to Christian martyrs at Roman hands, may have ignored the extent to which apostasy does occur. One of the major theological wrangles of early Christian times was over readmittance of the apostates to the Church. Donatism, the doctrine which refused to allow readmittance, was declared to be a heresy primarily because the numbers involved were too great. The enclaves *do* leak members during times of trouble, and abandonment of identification does occur in the face of disadvantage at any time.

This "leakage," however, is a matter of individuals at a moment in time; it is the persistence of the *system* of identity that is significant. The evolutionary perspective stresses that, just as an individual organism may perish while its species survives, so too individuals or whole segments of a total people may succumb in some way (through death, apostasy, or some other means) while the people as a structural system continues to exist over much time. Only a minimal membership must be maintained to support the necessary structural nucleus that provides continuity for the symbolic identity system. It may aid in understanding the phenomenon of endurance to realize that the identity matrix of a people may have large or small numbers of adherents in actual cooperating contact, depending on the environmental circumstances. This notion, something like the expandability of the segmentary lineage, suggests that during times of persecution a minimal membership is likely to be reached with entire local segments sometimes ceasing to be part of the system, but that the matrix can serve as the focal point for expansion of membership as the ethnic adaptive option becomes more workable and attractive. While persecution can serve to reduce membership temporarily, it also serves, as many have noted, to increase the strength of the identification of the post-persecution membership. As long as a minimal, "adequate" mechanism survives, suitable for the transmittal of the symbol sets to new members, the enclave persists — although many of its members may not.

The Tarascan communities, it appears, have become the beneficiaries of certain positive shifts in the structural pose of the larger Mexican society vis-à-vis Indianness; a predictable resurgence of identification by many persons and communities who had earlier been grateful to be recognized as Mexican has occurred. The native North Americans have shown signs, for similar reasons to be discussed, of revitalization and an increase in Indian identification by persons whose ability to avoid such identification is plain in the pains taken to display some of the material symbols associated with Indianness. Without these displays there would be nothing behavioral, linguistic, or racial to allow any immediate identification of such persons as being deviant from the characteristics of the general society. Their display is a conscious renunciation of such acceptance. The major goals of an interesting "North American Indian Ecumenical Movement," described by Stanley (1977:238) are "to revive Indian language and tradition in those tribes that are losing them" and "to educate Indian youth, especially city youth, in Indian history, culture, and languages." Obviously these objectives are not only a positive endorsement of Indian values but a recognition that many who might have some claim to an Indian identity are not in fact presently participants in such a system at an effective level. Such positive and active assertion of identity, I am obviously contending, is a phenomena of "good times," when the adaptive effectiveness of ethnicity is greater.

The nature and range of the structures which can effectively function to transmit the essential symbolic core of a persistent identity system is too vast a subject for this chapter, but a few words are necessary to indicate the structures associated with the two illustrative groups. Both the Tarascans of Cherán and the generality of reservation cultures have had relatively complete social structures approaching full societies during most of their encapsulated existence. For many persistent peoples the totality of the structure available for the maintenance of the symbol system may be reduced to isolated kinship structures or to some limited, often covert, ritual interaction. The regional network of Tarascan villages and the federal system of reservations provide a much more elaborate structure of boundary maintenance than these limited ones.

The closed corporate community is too familiar a mechanism to require discussion here except to indicate that until the first decades of this century it was the typical form of structure functioning to preserve Tarascan identity systems. The inwardly focused community pursuing its pattern of *costumbre* (the "way" of the community, a set of traditional or unique behaviors) and exhausting its economic energies in the service of the saints has done well until modern times in preserving ethnic boundaries even as the communities have changed. Never truly autonomous economically, the structure still provided minimum temptations for contact and involvement of its membership with the outside world by consuming surplus and setting high value, as Foster (1967) has suggested, on the "rewards of shared poverty." Few outsiders were likely to seek to claim their share of such rewards and, as long as the exploitable resource base in the regions of refuge was uninviting, the pressures from the outside were small. The key in the past has been isolation, both physical and in terms of degree of larger society interest. That isolation has now been broken and the inward-turned mechanisms have failed, or are failing, to preserve a total closure, but the identity system seems not only to be surviving the breakdown of closure but in some instances to be undergoing a renaissance.

For the native North Americans the range and variety of structures is great. The reservations are of course classic examples, as previously mentioned, of the preservation of a people through insistence as well as persistence. For much of their history the peoples were put into suspended social animation by confinement to isolated and reserved parcels of land where they were denied the means to follow their traditional ways of life, exhorted to undergo assimilation but also denied the means to achieve that goal or indeed any other. The reservation system is essentially a custodial mechanism which functions to maintain suspended societies while proclaiming its dedication to change (Castile 1979).

The essence of the reservation variety of the administered community lies in the process of decapitating once whole societies and replacing their decision-making structures with administrators from the larger society, responsible and responsive to that society, not to the peoples being administered (Castile 1978). Having prevented by this mechanism the Indian peoples from developing structures of their own for governance, the administrators have at the same time never seriously pursued in effective ways the avowed policy of individual assimilation. They have always been a "service" rather than an "action" agency. Inevitably, unable to influence the "service" areas under outside control, the Indian reservation peoples have tended to retreat into smaller-scale, family-community structures and there maintained the core symbol system, supported and suspended in other areas by the external system of administration. These miniature homelands have served not only as the keystone for the maintenance of Indian identity systems on the reservations but for the urban, non-reservation, and apostate populations as well.

YOU CAN ALWAYS GO HOME AGAIN

If the great chorus of social observers is to be believed, one of the major problems of the massive industrial nation-state is alienation of the individual from the whole, leaving him with a "quest for community" in the satisfactions of smaller-scale groups. Primary social identification for many, it seems, is not with their nation but with their club or neighborhood. The ethnic identity systems have always had the advantage of providing such harbors of "community" in complex states. If the question "Who am I?" is important to answer, then being able to say "I am of the people" is one potentially satisfying response which the enclaves can offer to their members.

Cherán was relatively anomalous as peasant communities go, according to the literature, in that while people left, often for years at a time, it was at least believed that they always returned. The dramatic population growth between 1939 and 1969 would seem to bear this belief out. The reservations are even more revealing in this matter of return since "relocation" programs (euphemistically called Employment Assistance today) have actively sought to uproot the peoples and submerge them in the great population centers of the larger society. The statements of many Indian peoples gathered in studies of the relocated are reminiscent of some of Steinbeck's "Oakies" who, retreating from California to their dustbowl "homelands," were asked, "Can you make a living there?" and responded, "Nope. But at least we can starve to death with folks we know" (1939:181). Hodge's (1969) study, *The Albuquerque Navajos,* is one example that shows clearly that the choice of reservation/non-reservation residence is not simply an instance of maximization of economic advantage but is tempered by considerations of community identification.

While I cannot fully agree with Lurie's (1966:10) observation that "the option to assimilate is far more open for Indians than for almost any other minority," I believe that the opportunities, pressures, and temptations are in fact more substantial than the results would seem to reflect. Part of this is surely related to the continued existence of the possibility of withdrawal that is provided by the miniature homelands of the reservations. Additionally, for those so thoroughly assimilated (those whom I have called ethnic apostates) that actual residence on the reservation (and pursuit of the poverty-level lifestyle there) is not possible, the "homelands" serve not only as centers for the preservation of the symbols of Indian identity but also as rallying points symbolically, if not in residential reality, for any resurgence of identity. Far more Jews are strengthened in their Jewish identity by the existence of Israel than live there.

Lurie (1966) also noted that if the curious American custom of regarding all who have any degree of black ancestry as black were extended to Indians, the million or so persons who are currently Indian would swell to some ten millions! I will not pursue here the thorny issue of who may be admitted to the status of Indian, noting only my agreement with Lurie's statement that "Indians are essentially an ethnic or cultural minority rather than a racial one" (1966:10), but I must add that virtually everyone seems also to agree that there must be some genetic claim, however vague, before one may be admitted to Indian identity. In Mexico or in the United States a quantum of Indian blood may not prevent majority membership status but it is seemingly necessary for minority membership.

Having previously criticized Barth's tendency to emphasize individual choice-making, I must note that much of what I am describing as adaptive rationality for the enclaves stresses something seemingly similar. My focus is, however, on systems and, although systems as systems serve themselves not their components (White 1975), the system advantage may be manifest in terms of individual advantage. If biological evolutionary success is ultimately describable in terms of differential reproduction, then the social evolutionary equivalent lies in the system's ability to attract, hold, and motivate its members. A discussion of the means by which enclaves do this can describe the system's adaptability as well as the more obvious individual advantages.

Barth, in his examination of those who may assume "inferior" Kohistani or Baluch identity rather than the dominant Pathan, points out that "to declare oneself in the running as a competitor by Pathan value standards is to condemn oneself in advance to utter failure.... By assuming Kohistani or Baluch identity, however, a man may, by the same performance, score quite high on the scales that then become relevant" (1969:25). In short, the enclave option suggests that there is advantage in playing in a game you can win, however humble the stakes might be, and that a forceful insistence on separate identity can let you avoid playing with the other man's dice. A Tarascan villager who in the city would at best be a "rube" with his obvious peasant dress, speech, and manner can, although poor and ill-educated by "Mexican" standards, achieve respect and dignity in his community by his adherence to costumbre and community service. The boarding-school children of the Carlisle era of Indian education retreated from the status of "marginal men" for much the same reasons, since their "education" prepared them for only the lowest places in Anglo society.

Given the existence of prejudice and negative stereotyping of which the enclaved peoples are fully aware, there exists an additional pressure to convert the negative self-image foisted on one by the outsiders into something positive. Foster (1967) spoke of "treasure tales" which served to reinforce the image of limited good, but in Cherán I encountered what I called "Mexican tales." These stories recognized the negative stereotype and to some extent accepted it while turning it around. I was gleefully told the story of the tractor salesman in Zamora who was scornful of an old Tarascan woman's inquiries. He was horrified when she promptly marched to a rival store and there bought a new tractor with gold nuggets taken from her worn bag. The myth of the same Tarascan gold featured in the treasure tales to explain away wealth has been used to ridicule the haughty Mexicans for their lack of judgment. A man may be scorned by the majority peoples when he is in their midst with little recourse. Safely among his own, he can return the laughter and derision. American Indian humor at the expense of intruders is legendary.

These matters of affording individuals psychological support in their dealings with outsiders are, of course, of variable significance depending on the cultural environment of the moment. While today the mestizo has inherited Mexico, there was a time when there was no place in the Spanish colonial system for him, and the assured status of the Indian, however low, was more secure and attractive. Since the revolution there has been a resurgence of "positive" advantage offered to the "Indigenes" by the Mexican government. Under the presidency of Lázaro Cárdenas (1934–40), the Tarascans, particularly the allegedly non-Tarascan community of Tzintzuntzan, benefitted greatly through preference in programs of road-building, electrification, and the like, precisely because of the high regard held by the administration for the elevation of the Indian past. The I.N.I. coordinating center buildings standing on the outskirts of Cherán reflect the reality of more tangible advantage in persistent identity, when it is recognized and supported by the larger society.

Obviously *the* adaptive problem for the enclaves lies in their relationship with the dominant peoples of the political state of which they are a part. Both the Tarascans and the reservation peoples appear to have attained, or may soon be able to attain, a viable, politically defined niche. In Mexico the individual communities still retain a special status ultimately derived from the Spanish colonial "republic of Indians," which in Cherán has taken on new importance in the administration of ejido programs. Collectively the "Indigene" and each identifiable segment have to some extent begun to take on the status of recognized "sectors" in the complex balance of forces that must be considered in the councils of the governing party, the Party of Revolutionary Institutions. The Tarascans had, at the time of my study, begun to be recognized as a political entity through such events as collective meetings of village leaders with state and national officials.

The reservation peoples have for a very long time had both a curse and a blessing in their special status in relation to the federal government. The tribes retain, as original possessors of the soil, some degree of residual sovereignty and political autonomy (see Spicer 1969c or Castile 1979). The autonomy has never been real and the levels of poverty make it evident that theoretical advantages, such as a nontaxable protected land base, have never been realized. Legislative and judicial moves, such as the "Indian Self-Determination and Education Assistance Act" of 1975 and Federal Judge Boldt's 1974 affirmation of Indian fishing rights in *United States* v. *Washington* indicate the existence of a trend that may realize some of the potential advantages, but in the past similar moves have led to little. The special danger is in the ultimate powerlessness of the enclaved peoples, revealed when their "rights" threaten some segment of the dominant society, as in the moves to abrogate Indian treaty rights provoked by the fishing decisions.

Very many of the advantages that would normally be brought forward in regard to Indians are essentially the "advantages" of being poor. I.N.I. operates its special loan programs and builds roads and sewers in order to bring the Tarascan populations into line with the general life conditions already possessed by the dominant sector. Indian "preference" in employment (an ancestor of the modern "affirmative action"), job-training programs, revolving loan funds, and the like similarly exist only because the reservation communities are the poorest of the poor and do not possess the resources to remedy their own condition. This kind of "advantage," although important for the development of the enclaves, is also a source of envy and irritation for members of the majority population, who tend to see it as privilege and a denial of political principles of equality of opportunity. This is logically the social equivalent of a healthy man's envying a tuberculosis patient his "privilege" of receiving treatment, but it persists nonetheless.

The positive identification with the ethnic "Indian" enclaves can be seen as yet another micro-temporal fluctuation in the unbroken continuity of these peoples. In the 1970s and 1980s, as at some other points in the past, such a resurgence has begun to reach levels that merit description by a term such as revitalization. Spicer seems accurately to describe not only the Yaqui, who were his subject, but the Tarascans and native North Americans as well when he says that "as long as a people's conception of themselves resulting from their unique human experience is not totally disrupted, they will be capable of revitalization. Their 'culture' may change in ways that make it impossible to describe it in the same terms over a period of years; there may be complete replacement of traits and complexes, but such cultural assimilation may not be accompanied by loss of identity" (1976:12).

An understanding of ethnicity will necessarily involve us in further examination of the general phenomenon of stratification and consequent resource competition in plural societies (Despres 1975). There is probably also considerable potential profit in relating the phoenix-like character of the enclaves to the theories developing to explain social movements. These, too, have long been oriented toward choice, an emphasis that does not fit well with deterministic human science. Views of revitalization that are systemic, such as Wallace's (1956) stress on the "organismic analogy," seem to offer hope of evading the temptations of psychological reductionism in this area that are inherent in the obvious issues of conscious perception of deprivation, charismatic leadership, and the like. One can hope that if something as profoundly "psychological" as relative deprivation can be treated in culturological rather than psychological perspective that the same may be accomplished for the phenomenon of persistence. If, as Spicer seems to suggest, revitalization is an intrinsic part of the adaptive strategy of the persistent systems, then perhaps the two problems are ultimately the same.

Spicer's work has shown us that *persistence* is not to be taken as synonymous with *static,* and that idea alone is sufficient to clear away much of the mystical approach to persistent peoples. The evolutionary adaptive perspective is at one with the Marxian assertions that it is stasis that needs to be explained and that change is the normal order of things. Once we can come to understand that enclaves are a variety of "entity that maintains continuity at the same time that it undergoes change" (Spicer 1976:1) then the systems cease to outrage deterministic logic. They are not marvelous collections of unchanging choice-makers thrusting against the currents of reality but simply another variety of adaptive system behaving, as all must, in accord with the necessities of sustaining themselves in a viable and adequate balance with their physical and cultural environments.

| 11 |

Anarchy, Enclavement, and Syntropy in Intentional and Traditional Communities

Charles J. Erasmus

In this chapter I wish to pursue in positive fashion some provocative leads in a pioneering work on the persistence of cultural enclaves. In *Pascua: A Yaqui Village in Arizona* (1940) Edward H. Spicer shows that the destiny of a culture and its system of symbolic behavior is dependent ultimately on the decisions of its constituents. Many Yaquis of Pascua village were resolving the conflict between American competitive consumption and Yaqui ceremonial collectivism by moving out of Yaqui society into lower-class Tucson society. Yaqui religious culture at this time and place was being maintained with little change, but the society supporting it was "definitely threatened" by defections.

In describing the decisions of individual Yaquis, Spicer is careful to avoid the teleological error of assigning motives and directions to entire social orders or cultures. As Liebenstein (1976) has pointed out in regard to the field of microeconomics, it is the incentives and efforts of the atomic constituents — individuals — that are crucial to understanding the "decisions" of the social molecules. Spicer's work is valuable because he has kept his microanthropology within the perspective of a macro-anthropology based on comparative analysis rather than an illegitimate teleology. In his "Persistent Cultural Systems" (1971) he compares ten different "peoples" widely scattered around the globe to arrive at identity-symbol generalizations. He begins, significantly, by divorcing himself from pattern concepts of the 1930s; and, while he is interested in collective — not individual or idiosyncratic — identity symbols, he stresses the fact that for him the essential feature of the symbol system he compares is its relationship to the feelings and motivations of individuals.

I shall examine a different set of groups to throw additional light on several of Spicer's key concepts and findings, comparing intentional and. traditional communities along a gradient of anarchic opposition. Of particular concern are Spicer's concepts of "peoples," "oppositional process," "spheres of participation," "high positive valuation of local community," and "enclavement." To these concepts I add one of my own — indoctrination of the young, a process vital to cultural persistence.

INTENTIONAL COMMUNITIES

With the exception of the Hutterites, the nineteenth-century North American communes fall far short of the longevity of the enduring peoples compared by Spicer (1971). Yet many lived under at least two states while resisting conformity pressures from the larger society. As deliberate countercultural movements they all developed well-defined identity symbols not least of which was their communal economy. Like many of Spicer's persistent peoples these groups favored community social controls rather than state law, a circumstance requiring some internal organization of their own.

Black's (1976) distinction between law and anarchy is useful for analyzing intentional and traditional societies. All viable groups, whether intentional or traditional, must have some degree of organization and social control. Black's fundamental dichotomy is between states, which employ the distinctive form of social control we call *law,* and all other groups and organizations, which rely on social control mechanisms of the traditional, pre-legal, and small-group kind — mechanisms that continue alongside law within the many groups and organizations persisting inside the state. To the extent that groups or peoples within a state can disassociate themselves from law and rely on their own social control mechanisms, they are anarchic. The more anarchic such groups are, the more oppositional we would expect them to be. We would expect, moreover, identity symbols and community to be important to the persistence of any such oppositional process.

To make this clearer I shall employ another of Black's distinctions, that between communal and situational anarchy. *Communal* refers to a little community of close, homogeneous, stable relationships and *situational* to a heterogeneous world of strangers rather than intimates. Because some of the anarchical groups dealt with in this chapter live or lived in communes, making *communal* ambiguous, I will substitute *community* for Black's *communal*. In community anarchy order is maintained by the social controls of intimates: ridicule, admonishment, ostracism, excommunication. In situational anarchy order is normally established by law; but law, by definition, replaces anarchy. Most of the persistent peoples studied by Spicer, however, are groups large enough to be both community and situational anarchists, a fact which helps explain the "high positive valuation of local community in some form" which Spicer (1971) finds endemic to them all.

Peasants, for example, have characteristically been traditional community anarchists to the degree they relied on social controls within the village to circumvent and avoid the law of the state. And characteristically they have remained fragmented unless united by social movements and revolutions. But when tribal, ethnic, or religious affiliations cut across communities, even those of peasants, these communities have some basis for a symbol-identity system that can extend the brotherhood of the community outward into the area of situational anarchy between community social control and state law. Persons who would otherwise be strangers can recognize one another as brothers. And for a short while at least, by extending the controls of community anarchy into the lawless realm of situational anarchy, they can extend their "spheres of participation." The more numerous and more widely dispersed a people, however, the more important will be some form of community to perpetuate the social controls of community anarchy as well as the identity system that allows those controls to expand situationally.

Tradition and the nature of the oppositional process set important conditions for the size of a people. In the case of intentional communities the oppositional process has a strong countercultural locus in the communities themselves whether or not oppositional hostility is directed at them by the larger society. Intentional community anarchy, however, is an essentially entropic process leading in many cases to rapid dissolution. Groups that survive must develop organizations, strong social controls, and effective indoctrination procedures. Few grow to the size of traditional peoples whose historical origins have often made them community anarchists by default.

Most successful nineteenth-century communes began as social movements with strong leaders. Shall we call these leaders charismatic?

Wilson (1975) feels that contemporary sociology has badly watered down the Weberian meaning of charisma, which emphasized the social milieu rather than the personality type of the leader. To correct this journalistic drift toward imprecision, he substitutes *charismatic demand* for the charismatic (inspiring) individual. He would thereby return the emphasis to those social conditions that create the willingness to believe and accept a leader of extraordinary supernatural power. In doing so, he returns the usefulness of the concept to those preliterate and less-developed societies with at least enough complexity for an incipient division of functions. With modernization, machine technology, and cumulative rationality, charismatic demand becomes less probable, Wilson believes. To judge from his examples, he is thinking of social movements that engulf entire groups or peoples. In more modern times charismatic demand may be widely dispersed within a population, and the leader or prophet may be a selective catalyst that draws his followers together and holds them together. But, unless he is superseded by a strong organization and indoctrination system, the social glue may not outlive him for long if at all.

Mother Ann, Father Rapp, Joseph Bimeler, Christian Metz, and John Humphrey Noyes — founders of the Shakers, Rappites, Zoar, Amana, and Oneida, respectively — all appealed to a dispersed charismatic demand. They selectively attracted their followers from within larger populations (Erasmus 1977). What was the nature of this dispersed need? How did it vary from one recruit to the next? Unfortunately, history does not provide these details. Only students of contemporary countercultural movements, such as Zablocki (1980), can collect the quality of data that may illuminate the nature of the personal conditions and decisions that once constituted charismatic demand.

The above leaders produced intentional community anarchies which, to persist, had to develop enough organization to indoctrinate new members and maintain their unique identity systems. In terms of longevity, they were not too successful compared to Spicer's "peoples." When Joseph Meachum took over from Mother Ann, he developed an organization that allowed the Shakers to outlast the other five movements despite the mortally damaging effect of celibacy on recruitment and indoctrination. In membership numbers the Shakers were in decline most of their two hundred years. Both celibacy and weak organization ended the Rappites within a hundred years. Oneida practiced group marriage, but its organization was practically synonymous with the personality of John Humphrey Noyes and failed to outlast him. Zoar failed to insulate its young from the outside and to keep them within the faith. After eighty years a new generation agitated to end "communism" (Erasmus 1977).

Amana was the most impressive of these five groups. It lasted almost a hundred years, and by the time it peacefully transformed into a joint stock company, its membership was nearly twice that with which it began. Not handicapped by rules of celibacy, it indoctrinated its young effectively during its early years and retained a high percentage of them. At its beginning Amana indoctrination seems to have been much like that of the Hutterites (Erasmus 1977).

The Hutterites moved to the United States just as the other five successful nineteenth-century communes had reached or passed their prime. As of 1980 the other five have long since dissolved or changed into corporations, yet the Hutterites are stronger than ever. In membership they are thirty times as numerous as when the original eight hundred arrived on America's western frontiers in 1874. Recruitment of new members has been almost entirely through successful indoctrination of their young. And if we add to the one hundred years of Hutterite growth and prosperity in North America their three hundred years of previous history in Europe, they come as close in longevity as they do in most other respects to what Spicer calls a "people." In fact, the Hutterites are one example of intentional community anarchy that has lasted long enough to become traditional as well. Having outlived the original conditions of charismatic demand by three centuries, their sixteenth-century leader had become much like a traditional culture hero by the time the Hutterites began their amazing period of expansion in North America—an expansion in no way dependent on charismatic leadership (Erasmus 1977).

With a four-hundred-year history the Hutterites combine tradition and intent through indoctrination of their young. They keep alive the history of persecution and injustice which their group has suffered at the hands of several different states. Yet today external opposition to Hutterites is minimal. Even in Canada, where for many years an objective of provincial government was to assimilate them into Canadian society, the policy of the 1970s was to strengthen—rather than undermine—the ethnic pride of all such minorities. Recognizing the danger of a benevolent, kindly state in reducing the oppositional process which helps maintain their community anarchy, the Hutterites increase their vigilance through a kind of traditionalized intent (Erasmus 1977).

If the Hutterites have experienced one of the most expansive periods of their long history under conditions of minimal external opposition, it is not too helpful in explaining their success (persistence and growth) relative to the other five community anarchies. Nearly all of them felt oppositional pressures from the larger society to some degree early in their histories, but they were never severe or long sustained. The three German groups (Rappites, Zoar, and Amana) came to the United States to escape religious discrimination, not bloody persecution, and in their new environment they achieved a certain amount of fame and respect. External opposition to Oneida was extremely mild, and the community became a popular nineteenth-century tourist attraction. During their proselytizing phase under Mother Ann, the Shakers were treated very roughly indeed, but once they settled down to community life they became internationally famous as an example of successful communism (Erasmus 1977).

To a large extent intentional community anarchists must generate and maintain their own oppositional process. The Hutterites' outstanding ability to do so is due in part, at least, to effective indoctrination and to the fact that — anything but celibate — they have always produced large numbers of new recruits to indoctrinate. In a study of nine colonies that varied in degree of economic success and effective management, Heiken (1978) found that "strong" colonies keep close control over public schooling and strictly limit its secular influence, use kindergarten for children between ages two and six to shift their individualistic tendencies toward "colony-mindedness," and insist on regular attendance at both Sunday school and the colony German school. At "weak" colonies, on the other hand, children tend not to be punished for willful behavior; given close adult supervision; taught hymns, prayers, and Hutterite history; sent to kindergarten; taught German before English; or strictly required to attend Sunday school and German school. Instead they are more likely to be indulged by their parents, given toys and bicycles, and enrolled in public schools off the colony where they establish friendships with non-Hutterites.

Strong, vigilant indoctrination is essential to the persistence of intentional community anarchy but by no means sufficient to explain it. Judging from Heiken's observations, weak Hutterite colonies have many characteristics in common with Amana just before it became a corporation. In addition to high rates of defection, individuals work off the colony or engage in independent enterprises to earn private income; establish friendships off the colony; rely increasingly on English rather than German; give up traditional dress; eat at home and generally participate less in collective activities; visit one another less or not at all; buy an ever greater variety of consumer goods for personal consumption; and even steal colony property or use it for illicit business purposes of their own. Why, however, do the strong Hutterite colonies overwhelmingly predominate after so many years while Amana went the way of the weak?

Anarchy, as we have already noted, tends naturally to be entropic. To persist, a community anarchy that relies mainly on an autochthonous oppositional process must develop and maintain some kind of dynamic growth pattern that will support — rather than undermine — opposition. Otherwise, it will die or change. Members not only must be indoctrinated to support the group at the expense of self, they must be given a rewarding way of carrying out those principles of indoctrination, a dynamic involvement which keeps the atomic constituents within the social molecule in such close harmony that they act almost as one. Only then can internal entropy be effectively checked.

Useful to our comparative analysis at this point is Land's (1973) distinction between the three major forms of growth that encompass all life systems. The first is simply growth in size and the second growth in numbers, as in cell division. Only the third involves the information exchange that is truly syntropic in its consequences. In an adaptation to the North American environment that was as much "traditional" (historical) as "intentional" (planned), the Hutterites have recapitulated the same dynamic form of growth that characterized most of man's primitive social past. Avoiding both entropy and syntropy, the Hutterites have achieved a remarkable growth of numbers through "cell" (community) division. Maintaining social isolation as much as possible through spatial and linguistic separation from the world and limiting education and external communication, they have resisted re-entry into the syntropic milieu of information exchange as well as its legal and state consequences. Amana, Oneida, Economy (Rappites), and even the Shakers (to some degree) industrialized and became caught up in market society. So successful were Amana and Oneida in their syntropic re-entry into market society that they survived as modern corporations within the contract law of the polyarchal state (Erasmus 1977).

Hutterites have remained farmers and eschewed industrialization. They enter the agricultural marketplace with a purpose that simultaneously restrains the market's influence upon them. Each colony works to accumulate the capital to "branch"—to start a daughter colony in fifteen years, by which time the colony population has doubled. This process provides a continuous and dynamic objective that also keeps the communal units small enough for social controls to remain primary and organization relatively decentralized. The opportunity for all adult males, at least, to participate fully in the building process is maximal. Given strong branching goals, efficient management, and effective indoctrination procedures (all of which reinforce one another), the members of a strong colony will be too involved in playing the Hutterite game to negatively appraise its "opportunity costs" vis-à-vis alternative games within the larger society. But when, for reasons often fortuitous, the branching process delays or breaks down, the atoms begin to behave like those outside the Hutterite molecule, a drift still relatively weak.

Members of an anarchic community can, however, be easily seduced by a polyarchal state. Under centralized authoritarian states, in which, according to Black (1976), the downward thrust of law tends to be highly punitive in the direction of marginal groups, the Hutterites had no difficulty maintaining an oppositional position. But, as Lindblom (1977) has argued, polyarchal states are the result of a long struggle to weaken centralized authority rather than to strengthen it. They encourage extreme pluralism through decentralization and the diffusion of power to individuals and small groups. One could say, therefore, that polyarchy encourages anarchical tendencies, a characteristic intimately associated with market economy. Market economy can and does join with a great variety of polities, but constitutional polyarchy has not been so flexible; it seems to need this particular form of economy. For one thing, the syntropic consequences of market economy seem to expand, rather than contract, under the anarchical encouragements of polyarchy. For another, market economy — despite the fact that polyarchy fosters an environment of pluralism permissive to differences and opposition — ties together all the diverse elements of the polity through their interdependence as consumers and producers. On the production side, Hutterites have controlled market participation very carefully through their mixed agricultural economy. Except, perhaps, where they have moved toward monoculture, they have been more susceptible to market seduction as consumers.

Amana and Oneida were seduced primarily through production (Erasmus 1977). As their industries grew, they hired increasing amounts of labor. Oneida members became managers of employees and finally succeeded as a corporation because of successful industrial management and unsuccessful communal leadership. Amana became a corporation out of desperation after a decline in both areas. As community leadership and commitment declined, members came to depend too much on hired labor. With the loss of their original enthusiasm and motivation, the conditions of what Liebenstein (1976) calls "x-inefficiency" prevailed, and membership effort moved toward entropy. Reorganized as a corporation under new management from outside, Amana became totally absorbed into the market economy with financially profitable results but with the end of community anarchy.

Communes, by combining collective production and egalitarian consumption, are an extreme form of community anarchy; their identity systems involve deliberate oppositional components in the economic as well as the political sphere. In a polyarchal environment of pluralism that politically indulges their oppositional character, they are susceptible to unintentional corruption by inexorable market processes. And owing to the collective nature of commune production, their duel with market corruption either turns them into corporations in the most modern sense or they self-destruct. A brief review of the Amish, on the other hand, shows how an identity "system" can persist although its constituent communities vary enormously in degree of market corruption.

The Amish are not communists. They are community anarchists who practice private farming. They help one another through various mutual-aid practices, but they do not produce collectively. And since they do not consume collectively, they differ unavoidably in wealth. What tends to keep them equal, in lifestyle at least, is the same anti-materialism and anti-progressivism they share with the Christian communists.

As Hostetler's (1968) studies show, the community unit of social control is the "church district," a group of thirty to forty households that form a congregation small enough to hold religious services in their homes on a rotational basis. Within this small community members are highly visible to one another, and social controls are tightly applied to maintain, as much as possible, Amish independence from state and world. To keep backsliders in line, the little community threatens them with the "ban"—excommunication and shunning. Once a person has been excommunicated, no member of the group can interact with him for any purpose—even marital relations are suspended. Like the Hutterites, the Amish limit their children's formal education to elementary school, a practice which reduces their chances of entering the outside job-world with any great success. The firm disciplining of children as well as their education in community ways and the German language is much like Hutterite practice except that among the Amish it is more a family than a community function. Like the Hutterites, too, the Amish must work hard to save the money necessary to buy farmland for their children. Again, they do it on a family rather than a community basis, but the effort helps them, too, in avoiding the temptations of worldly hedonism.

As land grows more expensive, however, the pressures to mechanize and commercialize their farming operations increase. And where communities (church districts) bend to these pressures, members must increasingly involve themselves in external contacts and the laws of the state. As they do, they also relax their anti-materialism and anti-progressivism. The result is that market economy corruption takes place by degrees along a spectrum of communities from those remaining highly conservative to those which no longer preserve enough identity symbols to remain within the Amish orbit. Cohesion of atoms within the community molecules may remain high, but the molecules drift toward re-entry into the economic syntropy of the polyarchal state. And as the distance between the molecules increases, so does situational anarchy among them. Members of communities that have drifted too far apart may no longer even regard one another as brothers.

INTENT WITHIN TRADITION

A similar spectrum of identity-symbol intensity exists among Jews on a broader scale. The Hasidic communities could be placed at the conservative extreme, and from there the spectrum might be said to move to orthodox, conservative, reform, and, finally, non-religious Jews. Here is a very large traditional group that meets all of Spicer's (1971) requirements for a "people"; it is, in fact, one of his type cases. It also illustrates what he calls "high positive valuation of the local community in some form." Just as Zionism itself helped to intensify the identity system of a whole people, the kibbutzim became a community movement that intensified in local form the spirit of Zionism. It is a case of intentional community anarchy that grew up within a very diverse people, and, significantly, at the non-religious end of the spectrum. As such it is also an unusual case of community anarchy dedicated from its inception to the accomplishment of goals quite the obverse of anarchy.

First, members of the kibbutz movement have always been too intellectual to fit the Wilson (1975) mold of charismatic demand, a fact congruent with their non-religious character. They are intentional communities within a tradition that has often been highly intentional in the values placed on community. In this case the form was sufficiently unusual to catch the attention and interest of the whole world. Although the early kibbutzim practiced mixed farming and endeavored to preserve their economic and social independence, they were only briefly anti-intellectual in the Hutterite and Amish sense of opposing higher education. Kibbutzim since their earliest countercultural phase have been characteristically open to the information exchange leading to syntropy. They have seldom opposed progress even on principle (Erasmus 1977).

Second, as community spearheads of Zionism, the kibbutzim began as pioneering groups helping to settle Palestine and transform it into a Jewish state. They were community anarchists working to create conditions of law and statehood. And once the state of Israel was established, they had to support it in ways that threaten eventually to destroy or radically change them.

The kibbutz movement grew during the period of maximal immigration of European Jews. Since this recruitment source has now dried up, the future of the movement depends upon retention of the young. According to Westerlind (1978), this is the biggest problem now facing the kibbutz. Unlike a Hutterite colony, the kibbutz, as we have said, is an open, information-exchange system. It cannot clip its children's wings through educational handicaps. And as a staunch supporter of the Israeli state, the kibbutz must send its children into military service like all good Israeli citizens. This period of compulsory service to the state abruptly ends the young person's communal provincialism and introduces him or her to a whole new world of attractive alternatives. Many do not return.

Unlike the Hutterites, again, the kibbutzim have been faced with limited land resources within their tiny state. Unable to expand their farm economies, they have achieved expansion through the development of industries. This forces them in the direction of Amana, not that of the Hutterites. They fail to perpetuate the pioneering, building spirit that Hutterites constantly renew through branching. Westerlind's interviews with kibbutz children and young pioneers showed a strong preference to join new kibbutzim where they, too, could build something for themselves, not just work at boring jobs in enterprises created and managed by others. Unfortunately there are almost no new kibbutzim to join.

The problems of profitability facing the kibbutzim twenty years ago have been solved in most cases by their very profitable industries. Well over half of all kibbutz income now comes from the industrial sector, while the agricultural sector, according to Westerlind, drifts steadily toward commercial monoculture. More and more a major goal of kibbutzniks has been the improvement of their living standards. And as they become more consumer-oriented, they tend increasingly, says Westerlind, to "rationalize" production toward profits. If, for example, it is most profitable to grow cotton, they tear up fruit orchards. But the fewer the work branches, the fewer become the positions of responsibility which younger members find challenging. The dissatisfactions that result are similar to those on a Hutterite colony that fails to branch.

As Rosen (1980) and Westerlind (1978) show in their analyses of kibbutz industrialization, the process radically alters the entire climate of the kibbutz. Pushed by market competition toward ever greater and more costly economies of scale, the kibbutz becomes more and more like a business corporation. Only the few capable of managing the operation understand what is going on, and they tend to become a special class apart from all those performing the routine, uncreative work. More and more the latter is assigned to the hired laborers who often outnumber the kibbutz workers.

Since all of this increases membership dissatisfaction and makes it more difficult for the kibbutzim to keep their young, the greater doses of hedonism and individualism that result only intensify the process more. Threatened by the prospect of diminishing numbers, the communities are afraid not to meet membership demands unthinkable twenty years earlier. When members want television sets, for example, they all get them. At least one kibbutz, according to Westerlind, has tried to provide all its members with cars. And so successfully have kibbutz mothers demanded a return to nuclear family living that in over half the kibbutzim of the Ichud federation members now live in family units. So much do its kibbutzim now resemble shitufim that one shitufi has actually joined the Ichud.

The kibbutzim fix an interesting point along our spectrum from intentional to traditional communities, for they began as a highly intentional movement within a traditional people. And no matter what further changes take place in these communities, their members and defectors will still be carriers of Jewish identity. The community movement had its own autochthonous oppositional qualities, but even these stemmed from external oppositional forces that exceeded anything in the history of the other seven groups. The Jews are a type case not only as a people but as victims of prejudice, discrimination, and even genocide. As an intentional community movement within a larger identity, the kubbutzim show not only the same vulnerability as our previous cases to market-economy syntropy but even a political vulnerability through their relationship to the larger identity. Whatever their fate, however, the enclavement which gave birth to them and threatens to reabsorb them will continue, and both the Jewish people and the world with which they interact will be all the richer for having shared this unique and instructive social experiment. And this bring us, finally, to Spicer's concept of enclavement and its place, as he sees it, in the process of cultural evolution.

TRADITIONAL COMMUNITIES

The final four cases on our continuum of communities illustrate traditional groups which are characteristically objects of an oppositional process rather than converts to one. The first and most extreme case might be called an enclave within an enclave or, perhaps, a people within a people. I refer to the Irish "Tinkers" or "Travellers" studied by George Gmelch (1977) and Sharon Gmelch (1975).

The Tinkers have been a separate Irish subsociety for several centuries, and they have carried their subculture with them as far as England and the United States. Although the Irish are one of Spicer's ten examples of a "people," this interesting Irish subsociety meets many of the same criteria. In fact, at least one of the Gmelches' informants regarded Travellers and settled Irish as distinct "nations."

According to Spicer (1966) a "cultural enclave is a part of a political society," a part which "places positive value" on the maintenance of its distinctive cultural traits. Two aspects of this definition require qualification. First, it would seem more consistent to speak of a cultural enclave within a larger political culture or a social enclave within a larger political society. My guess is that Spicer is referring to a social enclave maintaining cultural behaviors significantly distinct from those of the larger polity. This important qualification is necessary to avoid the mistake which, as we have seen, Spicer himself carefully avoids in practice — that of assigning motivation and volition to a culture. Second, and in the same vein, we must be careful how we assign positive affect to an entire "enclave." Like any social molecule it contains individual human constituents who can vary just as much in their commitment to enclavement as in their commitment to anything else.

Hutterites probably come as close to a "general will" in this regard as any of our groups. And although the kibbutzim are rapidly changing in cultural distinctiveness, their members are still united to an unusual degree in support of their own particular form of enclavement. Certainly many Amish communities are clinging steadfastly and deliberately to their identifying characteristics. It is only when we look closely and comparatively at communities within each enclave that we can detect different degrees of commitment to enclavement among the social molecules. And, as we do, we find these differences reflect the changing attitudes and choices of their constituents.

Commitment to enclavement seems much weaker among Tinkers and their community anarchy far more primitive and less deliberate than among any of our previous groups. As itinerant tinsmiths, peddlers, horse traders, chimney sweeps, seasonal farm laborers, scavengers, and beggars, the Tinkers traditionally moved in small bands of two to four families. Their nomadism was confined to relatively short distances covering at most three counties and consisted of repeated circuits through the same towns and villages each year. Although the nuclear families within a band tended to be related patrilineally, band composition was anything but permanent. So minimal was Tinker formal organization and social control that band fission was usually their way of resolving conflicts. Not only does Tinker anarchy closely parallel the form Black (1976) finds characteristic of very primitive peoples, the Gmelches (1975, 1977) compare it with the nuclear-family form of anarchy associated with lower-class poverty that some observers have labeled "atomistic." Tinkers, according to the Gmelches, apply the word *friend* only to close kinsmen and have no notion of friendship comparable to that of settled Irish. Among Tinkers situational anarchy is obviously predominant and community anarchy only rudimentary.

As we have seen in our previous cases, when the oppositional character of an anarchial group is largely autochthonous, it requires a strong sense of community, strong indoctrination of the young, and a dynamic opportunity for individual participation to preserve a lasting commitment to enclavement. None of these factors holds true in this case, yet the Tinkers persist because the oppositional process is so strong. But in this case the oppositional process is more a product of the group's social environment than its own intent. Tinker identity is not discretionary in the same sense as Hutterite, Amish, or kibbutznik identity.

Despite the fact that Tinkers are genetically Irish and physically indistinguishable from the rest of the population, they are readily identified by the settled Irish, who treat them as pariahs. They are identified by dress, carts, livestock, surnames, vocational practices, accent, and the secret argot they speak among themselves when dealing with settled Irish. Whether or not one could ever have said that Tinkers were as committed to their identity as Amish or Hutterites, such a conclusion would certainly not be true in recent times.

With mechanization of agriculture, consolidation of landholdings, and improved roads and communications, post-World-War-II changes in rural Ireland have made most of the Tinkers' vocations obsolete, a process reducing them to scavenging, begging, stealing, and living on welfare. Drifting into towns where they live in camps of twenty to thirty familes, Tinkers have become increasingly sedentary, dependent, and demoralized. Thrust into ever closer and more permanent contact with settled Irish, they are exposed to constant reminders of their social inferiority, for discrimination against them is strong and undisguised. Attempts to settle Tinker families in public housing provokes their working-class neighbors to picketing, protest marching, and even to destroying property. Pejorative labels such as "Gypo," "Tinker tramp," and "Knacker" follow Travellers everywhere. If identified, they may be denied admission to pubs and cinemas or even fired from jobs at which they have been performing well. Sharon Gmelch (1975) tells about a visit to a young woman who had "passed" into settled society, a girl related to Tinker informants who had provided her address. When the anthropologist brought up the subject of Tinkers, the girl burst into tears. Not yet fully understanding the reason for the visit, she thought something about her appearance or behavior had revealed her background.

Some Travellers try to pass, but most are resigned to their situation and dare indulge such hopes only for their children. They have little opportunity to shed the behaviors that identify and stigmatize them or to learn new vocational skills, for spatial mobility and pariah status intensify their social isolation. Most Tinkers are illiterate and perform only the lowest-paid, unskilled jobs. Here we come to a diagnostic difference between Tinker anarchy and that of the Hutterites or Amish. The latter groups deliberately limit their children's education to insulate them from contamination. Tinker children, on the other hand, fail to get an education because they are never in one place long enough and because Irish society has found the problem easier to neglect than to solve. While an autochthonous oppositional process clips the wings of Amish and Hutterite children to keep them in the nest, an external oppositional process of prejudice and discrimination keeps young Tinkers from fleeing theirs.

Where attempts have been made to settle Traveller families in public housing, they remain socially isolated because other Irish shun them or move from the neighborhood to avoid being identified with them. And when Tinkers settle on their own, they must keep their whereabouts secret from relatives. One way for kin to "level" an upwardly mobile family is to expose its Tinker roots to its neighbors by making a noisy, drunken visit. Even in camps or on the road, a family temporarily more affluent than its kin learns to avoid ugly gossip and even property damage by sharing its good fortune — often by buying drinks for all at some lower-class pub.

Only where a few Tinker families have been helped to buy their own homes, dispersed among the settled population, have they begun to break out of the vicious circle of Tinker poverty (Gmelch 1977). Improving their houses through their own work and savings, they have even started to consume competitively, a trend reversing the leveling process. They are replacing the old Tinker game of keeping the Joneses down with the settled-Irish game of keeping up with them. And, even more important, their children are attending school regularly and gaining acceptance among their settled peers. As these Tinkers successfully integrate with modern market economy, they try to shed Tinker identity and become settled-Irish members of the polyarchal state.

Does *enclave,* in the sense Spicer (1966) uses the word, apply to the Tinkers? Are these people trying to preserve their identity, or are they unable to shed it? Are they committed to enclavement, or are they the victims of some kind of enslavement? Certainly I do not mean enslavement literally nor in any simplistic Marxian sense of exploitation. The settled Irish are not trying to exploit Tinkers. In fact, a favorite complaint made against them is that they are economic parasites sponging off — and thereby exploiting — the rest of Irish society. Both Travellers and settled Irish have been locked into an oppositional process by social and economic conditions that are discriminatory and counterproductive for the subordinate people. This is what I mean here by *enslavement*.

When we contrast peoples from both ends of the oppositional spectrum, the difficulty of applying the word *enclavement* to some pariah groups is relatively clear. But what about the great majority of cases that lie between? What about subsocieties in Latin America, for example, that not only appear committed to a distinctive way of life but endure the stigma of ethnic or class prejudice along with economic and social discrimination? When is their situation enclavement, and when is it "enslavement"?

In the late 1950s, as part of my regional study of economic development and culture change in northwest Mexico, I found striking differences between Mayo and Yaqui opposition to Mexican society and culture (Erasmus 1961, 1978). The source of those cultural differences I attributed to historical differences largely of a demographic and topographic nature.

As a consequence of their history Yaquis were concentrated in their own communities on their own tribal land and had preserved enough cohesion and organization to tax Mexicans within their reserve, police themselves for misdemeanors, and lobby for political and economic favors in Mexico City. In addition, they effectively maintained group identity through their language, ceremonial participation, and informal social controls. I compared them to Hutterites at the time because they were so intentionally committed to maintaining their boundaries against the outside that, like Hutterites, they deliberately kept alive—through oral tradition and indoctrination of their young—the memory of past and current injustices perpetrated against them by the dominant society. And while they did not actively oppose or limit formal education, most did not consider regular or sustained school attendance by their children worth advocating or supporting.

Mayos, on the other hand, had no communities exclusively their own but lived everywhere in close association with Mexicans and assimilated Mayos. Identity symbols had become so scrambled that many worried about how to identify other Mayos when away from their own village. Some concluded it was better never to initiate interaction with a stranger; let him be first to identify himself. Their only organization was ceremonial, and it seemed weak compared to Yaqui organizations. Although many Mayos had even shifted to keeping up with the Joneses, none were effectively keeping the Joneses down. Economically successful Mayos no longer participating in ceremonial life might be envied, but they were seldom if ever ostracized, for this kind of social control was losing strength. Enough families were changing to find safety in numbers everywhere. Not even those joining Protestant cults were effectively intimidated. Most wanted more education for their children, and increasingly families were making a special effort to get their children through secondary school.

The community anarchy of the Yaquis resembles that of Hutterites and Amish to the extent they have made the oppositional process their own and to the extent they try to maintain their identity system through social isolation. But if the Hutterites are a case of traditionalized intent, the Yaquis are a product of intentionalized tradition, for the latter are not nearly as sophisticated as the literate and prosperous Hutterites. The Mayos, on the other hand, resemble the Tinkers in their weaker sense of community and their close contact and interaction with the dominant society. Since deliberate discrimination against Mayos, however, is neither as vicious nor intense as that directed at Tinkers, their assimilation rate is understandably much higher. Yet both groups are economically disadvantaged and at the bottom of their respective social ladders. Under the circumstances one might be tempted to label the Yaquis a case of enclavement and Mayos one of "enslavement," but this would be an oversimplification. To show why, I turn now to the last case on our continuum, the Maya Indians studied by Smith (1977) in Guatemala.

In his comparative regional analysis, Smith found a rich ceremonial life being preserved by Maya communities still relatively isolated and economically self-sufficient. But in the Indian town of San Pedro Sacatepéquez, a high concentration of Indians (more than 10,000) in a single community had resulted in a dynamic and unusual form of enclavement. In this prosperous town so many Indians had become successful in business and the professions that they were leading the entire population away from fiesta sponsorship and other symbols of Indian identity in areas of dress, language, consumption patterns, and education. Yet while this community was deliberately shedding traditional symbols of Indian identity, it was vigorously proclaiming its Indian roots. The prosperity of San Pedranos and their dynamic entrepreneurial economy were the result of competitive forces that were collective as well as individual. San Pedranos no longer had time for the old Indian game of ceremonial consumption and service because they were out to beat their Ladino neighbors at their own game of competitive production and consumption. They now looked down on the adjoining Ladino town of San Marcos as an object of ridicule. "We are through with mistreatment from those *españoles* with their white faces," was one typical cry of defiance during a confrontation between San Pedranos and San Marquenses over a disputed boundary between the communities.

Here is a living example of the kind of extreme enclavement Spicer (1971) alludes to when he suggests that a "people" can lose or abandon most identity symbols in the usual areas of dress, language, and ceremony and still retain their identity. The expression which group identity takes in any particular case is highly variable; there is no intercultural symbol system.

San Pedranos are a crucial example of enclavement for at least two reasons. First, they show again how an oppositional process originating in a dominant group can inspire a countermovement within the subordinate. When it does, the oppositional process takes on autochthonous characteristics within the subordinate community as it moves from the traditional toward the intentional pole, thus bringing us at the close of our section on traditional communities full circle to the subject with which we began—intentional communities.

Second, the move toward intentionality takes quite a different form in the San Pedrano case than it does among Hutterites and Amish, for example. San Pedranos are defiantly and successfully competing with their Ladino oppressors in both market economy and polity, for they are developing civic organizations, neighborhood improvement committees, youth clubs, and even a political lobby in Guatemala City. Proudly affirming their Indian identity, they are leaving community and situational anarchy to become full economic and political participants in a plural society. They are not maintaining defenses against syntropy either by intention or default. Education of their children has become a major route to higher status and the power to expand their spheres of participation. Like the Hutterites, San Pedranos have found a way to increase opportunities for individual participation in a dynamic fashion, but unlike the Hutterites they are doing it through full entry into the larger society rather than through a partial re-entry that is heavily monitored and restricted. They are claiming their right to full participation in a plural society while retaining their ethnic identity. San Pedranos clearly support Spicer's (1966) contention that enclaves are not just "backwashes of civilization" but potentially a major stimulus for the evolution of higher forms of cultural and social integration.

I do not wish to imply by this statement that peoples such as Hutterites and Amish are backwashes that do not contribute to cultural evolution. All such voluntary social experiments teach us much about the limits of human social organization. And even though growth among a group such as the Hutterites is more "cellular" than syntropic, future interaction between Hutterites and external society promises a rich learning process for both. At their customary rate of growth, about 100,000 Hutterites should occupy 1,000 North American communes by the end of the century; by the middle of the next, some 10,000 colonies will contain a million Hutterites (Erasmus 1977). Competition for resources will inevitably disrupt this pattern, forcing mutual accommodation of Hutterites and non-Hutterites within polyarchies that place high value on independence and self-determination at the local level. This mutual accommodation of syntropic forces and antisyntropic intentions will provide the entire world with a learning experience far greater than any designed experiment could possibly provide.

Not only must research be continued among the Hutterites by experts with a variety of skills and theoretical approaches, it should be continued among groups within such readily accessible and rapidly changing areas as northwestern Mexico. To understand commitment to enclavement and the form it takes in any particular case, we must elevate it within its total social context. Unlike San Pedranos, whom they resemble in their ethnic pride, most Sonoran Yaquis in 1958 were poor, illiterate, and ill-equipped to pursue alternatives. Can one be sure under such circumstances which identity symbols persist by default and which by real membership commitment?

And while some Mayos are still participating in ceremonial life and giving some support to new cult movements, more than half of each generation is assimilated into Mexican society (Erasmus 1961). As we have seen, strong participation is associated with an oppositional process autochthonous to dynamic intentional communities, and we would expect it to be weaker when associated with the external constraints characteristic of traditional, class-conflict opposition. In the latter case, high rates of defection should not be surprising. For this reason persistence within a context of mass defection must be studied in relation to that defection, not apart from it. A situation may be relatively open without being totally so. Commitment may be given more weight than lack of alternatives not only by the observer but by the subjects themselves. Some of the poorest Tinkers defend their Traveller life as "in their blood" and a means of remaining their "own boss" just as many Yaquis and some Mayos in 1958 preferred to eke out a meager subsistence by exploiting the native thorn forest rather than work for Mexicans and become "a white man's dog."

There is a romantic tradition in anthropology closely tied to cultural relativism that values positively all ways of life. Thus, some anthropologists come to love cultures even more than the people who carry them. By creating an enclavement "model" based on a mass tension-reduction hypothesis based in turn on a metaphorical comparison between a transitional phase in the history of an entire society and a stage in the life cycle of individuals, it is possible to portray a way of life that seduces its constituents through the sheer power and beauty of its "logico-aesthetic integration." Thus can symbolic analysis employ the same teleological mentalism as the old culture-pattern approach. It can also follow the same trail blazed by functional analysis. It can convey a metaphor of village cohesion inspired purely by self-protective and self-generating internal forces. For example, as Smith (1977) has argued, the fiesta system of Latin America was very much a part of colonial society. In Sonora as in Guatemala, hacendados encouraged ceremonial service and consumption on the part of their Indian labor. It kept their labor force fragmented, in debt, and more easily managed.

The oppositional process underlying most cases of enclavement is likely to stem from dominant-subordinate social conflicts which cannot be separated from questions of social justice. We must be careful not to justify the social privileges of dominant groups by painting over social injustice and human misery with the jargon of functionalism and symbolic analysis.

There is another danger to symbolic analysis through metaphor. It can too easily be based on what I call "deep throat" anthropology — intensive interviewing of a few esoteric individuals while neglecting exoteric variation. Boas (1902) warned us against this methodological error more than seventy-five years ago. Through a metaphorical interpretation and a selection of informants most likely to fit it, a social molecule may be delineated that is as much fiction as reality. In an area as complex as southern Sonora, one has to observe and count a lot of atoms before delineating social molecules. And as O'Connor (1980) discovered in her research among the Mayos, these atoms are diverse enough to comprise a molecule which is not only complex but also in a state of almost constant structural, ethnic, and cultural change.

Such studies are worth our time and diligence. For the cultural evolution to which enclavement processes contribute is one closely bound to the moral ecology unique to human culture. Any drift from community and situational anarchy toward the social pluralism of polyarchy can have tremendous consequences for the evolution of human rights. Many astute observers of the Russian scene believe a severe internal crisis in that country is more likely to come from the various enclaves within its borders than from intellectual dissidence per se (Meyer 1978). The Ukrainians, Byelorussians, Moldovians, Estonians, Latvians, Lithuanians, Georgians, Armenians, Uzbeks, Kazakhs, Tarters, Turkmen, Tadzhiks, and many other peoples are pressing increasingly for greater economic self-determination. It is not impossible that this great patrimonial empire will eventually give way to the centrifugal, anarchical forces inherent in the suppressed nationalism of its many peoples. As these get caught up in the expanding market economy and seek a greater share of the action, they become pressure groups for a more equitable distribution of living standards and political power. Conceivably their combined oppositional processes could be crucial in replacing patrimonial statism with the economic and social pluralism of polyarchy.

| 12 |

Enclavement, Fusion, and Adaptation in a Tzeltal Maya Community

Robert C. Harman

Cultural groups do not necessarily disappear when subjected to pressures for change in contact situations. Societal integrity may be expected to persist under conditions of intensive contact (Barth 1969:10). Indeed, politically weak cultural groups under the domination of more powerful political units often attain a high degree of cultural cohesion and social solidarity. Spicer (1971:797) has identified several cases in which the opposition between two such societies has been essential to the formation of a persistent identity system. Studies of acculturation reveal that the identity of a people is long retained in most contact situations even though cultural changes occur after any considerable period of continuous, face-to-face interaction by individuals of different societies. The popular assumption that rapid cultural replacement and social assimilation are the most likely results of directed acculturation is not tenable, although these processes sometimes occur. A number of complex variables, incompletely understood and partially unique in each situation, determine whether an ethnic group shall retain its identity or be absorbed by a larger national society (cf. Gregory 1976:705). Whenever an ethnic group maintains a culture distinct from that which is dominant in a nation-state and places positive value on the differences, enclavement is occurring (Spicer 1966:267). Each modern-day enclave, such as the Basques, Welsh, and numerous American Indian groups, is the result of a particular series of events that have occurred during its existence within a state system (cf. Spicer 1966:269).

A cultural process of fusion usually dovetails with that of enclavement in determining the form and meaning of traits that characterize the ethnic enclave. A subordinate people may adopt many new cultural elements and institutions without loss of either the culture's integrity or their social identity. According to Spicer (1961:532), "The essentials of fusion are that elements of two or more distinct cultural traditions be involved, that they be combined into a single system and that the principles in terms of which they combine not be the same as those governing the cultural systems from which they come." The vast change in Yaqui culture after contact with Jesuit missionaries involved the adoption of European agricultural technology, a nuclear settlement pattern, the Spanish ritual kinship system, and Catholicism without a corresponding cultural reorientation (Spicer 1954*b*:670–74). Fusion is an adaptational process that enables the members of a society to modify their existing culture by utilizing more effectively new combinations from elements which are available and desired.

The fusional process of cultural integration has long been recognized as the dominant process of change in the religion of many peoples and elsewhere after European contact (cf. Wolf 1959:166–75; Herskovits 1964:190–92; Madsen 1967). Spicer (1954*b*, 1961) provided a systematic approach and a much clearer understanding of the process, as it has operated among American Indian groups, by establishing that particular contact conditions gave rise to fusion in all aspects of culture. Fusion was found to be the dominant cultural process occurring in the realm of medicine among the highland Maya Indians of Chiapas during the 1950s and 1960s, as they began to adopt Western medical practices even as the causes of illnesses were still conceptualized as magical (Holland 1963:238). Similar findings have been made elsewhere.

Adaptation encompasses modes of accommodation to sociocultural, biological, and physical environments. At the same time, it often involves alteration of the environment to meet human needs or wants: "Adaptation refers to the processes by which a population or group alters its relation to its habitat" (Cohen 1968:3). Until about 1960 most work in anthropology that focused on adaptation was carried out by physical anthropologists. However, since then a number of cultural anthropologists have used an approach that views mankind in a total biological and cultural context, and this trend is perhaps most notable in the field of medical anthropology (cf. Alland 1966, 1970).

In medical anthropology an ecological model now explicitly recognizes the critical importance of the adaptation of populations, biologically and culturally, to given natural environments, and the approach is providing explanations of important evolutionary and synchronic issues that were previously ignored (Wellin 1977). Bennett (1976) suggests that the idea of adaptation, for its explanatory power, is a worthy concept to replace that of culture. Adaptation implies process, with concern for the identification of specific events that lead to particular cultural, social, and biological results:

> ... it focuses on human actors who try to realize objectives, satisfy needs, or find peace while coping with present conditions. In their coping, humans create the social future in the sense of generating new problems or perpetuating old ones and may even modify the biological constitution of the population in the process.... By analyzing the factors that guide the choices of strategies, one gains knowledge of the possibility and direction of change and the relation of human behavior to the milieus (Bennett 1976:847).

AGENTS OF CHANGE IN THE COMMUNITY

The setting for my research on medical change was the Tzeltal Maya township of Oxchuc. When investigated by Villa Rojas in the early 1940s, the inhabitants comprised a tight-knit cultural enclave. The township fit quite well the model of the corporate community (Wolf 1955:456–61) with characteristics of extreme poverty, strict edogamy, marginal land, traditional technology, communal land ownership, distinct local dialect and dress, mandatory participation in community affairs, and strict boundary maintenance based upon effective social control sanctions such as institutionalized envy and witchcraft (cf. Villa Rojas 1946).

After the departure of Villa Rojas in 1944, a pair of dedicated, young, female Protestant missionaries entered the community and one, together with other working partners, stayed for several years. By the mid-1950s an estimated fifty percent of the township had converted (Slocum 1956:491), and a number of remarkable changes had begun to occur that were directly stimulated by conversion of a segment of the Oxchuc society from the preexisting Maya-Catholic religion. The Catholic Church began to administer a directed culture change program in Oxchuc. The Catholic program, effective since 1950, will not be examined here because its effects on community life are less signficant than those of the Protestant program; also, it has been covered elsewhere (Harman 1974; Siverts 1960). In the early 1950s an agency of the Mexican government, the National Indianist Institute, began operations in the region and soon had considerable influence on life in Oxchuc. It is not coincidental that these Western agencies were all accepted about the same time, after a long period during which the Oxchuc Indians had rejected the outside world. By the 1940s the people were suffering from rampant poverty, ravishing epidemics, and exploitation by a dominant Ladino group. Conditions existed which would facilitate major social and cultural changes in a heretofore extremely conservative community.

The Protestant Church is a social group whose members adapt to the sociocultural milieu by a process of fusion, as individual members readily accept culture elements introduced from outside the community. It is a new kind of social group in Oxchuc, the first voluntary association. The rate of sociocultural change among Protestants is higher than within other groups in the township as the Church endorses and promotes rapid change.

The Protestant Church of Oxchuc exercises considerable influence beyond its membership, which comprises nineteen percent of my sample. An important factor here is a high rate of membership turnover. Many individuals revert to the Maya-Catholic faith, and some of these later convert again to the Protestant religion. There is a tendency for individuals who give up allegiance to the Church to continue to be advocators of rapid cultural change. An example of how the initial conversion commits a person to change pertains to the traditional Maya-Catholic housecross. Prior to 1944 a large wooden housecross was part of an altar in every household. The cross facilitated prayer to the deities, and it served as a focal point for healing rites. Protestants, upon joining the Church, are required to destroy their housecrosses. Those who subsequently leave the Church are disinclined to replace them because of the expense and inconvenience of proper installation. As a result, without the housecross few if any traditional rites are held at the domicile. This condition, in turn, motivates these former converts to seek cures through Western medical sources such as Western-trained practitioners in the community as well as physicians and pharmacies in the city.

A serious shortage of land existed in Oxchuc (Villa Rojas 1962:57), where nearly all the men are peasant farmers. An individual, in determining how to allocate time and resources, was limited to a meager share of the corporate land available to him for slash-and-burn farming as a member of a lineage and of the township (1969:114). In the past there had been little opportunity, and apparently no desire, to resettle outside Ox-chuc. In the 1970s, however, some Oxchuc families began to sell their land and houses to relocate in Ocosingo, a township lying some three days' walk to the east. Why are they doing this? The economic motive is strong as there is abundant land in Ocosingo, and it is said that the soil is rich enough to yield three harvests of corn per year compared to only one in Oxchuc. Contributing to this migration is the fact that the Protestant Church has encouraged its members to seek economic prosperity, and those who choose to emigrate find camaraderie among Church brethren in Ocosingo. Identification of individuals with a new social group, the Pro-testant Church, exceeds that with the preexisting township and lineage groups. This involves a breakdown of township boundary maintenance and certainly runs counter to the enclavement process. Since 1970 the Indianist Institute has had a coordinating center in Ocosingo to further promote Indian migration as a measure to relieve the Oxchuc land prob-lem, and these efforts, too, have no doubt fostered a decline in township identification.

The Indianist Institute began to operate among the highland Maya in 1951. Since then a number of Oxchuc Indians have been employed at respectable salaries as bilingual-bicultural promoters of education, health, and economic improvement. Some promoters have attained considerable economic and political power. These new leaders of the community have chosen to remain Indian rather than become Ladino, that is, to retain township identity rather than try to assimilate into the national society (cf. Siverts 1964:373). They are contributing toward the process of en-clavement to the extent that their actions continue to reinforce identity among members of the Oxchuc township. Most of their social interaction is still with individuals of the community, and transactions with outsiders appear to be means to enhance their community roles. All continue to own and farm land within Oxchuc and to speak the Oxchuc dialect of the Tzeltal Maya language, thereby using two of the major symbols that promote enclavement: traditional land and language (cf. Spicer 1971:798).

The majority of indigenous government employees are schoolteachers and health promoters. The schoolteachers conduct regular classes in the Spanish language, speaking Tzeltal Maya for explanation when the stu-dents have difficulty, and they teach all the preparatory preschool classes in which the students learn to read and write solely in the native dialect (cf. Modiano 1973). The health promoters work sometimes as autonomous practitioners conversing with patients in the native tongue, and some-times as assistants and interpreters for monolingual Spanish-speaking physicians. In either type of situation there is reinforcement of the com-mon identity shared by residents of the township and positive value placed on the traditional language, gestures, and sentiments regarding topics that arise.

PROCESSES OF HOMEOSTATIC AND CENTRIFUGAL FUSION

Fusion is the dominant cultural process in Oxchuc. Yet fusional integration, as the Indians adopt new Western forms, does not occur evenly throughout the township. Consistent differences in the rate and extent of cultural modification correspond to contact with different agents of change, and at least two subprocesses or subtypes of fusion can be identified.

One subprocess of fusion emphasizes a gradual reworking of outside culture elements with preexisting ones. The label *homeostatic* fits this subprocess inasmuch as a relatively stable state of equilibrium characterizes those areas of culture affected by it. Homeostatic fusion is more widespread than another type, which I call *centrifugal* because it manifests rapid change that draws away from a stable core. Homeostatic fusional change occurs slowly and does not threaten or destroy the core of traditional culture.

In Oxchuc homeostatic fusion is associated largely, although not exclusively, with the National Indianist Institute. That agency, through its goals and methods, promotes the subprocess more than other outside agencies. The Institute is oriented toward moderate change that permits the preservation of fundamental values and core customs (Instituto Nacional Indigenista 1964; Spicer 1969a:19). Homeostatic fusion in Oxchuc is present in school activities, prestige-ranking, personal names, and aspects of medicine.

The government school system is an important institution in Oxchuc, where an estimated four-fifths of school-aged children are enrolled (Modiano 1973:96). Schools were not well attended until the Protestant and Indianist Institute programs went into operation. Prior to that time there was considerable resistance to schools (cf. Villa Rojas 1946:580). Modiano (1973:83) indicates that at home the Oxchuqueros learn by reasoning rather than rote, whereas at school they are confused by a teaching emphasis on memorization (1973:101). Students and former students appear to have little comprehension of the subject matter covered at school. Indeed, they are utterly confused about topics that are not within the spatial and temporal confines of whatever they, personally, or their Tzeltal acquaintances have directly experienced. So, even though they attend school, they are not learning in a traditional Tzeltal mode nor are they learning like other Mexicans.

Schools have become focal points for Oxchuc communities (Siverts

1958:182). The school is a center for various community activities, including public meetings, adult education, and festivals. Independence Day and Mother's Day festivals draw a large turnout. Activities on those days center on the basketball court, and hundreds of spectators observe even though they do not understand the game. The festivals are legitimized events, and the people feel free to leave their work in order to interact socially with relatives, neighbors, and friends. Formerly, community religious rites fulfilled this function, but they are no longer well attended. Two symbols that have become part of the new school festivals are the Mexican flag and nationalistic speeches. Students do not understand the historical significance of the flag, nor do they understand their own speeches, which are memorized and given in the Spanish language. At the same time, basketball games are not associated with the meanings that exist elsewhere.

Prestige-ranking of community members is affected by homeostatic fusion. In the early 1940s the men of high prestige were those who provided bountiful service to the community through the civil-religious hierarchy or through healing. Concomitant with either of these part-time specialties, usually, was the attainment of middle age. Many young men with Spanish language skills and other attributes acquired through contact with outside agents of change have now achieved positions of high prestige as schoolteachers, Western-trained health promoters, or state-recognized political officials.

In Oxchuc it is still possible for Maya-Catholics to attain prestige through civil-religious service and traditional healer roles. Former incumbents in civil-religious offices that no longer exist are respected by many members of the community for having served. Ambiguity and confusion sometimes exist, however, when new standards conflict with earlier ones. For example, on the footpaths within Oxchuc it is customary, when two individuals approach from opposite directions, for the subordinate to step aside and say *kashan mam* ('pass, honored sir'). Now it is not always clear who is dominant. This is especially true at times when a high-ranking Maya-Catholic meets a high-ranking Protestant and neither party considers himself subordinate due to the different criteria used to measure prestige within the two distinct, religious social groups.

Personal names are affected by homeostatic fusion. When Villa Rojas (1946) was resident in Oxchuc all the inhabitants used a personal name system that was well established and effective. Since the 1950s the Mexican government, through its official agencies such as schools, clinics, and civil offices, has attempted to introduce the Mexican national system of naming. Tomás Gómez Nimail, according to the traditional system, would become Tomás Gómez Méndez, according to the Mexican system, in which Gómez is his father's Spanish surname, Nimail his father's Indian surname, and Méndez his mother's Spanish surname. There are only six Spanish surnames in the township and more than a hundred Indian surnames. Anybody who has tried to identify individuals in Oxchuc by the Mexican system knows that it does not operate effectively because too many individuals have the same name. On an everyday basis individuals within the community use the traditional system, with the exception of some men who have introduced a fusional name system. In the fusional system the individual uses his baptismal name, father's Indian surname, and mother's Spanish surname: for example, Tomás Nimail Méndez. This mode of identification is more efficient than either the traditional or the Mexican system. Most men who use it have had considerable contact with non-Indians and are young community leaders. The fusion is an adaptive solution to the Mexican government's efforts to have Indians adopt the mother's surname, a practice which is standard throughout the country. It enables the user to avoid being lost in the multiplicity of identical names that the Mexican system imposes (Harman 1975:120).

The Indianist Institute has clinics which are well equipped and staffed by full-time, salaried physicians or promoters. However, the Institute has no way to compel individuals to follow its recommendations on health-related matters. This problem became clear when I spoke with members of the community about an Institute-sponsored puppet theater in which characters act out humorous roles that delight the audience. The purpose of the puppet theater is to instruct viewers to employ Western medical practices and beliefs in order to promote better health. Beliefs in witchcraft and other "superstitions" are ridiculed by the puppets, but, while the viewers recalled that they enjoyed the performance, they did not remember the import of the health topic messages. As a result of the puppet theater and other education many of the Indians have adopted the term *microbios* ('microbes') into their vocabulary, but none appear to associate with the word meanings that resemble those of the Western world.

The role of the Western-trained health promoter is well accepted in Oxchuc. In one hamlet there are several, but the position of most prestige is held by the full-time Indianist Institute promoter. He and the religion-affiliated promoters treat far more patients than the physician resident in Oxchuc. The presence of promoters must be considered adaptive for the community since they save lives and alleviate suffering. The context within which the promoters, including the Indianist Institute promoter, practice medicine is one of fusional change. Patients share with the promoters a world view different from that of physicians. Together they adopt and modify Western medicine as it enters the community. Patients often request that the Institute promoter give an injection at the location of whatever discomfort they are experiencing. Of course, these requests must often be denied, but one pattern of treatment that is popular is to receive injections on four consecutive days. Accordingly, the promoter gives the shots in upper arms and hips. The same promoter believes that the people get sick frequently from winds and microbes, and that the intravenous feedings he administers for serious cases of diarrhea have the effect of drying up the body. He uses his affluence to support three wives, polygamy being a traditional symbol of wealth and prestige in Maya society. He tells patients to avoid "hot" foods on the day they receive an injection with the rationale that it would interact unfavorably with the "hot" medicine. He speaks with conviction about the clairvoyance of a local shaman and about the peopling of Oxchuc by distant ancestors as recorded in the *kawaltik,* a sacred book which is actually a legal document written by a Spanish administrator in 1674. The health promoter is able to innovate effectively while occupying a status that has ambiguous role privileges and obligations (cf. Press 1969). This ambiguity is reflected in terms of address: while other men of the community are addressed by a kinship term, if applicable, or by the term *tat* ('sir') the promoter is frequently called by his first name; I have also heard reference to him as *loktor* ('doctor'). Clearly, fusion is occurring as forms from another culture are being adopted and given new meanings.

Patients often have the traditional healers treat a condition that has been diagnosed as witchcraft in order to eliminate the cause of illness, followed by injections from the promoter. The forms of Western medicine have been accepted, but by themselves they are considered valid only to alleviate symptoms rather than to treat the underlying cause of sickness.

Maya-Catholics and Protestants are often involved in social conflicts, and considerable ideological differences separate the two groups. Nevertheless, the Protestants are still integrated within the municipal ethnic enclave. An interesting phenomenon that supports this contention involves the practice of witchcraft, the existence of which on most occasions the Protestants vehemently deny. Maya-Catholic diagnosticians often identify as witches some of the spiritually powerful Protestants who formerly served the community. They are said to be unable to rid themselves of their illness-inducing *lab* ('animal transformation') spirit. Thus, individuals who have been Protestant for years and who do not participate in the traditional healing system any longer are brought into that very system in the conceptualization and practice of the larger community. Even some Protestants concede that those individuals still possess a lab. Denial of the new social role of former witches may be an adaptation that minimizes the amount of social disruption that has occurred since the mid-1940s.

Centrifugal fusion in Oxchuc is associated most often with the Protestant Church. Adherents to the Protestant program are pulling away from custom and from former social group affiliations. Indeed, the Protestant leader cites the rejection of witchcraft and of drinking by Church members as two of their major accomplishments (Slocum 1956). Those cultural complexes were essential to the social order prior to the missionaries' arrival in 1944. Protestants and former Protestants have given up other symbols important for ethnic persistence: appeals to the Catholic saints, service in those aspects of the civil-religious hierarchy that have connection with Catholicism, and, in at least some hamlets, the communal ownership of land by men of the same lineage.

The Protestants use the same Oxchuc dialect of Tzeltal Maya as do other people of Oxchuc in their everyday conversation, and they use the vernacular exclusively for church services. However, with the traditional moral sphere (cf. Spicer 1971:799) the Protestants have less intensive participation as a consequence of their Protestant Church membership. In many everyday affairs and in township and hamlet activities such as religious festivals they do not use traditional culture elements (from behaviors and artifacts to beliefs and sentiments).

As part of the centrifugal process Protestant leaders have been staunch opponents of Indian participation in seasonal labor at the lowland coffee plantations located approximately 150 to 200 miles from Oxchuc. At these plantations the wages are low and living conditions deplorable. Many men from Oxchuc continue to spend time there each year in order to earn additional cash income, but almost no Protestants are among them. The Maya-Catolic men averaged 8.1 weeks there in 1967 compared to 1.7 weeks by Protestants. The Protestants have adopted the practice, and, to all apparent purposes, the belief, that work on one's own land is superior to labor under the exploitative practices of plantation owners. The Protestants invest most of their capital into crops, tools, and nutritious foods. Health improvement is a payoff, an adaptation, in the Protestant sector. Maya-Catholics who continue to work at the plantations squander most of their meager earnings on rum, and frequently they return home financially insolvent and sick as well (malaria is one of the diseases frequently contracted at the lowland plantations). The process here appears to be somewhat like that of replacement, yet it is inconceivable that the Indians perceive the process as did their Anglo missionary teachers. Individuals are making decisions to engage in activities that provide more advantages for them than those conducted at the plantation. The decisions are made consciously, and there are only mild sanctions—approval from missionaries and Indian brethren, and disapproval for going to the plantation.

The Protestant Church in Oxchuc has introduced a number of new beliefs and proscriptions regarding curative and preventive health-related behavior. Some positive adaptations are certainly part of the process of centrifugal fusion in the medical realm. The Protestants, more than others in the community, attend clinics and pharmacies to receive Western treatment, which is more effective than the traditional medicine in combating physiological disease processes. Also, with their consumption of improved foodstuffs in place of alcoholic beverages, the Protestants have better diets (Turner 1978:6). On the other hand, data indicate that some Protestants endure additional emotional stress as a result of the official Church proscriptions on seeking traditional native healers for such illness conditions as witchcraft and fright.

Protestant elders and health promoters are foremost among the Church members in respect to their acceptance of Western culture elements. In the medical area, however, even the health promoters reinterpret much that they adopt. Epidemics are sometimes attributed to the season and to evil winds rather than to disease agents. A concern with the traditional hot-cold balance exists; one promoter explained to me that after an injection (hot) one should not use the sweatbath (hot), eat chili (hot), or be exposed to winds (cold) lest the balance be disrupted. The same restrictions do not apply after taking pills because these are not conceptualized as mixing with the blood as does injected medication.

Centrifugal fusion should not be mistaken for the process of cultural replacement. My data, focused primarily on the medical system, indicate that most ideological phenomena of the 1940s still persist within the Protestant group. Replacement does not characterize the changes that are occurring. In the process of replacement, "the distinctive feature consists in the acceptance and replacement of cultural behaviors in terms of the dominant society's cultural system. This means an absence of modification which harmonizes what is accepted with a divergent system. Individuals select among alternatives in the contact situation as if they were participants in the dominant culture" (Spicer 1961:531). Sometimes fusional integration among Protestants bears the appearance of replacement. Sanctions exerted by Protestant agents of change enforce the overt adoption of some Western elements that actually have gained only tentative acceptance. Rigorous enforcement of new standards by indigenous leaders within the Church encourages a high rate of overt change. Much of this is not real cultural change, however, as described above, and even when real change occurs it involves modification since the indigenous Protestant leaders themselves do not fully comprehend the dominant society's culture.

The indigenous leadership of the Protestant Church—elders and deacons—is an authoritarian body that resembles in structure the indigenous civil-religious hierarchy of the 1940s, when inhabitants were living in perpetual fear of witchcraft-caused illness for any *mulil* ('sin'). The head administrators of the township were spiritually powerful men who had the ability and the privilege to send misfortune, usually in the form of illness, to any Oxchuquero who had violated the cultural norms (Villa Rojas 1947:584). The forms of mulil and the means to punish wrongdoers have changed considerably among Protestants. The traditional system emphasized social misdeeds, so that punishable acts included failure to buy elderly men sufficient rum at the Saturday market, gossip about other members of the community, and refusal to carry a father-in-law's burden on the road. Analysis of the mulil behaviors that provoked witchcraft indicates that the most sacred of traditional values was maintenance of the moral order and, in particular, subservience to the elderly men.

The content of mulil among Protestants has changed in accordance with Church proscriptions on traditional concepts dealing with the supernatural. Today's Protestant Church leaders act as an administrative and judicial body. As an administrative body they make many suggestions as to how congregation members should conduct their lives. Occasionally they refuse to endorse a marriage between two members of the community. As a judicial body they can and do expel from the Church individuals whose behavior is deviant. One woman who had an illegitimate child was expelled for three years, and other members of the congregation were told to avoid her during that period, and they did, even while she gave birth. The content of leadership behavior, like that of mulil, certainly differs from the days of witchcraft-wielding elders. The power of Protestant leaders derives from their exemplary religious and secular behavior and knowledge of the Bible. Consequently, not many of the elderly men, steeped in the old traditions and illiterate, are part of the current leadership. Fusion is occurring as new forms, standards of correct behavior and social roles, are adopted within the preexisting context of harsh authoritarian leadership legitimized by a culture which stresses obedience (cf. Modiano 1973:101).

Protestants of Oxchuc are choosing to emphasize their church group identity at the expense of township identity. A speech symbol frequently employed by Protestants, especially upon greeting one another, is *kermano* ('brother'), and no equally strong integrative greeting is used by Maya-Catholics. Vocal identification of another individual as kermano establishes immediately a level of intimacy that never existed in earlier times among non-kinsmen. The intimacy among Protestants extends across township boundaries when members get together for Church activities, informal gatherings to sing hymns, and other encounters such as consultations by Protestant health promoters.

OUTCOMES OF ADAPTIVE CHANGES

Oxchuc inhabitants of the early 1940s were a people who maintained a persistent identity system as defined by Spicer (1971:796). The Indians perceived themselves as *bats'il winik* ('true man'), apart from other peoples, sharing a common heritage purportedly described in their sacred book, the kawaltik. The moral order was enforced by witches who sent sickness to anybody who deviated from the norms. Suspicion was high within the community, and it was even greater toward outsiders; strict endogamy was practiced. Moreover, members of the community shared a common dialect and mode of dress, and there was only one style of house. It was a kinship-based society, and the kinship group leaders were also the high officials in a civil-religious hierarchy that ran the affairs of the township.

Two types of fusion have been operating simultaneously in Oxchuc since the mid-1940s. Homeostatic fusion is characterized by a slow to moderate rate of cultural change that does not threaten the preexisting social fabric. There is just enough change to adapt to sociopolitical and demographic conditions without having to give up core values and customs of long standing. In contrast the operation of centrifugal fusion does not occur entirely within the framework of the existing order. Wherever centrifugal fusion is dominant, tradition is dispensable, and, while some of the core customs are retained, others are vigorously rejected. The events of centrifugal fusion often rupture the former integration of culture elements and of social relations among individuals. It threatens the persistence of an identity system and the social solidarity among a people.

Centrifugal fusion promoted by the Protestant program involves a pull away from the enclave and resembles to an extent the process of replacement. Protestant agents of change have stronger sanctions at their disposal than do the Indianist Institute employees, and this factor contributes toward the effectiveness of their program. Church elders meet regularly and commonly expel or threaten to expel members who have violated the norms. As a result of negative sanctions for seeking the services of traditional healers, Protestants use sources of Western treatment more than other members of the community. At Protestant weddings the groom is required to provide large amounts of food instead of rum, which is the major expenditure at Maya-Catholic weddings (cf. Villa Rojas 1946:168). Church members are directed to invest time and money in their fields, better diets, and Western health care instead of alcohol, and these things they have done. Some Protestants have even left their small and relatively unproductive fields in the ancestral homeland in order to seek economic prosperity elsewhere. These new activities are adaptations to the existing natural and social environment.

Homeostatic fusion is more widespread than centrifugal fusion in Oxchuc. It appears to be the same process of dominant culture change documented for the highland Mayas since initial contact with Europeans (cf. Trens 1957; cf. Vogt 1969). Homogeneity of values and social roles within each township was strongly enforced through internal sanctions such as witchcraft and a civil-religious hierarchy, which promoted enclavement along with fusion. Social cohesion within the township is not threatened where this subprocess occurs despite the acceptance of extensive change.

The fusional process as it interacts with that of enclavement is adaptive in many respects. Reproductive success is considered by biologists to be the ultimate measure of adaptation, and by this criterion Oxchuc is doing well with a population increase of approximately 100 percent— from 5,411 in 1950 (Villa Rojas 1962:67) to 10,000 in 1969 (Siverts 1969:3).* Most of the increase must be attributed to Western medical treatment and newly accepted modes of preventing disease, such as declining participation in the plantation labor force and improved diet.

Farming practices from outside have been borrowed, and new crops as well as innovative techniques such as terracing are making an appearance (cf. Turner 1977). Oxchuqueros have instituted new marketing procedures, with women as well as men acting as intermediaries between the local producers and buyers in the city. Some entrepreneurs have begun to sell items manufactured in the city to other members of the township. A number of these operations have expanded to the size of small stores in which storekeepers sell from a small stock consisting of candy, soft drinks, thread, medications, candles, and other inexpensive items that are frequently in demand. Indianist Institute promoters might also be considered entrepreneurs in that they are engaged in new roles that have favorable economic and political payoffs and that enable the individuals to live healthier lives with more control over their destinies than in the days of oppressive Ladino exploitation. All of these adaptations involve increased contact with people outside the native community. The changes are beneficial to the Oxchuqueros' standard of living as forms have been adopted and modified to fit Oxchuc cultural orientations.

Enclaves or persistent identity systems appear to develop where there is opposition between the enclave and a state's political system (Spicer 1971:797). Without such opposition the enclave may not persist, and a major distinction between the Indianist Institute and Protestant programs is that the latter lacks opposition between the dominant and subordinate

---

*These population figures may represent considerable underestimates at both periods of time (cf. Turner 1977:169, 173). Nevertheless, the rate of growth has been extremely high.

society. There has been no history of conflict between the Oxchuc Protestant community and the missionaries or Indian Church elders as there has been between the Indians and the Spanish and, subsequently, the Mexican government. The opposition between Protestants and other segments of the community today is on a horizontal rather than a vertical plane, and, while one result could be the formation of a new enclave, that does not appear to be happening. The question of whether the centrifugal pulls affecting the Protestant social group may eventually result in the formation of a new enclave must remain unanswered for the moment.

The lessons to be learned from Oxchuc may have practical application in other parts of today's shrinking world where overpopulation, widespread disease, malnutrition, and sometimes starvation are found among many peoples. Within ethnic enclaves as well as other types of societies it is not unusual for intrusive social groups with new social roles and new values to be introduced, and when this occurs the presence of conflicting ideologies as well as social conflicts sometimes characterizes such communities. People will institutionalize different forms of behavior, depending largely on ecological constraints (Barth 1969:12); for example, new behavior can be expected of peasant farming people whenever their land is not sufficiently productive.

Conservative community development programs, which favor gradual change without social and cultural disruption, have been severely criticized for accomplishing too little (Bonfil Batalla 1966). The Mexican Indianist Institute program is conservative and appears to be adaptive culturally and socially for the people affected as they gradually accept changes in a process of homeostatic fusional integration, although the changes may not be radical enough to solve the basic economic problems. The Protestant program is accomplishing what critics of the conservative approach advocate — that is, rapid change that strikes at the heart of economic problems and whatever factors may impede their solution. In seeking to determine what type of program provides greater overall adaptation for the recipient population, the tangible benefits to the people served must be considered the most sound criterion of success. Many adaptations in Oxchuc have been discussed here in a context of two subtypes of fusion: homeostatic and centrifugal. The homeostatic changes occur in familiar contexts and may be more permanent; the centrifugal changes occur more rapidly and rupture the preexisting order, which at the same time had provided cohesion and prevented economic progress. These are potential outcomes that program administrators should evaluate when planning projects directed at enclaves. The advantages and disadvantages of each for a target population need to be considered.

ACKNOWLEDGMENTS

I am grateful to David Cundiff, Patricia Etter, and Robert Gregory for their comments on an earlier draft of this chapter.

The data on Oxchuc were collected under the support of NIMH Predoctoral Fellowship MH-31,944, Wenner-Gren Foundation for Anthropological Research Grant 2549, and NIMH Small Grant Mh 20604-01.

| 13 |

Persistence With Change

A Property of Sociocultural Dynamics

Janet R. Moone

The historical continuity of cultural systems of peoples who have otherwise changed and adapted to variable environments confronts anthropology with an important challenge. To recognize inadequacies among concepts that guide the study of sociocultural dynamics, we must overcome a particular conceptual limitation which retards full understanding of dynamic process. The phenomenon of persistent cultural systems dramatizes the need for a conceptualization of process more valid than that which focuses exclusively on change. A concept is required that incorporates and integrates maintenance with change and honors the role that maintenance plays in shaping change.

Order is the essence of culture, and change is its temporal prospect. Together, order and change in culture and related social action comprise the paramount object-process, the ultimate focus for explanation in much of the anthropological endeavor. Yet therein functions the resident paradox, a fundamental dilemma upon the horns of which cultural and social theorists become repeatedly impaled. When it is believed progress is being made along one of the conceptual dimensions, the other intrudes with valid qualification, and ensuing debate does little more than maintain the theoretical impasse. Whether explicitly confronted or expressed through its often complex implications, all versions of the dilemma reduce to essentially the question of how to conceptualize order and process, maintenance and change, as concomitant properties of the same system. By what analytic means can we correctly interpret our perceptions of form, structure, the continuity of pattern, the order in sociocultural phenomena, while simultaneously honoring our recognition of the constancy of process, of variation formation and change affecting the selfsame cultural and social forms?

In practice, generally applicable constructs singularly capable of guiding analysis and generating explanation of order with process are disciplinary rarities. The history of anthropology is largely the history of separation, opposition, and alternating shifts between preferences for dealing with order, identifying structures and explaining their maintenance, and preferences for defining processes, describing outcomes, and explaining change. Within this latter orientation, the paradox has been bypassed largely as a result of conceptualizations of process which do not raise the need to integrate maintenance with change. Concepts of process are commonly derived from change and defined as change. When maintenance has been included, it has been viewed primarily as a property exclusive to sociocultural systems as wholes. Here the concern is not with persistence in and among parts of a system but rather with the continuity of systemic relations or integrity through time, the explanation of which is sought in adjustive change in parts of a system. The idea of maintenance as an aspect of process within systems has suffered analytic neglect as a result of its misidentification with the controversial concept of equilibrium as envisaged by early functionalists.

The dilemma reaches beyond the apparent antithesis of order and process to involve the question of the role of culture, the system of meanings, as an instrument in its own as well as in social structural maintenance and change. Among those preoccupied with the dimension of order, there is a tendency for culture to become transcendent: the simultaneous object of and accountant for all aspects of order and its maintenance. Among those concerned with change and process, as dependent variable or epiphenomenon, culture at times has been totally excluded from the domain of factors evoking order and pressuring for maintenance. Rather, culture is viewed as an inert derivative of behavior constrained, structured, and restructured by the interplay of social and environmental forces. Thus the dilemma ramifies as a breeding ground of theoretic extremes.

Realistic attempts to resolve the paradox, however, have appeared and reappeared in a cumulative if somewhat diffuse manner. The recurrent efforts to bring some combination of modified historical, structural, functional, and ecological-evolutionary concepts of culture into productive synthesis represent the exemplary approach (cf. Barth 1956; Eggan 1950; Geertz 1963). Synthetic solutions have unquestionably advanced the recognition of maintenance with change in sociocultural dynamics. On the theoretical plane, some of the arguments of the 1970s promoting the synthetic approach or exposing many implications of the paradox have been elegant (Keesing 1974; Murphy 1971; Sahlins 1976). However, synthetic conceptualizations of process quite often have been highly abstract and open to wide variance in interpretation. In the effort to arrive at the general principles of sociocultural process, the single most compelling need remains the development of a working construct: a set of conceptual tools capable of examining maintenance with change in process on the empirical level. But we *are* heir to concepts that long since should have served as models for what is required to further this cause and finally dispel the order-process dilemma.

MAINTENANCE WITH CHANGE

Resolution of the paradox lies in reviewing a conceptual framework which has provided a modest answer to the obvious questions: how much order is there in process? How much and what kinds of pattern maintenance occur in change? The idea that persistence is a part of change, that forces for maintenance and forces for change effectively coexist in single processes, is not new. The idea was given early and explicitly analytic development in works of Barnett (1942, 1953) and Herskovits (1945, 1964). In particular, the concept of syncretism, as formulated by Herskovits (1964:190–98), was the most concrete and analytically useful definition of a specific process involving maintenance with change. Since that time, however, few researchers have induced comparable formulations, that is, concepts which direct analysis toward identification of the mechanisms and relative strengths of maintenance and change in process, or toward their respective qualities and quantities in outcomes.

To the contrary, the vast majority of research on culture and social change has followed the dominant model of process developed out of the assumption that that which is changed during a given process changes in its totality and is the direct result of forces for change unstructured by the intercession of forces for maintenance. Maintenance becomes objectified only in relation to system continuity or successful resistance to change, whereupon the effects of maintenance on change in process, and the dimensions of persistence in outcomes, are not open to the tests of empirical reality. One formulation that encompasses the idea expressed by syncretism, but goes beyond it to define other processes, will be used below to demonstrate one way by which closed models of change and process can be opened.

What follows is an exercise in conceptual logic designed to support the thesis of maintenance with change in process. At the same time, the exercise will serve as a review of what can be achieved by an analytic construct formulated on the principle of persistence with change. The concepts used in the exercise were drawn from the culminating effort (Spicer, ed., 1961) of what may have been the most concerted and organized attack on a specific problem area that cultural anthropology has yet produced, or seems likely to produce again. The reference is to the series of working sessions and seminars on acculturation sponsored by the Social Science Research Council in 1935, 1953, and 1956, as well as to the many substantive studies that derived from and in turn contributed to this series of deliberations (Spicer 1961*a*:1–6).

The recommendations and cumulative conceptual refinements which resulted from these efforts have had wide-ranging influence on subsequent studies of change occurring under conditions of culture contact. Although frequently cited, the full significance of the findings of the final seminar of the series (Spicer, ed., 1961) has not been generally recognized. In large part, the cross-culturally recurrent processes identified by the seminar participants and summarized by Spicer (1961*b*:517–44) diffused outward only to have the dominant view of change remain implicated in acculturation. To the detriment of the seminar's definitive contribution, the commonly shared, change-filled idea of acculturation was soon to become a concept *non grata* during the reinvention of anthropology (cf. Clemmer 1969). The frequent over-association of the seminar-identified processes with absolute change is in disregard of the fact that, collectively, these processes have as much or more to do with maintenance and persistence as they do with change. This fact is precisely what the present exercise is intended to demonstrate.

My narrative descriptions of processes are based on the logic of what I understand to be the major analytic concepts employed by members of the seminar in identifying and developing definitions of four distinct, cross-culturally recurrent processes, each involving different degrees of maintenance with change. For two reasons a reading of the original presentation, with its case studies providing substantive examples, will be essential to a full understanding of the seminar's conceptual framework, its applications, and the resulting process definitions. First, it has not been possible to include examples of processes in this limited space. Second, I have assumed considerable license in inferring the use of concepts and interpreting process descriptions. What is more, in the definitions which follow, I have intentionally attempted to disassociate the processes from the context of acculturation. For it is my belief that the four processes are generalized in sociocultural dynamics; that is, they can be initiated and controlled by forces unrelated to contact with another society as well as by those that are. I therefore have taken the liberty to phrase definitions using terminology that differs considerably from that used in the original presentation. The translation has been difficult and is incomplete at times. Where ambiguous, unqualified terms are present, as in "new" or "entering" forms or the "receiving" system, they should be taken to mean that the process in question can occur in response to forces internal to a society and its noncultural environment, as well as to forces emanating from another sociocultural system. An external sociocultural system is viewed here simply as one of several kinds of environments generating forces which, in interaction with internal forces, have the potential to produce or control process. If I have erred in taking this broadened perspective, or in my inferences and interpretations, the fault is mine alone.

The Analytic Construct

Although not explicitly cited as such, it is easily inferred from Spicer's summary (1961*b*:528–37) that a principal construct employed by the seminar participants in sorting, comparing, and classifying the data of their case studies was Linton's (1936:401–21) analytic division of the observable dimensions of any social or material, and culturally significant, phenomenon: that is, the triad of *form, function,* and *meaning,* with Linton's fourth dimension of *use* apparently included in *function.* A few supplementary attributes attached to the three lintonian dimensions appear to have been derived from Malinowski's (1944:52–66) similar but more comprehensive construct of the *concrete isolate.* It has also been inferred from Spicer's summary how, in an ideal sense, the analytic triad was used. In brief, by systematically applying the three concepts to serial outcomes of the many instances of process in their data, the analysts determined which of the three dimensions of involved elements or complexes represented a qualitative change and which did not. From this vantage point, it was then possible to compare the trisected outcomes, identify the dimensional regularities of maintenance and change among them, and thereby discern four clearcut types of process.

Equally important, and explicitly related to Linton's (1940) and Malinowski's (1945) earlier discriminations among types of contact situations, this analysis led to identification of different, recurrent combinations of interacting internal and environmental conditions affecting the specific dimensions and degrees of maintenance and change in each type of process (Spicer 1961*b*:517–28). These distinctive sets of associated conditions further strengthened the differentiation of processes and, with regard to the identification of causal forces, constituted another major contribution of the seminar. In developing the exercise, however, the present definitions are based only on the identifying dimensional qualities of each process without discussion of related environmental conditions.

What the use of the analytic triad accomplished toward the differentiation of processes will become clearer as each definition is provided below. But first it will be well to briefly review the referents of form, function, and meaning as they have been interpreted and used in the exercise.

Form refers to the observable patterns, structures, or organization in social relations — in an activity, event, social unit, or subsystem. Or, in the case of material objects, form refers to their physical patterns or structures. The term applies as well to complexes of combined social and material elements. In the present usage, form does not include the cognitive or ideational patterns, the structure of symbols and significance that are or come to be associated with social and material forms. These cultural forms constitute the dimension of *meaning*. Thus social structure and material elements are analytically separated from their corresponding cultural forms. However, the relationships between form and meaning, as well as between function and meaning, are far from ignored in the final analysis.

Function is used in the sense of the nature of a social or material form's integration or articulation within a sociocultural system. The nature or type of a form's integration is determined by the kind and quality, and sometimes the number, of structural linkages and operational dependency relations that are or are not established with other social and material forms of the system. The kinds and qualities of linkages established by a form are closely related to the meanings associated with or assigned to the form. The functional integration of a new social or material form, whether entering or developed within a system, varies in accordance with its assigned meanings and, in turn, with the character of the forces behind its entrance or internal development. Function, in the above sense, is the most diagnostic of the three dimensions in distinguishing one type of process from another. One of the fullest, most operational, and least ramifying types of integration occurs when a new form is an addition to an existing form, does not displace anything, establishes internal linkages and other relations identical or compatible with existing forms and their functions, and derives its significance from existing meanings.

Meaning represents the cultural dimension and refers to subjective domains of significance directly or indirectly, consciously or unconsciously, associated with social and material forms. The symbolic, socially constituted significance of a social or material form is itself an observable form, manifest in norms for action, technical concepts, beliefs, evaluations, attached sentiments, or other shared meaningful expressions. With regard to new forms, meanings can become associated with them in a number of different ways. The meanings of a new form can be newly derived or assigned from the existing system of meanings; they can be acquired meanings, transferred in from an external cultural system; or they can be developed as a fusion or synthesis of elements of meaning from differing internal, or internal and external, sources. That differences in constituting the significance of new social or material forms are highly correlated with differences in the type of operational integration they establish is amply illustrated in the substantive examples provided by the seminar's case studies.

The Processes

Figure 13.1 summarizes the processes and is designed to facilitate comparison of their different dimensional effects. Each of the four seminar-identified processes is depicted in accordance with its narrative definition below, that is, in accordance with its distinctive pattern of change relative to maintenance across the three dimensions of form, function, and meaning as I have interpreted that pattern to be. For the sake of logical consistency in constructing the diagram, each process was viewed as involving a complex of elements of form, elements of function, and elements of meaning. As a consequence of a given process, some elements will constitute change in one or more dimensions of an involved complex and some will not. Black areas, therefore, indicate that some or all elements of a dimension represent change in that dimension, and white areas indicate maintenance or persistence of elements in the same or other dimensions of an involved complex. In the case of *addition,* for example, the area of change is only in the dimension of form and is representative of the addition of new elements of form to a maintained complex of forms, functions, and meanings. In *replacement* all elements in the dimension of form and, conditionally, in those of function and meaning represent change as a consequence of the displacement characteristic of this process. The special treatment of *fusion* is explained in the definition of that process. The row depicting a process of total maintenance has been added merely to indicate the existence of such a process and will not be defined. Although discussed only briefly in the definition of replacement, the

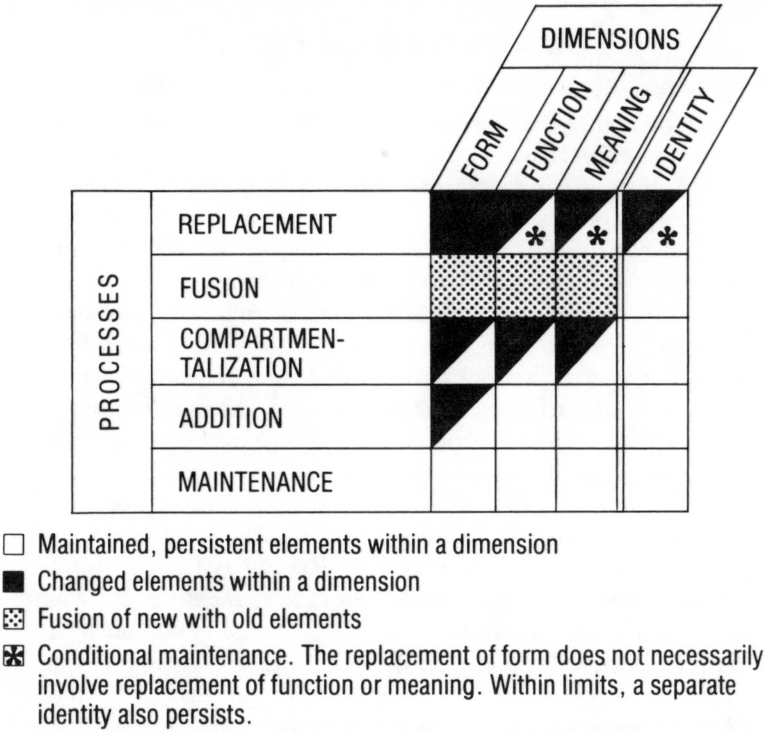

DIMENSIONS

PROCESSES	FORM	FUNCTION	MEANING	IDENTITY
REPLACEMENT	■	*	*	*
FUSION	▨	▨	▨	
COMPARTMEN-TALIZATION	◪		◪	
ADDITION	◣			
MAINTENANCE				

□ Maintained, persistent elements within a dimension
■ Changed elements within a dimension
▨ Fusion of new with old elements
�֎ Conditional maintenance. The replacement of form does not necessarily involve replacement of function or meaning. Within limits, a separate identity also persists.

Figure 13.1 Summary of the dimensions of maintenance
with change in dynamic processes

fourth column, *identity,* was appended to suggest the relationship each process holds with the persistence of a separate identity system in those situations in which a process is one of transference of form or meanings from another society.

I must hasten to add that the processes entering into the exercise do not cover the total compass of similarly conceptualized process types in sociocultural dynamics. Other processes involving other combinations of maintenance with change among the three dimensions are quite possible. Some obviously do occur, as in instances of an unchanged form taking on new elements of function and meaning in addition to its·existing and maintained functions and meanings. The present incomplete coverage stems from the scarcity of studies with process identifications equal to those documented in the seminar's presentation. However, a lack of comprehensiveness presents the challenge to add to or logically complete the exercise.

PROCESS DEFINITIONS

ADDITION (synonyms: elaboration, augmentation, incorporation)

During the process of addition a preexisting and stable social or material form takes on an additional element or elements of form. There is no displacement of existing elements, and no loss is involved. The added form is developed or may be modified to fit the receiving form and its functions. The linkages and operating relations of an added form are congruent or consistent with those of the receiving form. Further, they often reinforce or augment the receiving form's functions. Linkages required to sustain the new form do not exceed the structural capabilities of the receiving or related internal forms. The functional integration of an added form is easily achieved without systemic disruption. Meanings associated with an added form are entirely in keeping with the existing meanings of receiving and related forms. Elements of meaning necessary to an addition are either derived or assigned from existing cultural domains and are arrived at without ensuing conceptual conflict. By virtue of this type of process, an added form does not give rise to derived changes in other dimensions of a receiving complex nor in related parts of the system. Although it is possible that subsequent, uncontrolled development of an added form or forms will ramify, resulting in initiation of another type of process, this event does not occur during a primary process of addition.

In accordance with this definition, and in comparison with other processes depicted in Figure 13.1, it is clear that the addition of a new form is the least disruptive of the change-involving processes. The change an addition represents is not change of any part of an existing sociocultural system but rather is simply an accrual of social or material form to that system. It is a process during which the forces of maintenance dominate. The forces for change are mediated and channeled entirely in terms of a society's antecedent meanings and prevailing structural, functional order. During addition the integration of change is achieved in conjunction with persistence of the receiving complex and, barring other ongoing processes involving change, the system as a whole. It seems evident that factors within a society's existing system of meanings are not only maintained but must play a major role as forces in the initiation and control of this type of process. Lastly, as defined here, addition is not a process necessarily limited to contact and the transfer of forms from one society to another. The process applies as well to the independent generation and integration of new additions to existing forms.

COMPARTMENTALIZATION (synonyms: isolative integration, isolation)

Upon initiation of the process of compartmentalization, a complete complex of elements of form, function, and meaning develops or enters as a variant of an existing social, or material, and cultural complex. This process occurs without replacement or loss of elements from the dimensions of the existing complex. Quite unlike the actual process of addition, however, compartmentalization does not proceed to the full functional integration of the new form or the meanings it carries. Rather, the new variant elements of form and meaning enter or internally develop largely in operational isolation from the existing complex. Although it pertains to the same general area of function, the variant complex fails to establish strong linkages with the existing complex or related parts of the system. It does not reach its potential as either a fully functional addition to, alternate, or substitute for the existing complex of maintained forms, functions, and meanings. Nor does the new complex directly contribute to the operations or internal integration of the maintained complex. Linkages are established with an isolated social or material form to the degree that it is participated in or used. But the number, kinds, and qualities of these linkages are limited and definitively controlled by cultural and social mechanisms within the prevailing system.

Meanings necessary to participation in or use of an isolated social or material form are acquired through participation or use, or are internally and differentially developed as the forms and functions of the new complex develop. Participatory and use meanings do not correspond in any substantial way to existing meanings. As they are acquired or developed, these necessary meanings become specialized and circumscribed, coming into play only when and to the extent that the compartmentalized form is participated in or used, thereby becoming isolated from the meanings of the existing complex. In sum, during this process all dimensions of a new entering or internally developing complex are compartmentalized in relation to, and under the control of, a maintained cultural and social order.

In isolation the distinct and specialized linkages of a variant complex do not seriously interfere with nor do they augment the operations or systemic integration of the existing complex. This fact is especially clear in contact situations in which an externally imposed but processually isolated variant is unable to duplicate or take over the operations or the internal integrative functions of the centrally established complex. Use of or participation in an isolated complex, however, may serve to maintain the operations and internal linkages of the central complex through the provision of resources. Given the controls of a central system, such services are carefully managed in order that disruptive dependency relations do not become established.

In cases of this type of change by isolation of a variant complex, disruption or derived changes in a central system do not occur as long as internal controls remain effective. It is quite possible for a compartmentalized complex to become stabilized and maintained as such over long periods of time. It is also possible for controls to weaken or be overpowered by subsequent forces for change. Either of these occasions will trigger another type of process affecting an established compartmentalization. Finally, with specific regard to the internal dynamics of a sociocultural system, a retroactive version of the compartmentalization process can take place, resulting in the separation of formerly well-integrated parts of a system. A retroactive process of isolation affects preexisting and functionally related complexes in the ways described above. Its forms, functions, and meanings of one complex becomes differentiated, specialized, and essentially isolated from those of a related and internally maintained complex.

FUSION (synonyms: syncretism, synthesis, recombination)

The process of fusion involves the three dimensions of two different and previously disassociated complexes. The two complexes consist of differing forms and meanings, but both pertain to the same general area of activity and experience. In response to a near balance between forces of maintenance and change, elements of an entering or internally developed complex are pressured into conjunction with elements of an established complex. In a figurative sense, the process proceeds as follows. The dimensions of form, function, and meaning of each complex are factored into discrete elements. Then, selections of elements from each of the differing dimensions are combined to reconstitute a new and distinctive complex, reintegrated within the system. Building a simile from the depiction of the process in Figure 13.1, some new elements (black) and some old elements (white) fuse to produce something that is neither black nor white, but a shade of gray. By virtue of this process of reciprocal transformation, taken as wholes, the form and meaning dimensions of the resulting complex bear little resemblance to either of the original complexes. However, in terms of the constituent elements of the new complex, neither of the originals has suffered total replacement or loss.

As an outcome of the fusion process, reconstituted forms and meanings are integrated within a system in the functional areas occupied by the prior complex. By and large, fusion in not a disruptive process. The operations and linkages of newly constituted forms and meanings are compatibly generated during the process. That is, dysfunctional forms and inconsistent meanings are automatically omitted from the synthesis. Moreover, the fusion process can lead to strengthened and expanded internal integrative functions. Fused forms and meanings often develop stronger and broader areas of linkage and other operational relations within a system.

Although fusion represents change with respect to a former integration of forms, functions, and meanings, it is not thoroughgoing change, devoid of the effects of maintenance or of persistent elements. In a reintegration of the old with the new, something of the old remains. Old elements of form are combined with new elements of form under fused meanings. Even in fused meanings there are old, persistent elements and themes. What is more, prior to actual fusion the new entering or internally developed elements of both form and meaning were subjected to interpretation, selection, and reordering by an existing, established, and maintained system of meanings.

The process of fusion can be pervasive. It can transform whole subsystems, even whole systems. Further, there seems to be an increment in synergy created by the process. Fused forms and meanings, themselves, are tightly integrated; they are functionally capable of increasing areas of systemic integration; and, once in operation, they are highly resistant to further change. The number of syncretisms or fusions reported in the ethnographic literature attests to the high frequency of this process in association with certain types of contact situations and sociocultural transfer. But clearly the process of fusion applies as well to the synthesis of preexisting, differentiated complexes within a sociocultural system.

REPLACEMENT (synonyms: assimilation, substitution)

On the surface, replacement is seemingly a simple, straightforward process. Indeed, it is often portrayed as merely the substitution of a newly acquired or internally innovated form for an old form, an iron pot for an earthen pot. In reality, the process is a good deal more involved than such descriptions would indicate. Moreover, genuine replacement occurs far less frequently than is generally assumed. The supposition of high frequency is largely due to the mistaken labeling of additions, compartmentalizations, and elements of fusions as replacement. Considering the widespread lack of careful discrimination among dynamic processes in terms of differential qualities and qualities of maintenance with change, the members of the 1956 seminar did yeoman service, particularly with respect to their pinning down and clarification of the ambiguous concept of assimilation in relation to other processes of acculturation. By equating assimilative change with the process of replacement, the concept is given a concrete reference point in contrast to its usual indefinite and confusing use as a synonym for acculturation in general. In turn, the concept of acculturation takes on a different significance when assimilation is seen to be merely one of several of its possible outcomes.

The process of replacement involves a complete substitution of form, function, and meaning. The social or material forms, functional relations, and meanings of an existing complex are disengaged from a system and replaced by a different entering or internally developed complex. The replacement consists of different and unaltered elements of form, carrying their own meanings and having their own functional requirements. As the process proceeds, the replacing complex, on its own terms, becomes directly and fully integrated within the receiving system. The distinguishing characteristics of replacement are the unmodified nature of the displacing elements of form, their full integration, and the consequent social or material and, at times, cultural loss. The preceding caveat covers those cases in which the replacing forms have functional relations and meanings similar or identical to those of the displaced complex. When this situation is not the case, the replaced complex ceases to exist as an integral of a system in the event that it does not itself take on revised form and meaning as well as different or greatly reduced functions.

During the replacement process an entering or internally developed form is not adjusted to fit related parts within the receiving system. Rather, related complexes may be forced to adjust or change in order to meet the functional requirements of the entering complex. To the extent that a replacement does not entail the same or similar meanings and operational needs as did the displaced complex, its full and direct integration will involve accommodations or lead to other derived processes. Excepting meaningfully similar and functionally neutral replacements, the forces of maintenance emanating from and in behalf of the retained aspects of the cultural and social order may be dominated by the forces of change associated with the replacement. This dominance, however, does not mean that the existing order is passively receptive of derived change. Most particularly, derived change does not necessarily involve the remaining system of meanings. Within limits, change among these meanings is preceded by accommodation of their related social or material forms; that is, related forms may be adjusted or partially changed to fit the requirements of a replacement, allowing their meanings and functions to remain essentially intact. Consequently, cultural persistence, if not the total maintenance of remaining social and material forms, is possible even in cases of disruptive and ramifying replacements.

With regard to both internal innovation and assimilative change, only when the number or accumulated impact of replacements reaches some as-yet-unknown critical level will the retained meanings of a traditional cultural order break down, making way for the final establishment of a replacive order. In relation to assimilative replacement, the literature on pluralism and ethnicity provides sufficient evidence to hypothesize that this critical level is extremely high. The long-term persistence of separate identity systems, based on small but central and vital cores of traditional meanings, amidst massive replacement and accompanying revisions of traditional social and material forms, is a well-documented phenomenon. It remains, however, for us to understand the contextual relations and internal mechanisms which integrate and sustain the functioning of these long-lived cores of traditional meanings. A study by Spicer (1971) concerned with persistent identity systems points to several potentially fruitful focal areas for research in this regard.

Consistent with the other process definitions, replacement need not be limited to sociocultural transfer. Obviously, replacements in the form of independently generated, social and material innovations occur within societies without benefit of transferred ideas or forms. An independent replacement process has all of the characteristics and possibilities described above. The replacement is facilitated by an existing cultural order; it is fully integrated within a system which suffers some loss; it can be functionally nonequivalent to what it replaced and ramify accordingly; but, within limits, it will not undermine the maintenance of retained, traditional meanings.

An observation embedded in the definitions and drawn from the substance of the seminar's case studies deserves emphasis. Through the analytic division and controlled comparison of complexes incurring change, it emerges that the dimensions of meaning and function are less affected than the dimension of form. It has not been too difficult to accept this observation as support for the oft-repeated anthropological contention that it is the system of meanings, the existing cultural order, from which major forces for maintenance arise to interact with cultural and noncultural forces for change. In turn, these cultural forces for maintenance are supplemented by those deriving from the functional dimension, that is, maintenance forces that arise from the recognized functional incompatibilities of forms and meanings representing and driven by forces for change. Acting together in a process these two varieties of maintenance forces are capable of mediating and powerfully channeling forces for change, shaping outcomes and giving order to process.

THE REVISED IMAGE OF DYNAMIC PROCESS

The goal of the exercise has been to illustrate the existence of forces for maintenance in dynamic processes as well as the variable contributions they make to persistence in outcomes. Once the validity of this demonstration is accepted, the most generalizable conclusion to be drawn holds a great deal of significance for the study of sociocultural change. I shall venture to state this conclusion in the form of a proposition: *If a dynamic process gives rise to observable change within a sociocultural system, then that process will have derived from an interaction of both forces for maintenance and forces for change.* It follows that the specific qualities and quantities of that change will have been determined by the nature and intensity of the two

242   *Adaptive Perspectives*

sets of opposing forces relative to one another. Relating this statement to anthropology's repeated attempts to resolve the antithesis of pattern maintenance and change, a broader recognition of the inevitable unity of opposites within sociocultural process is essential. To assist fuller recognition of the unavoidable dialectic, it is possible to think of process in sociocultural dynamics as, in some ways, similar to physical process. The similarities can be described metaphorically with terms drawn from mechanics.

In sociocultural systems all dynamic processes comprehend mechanisms and associated forces of maintenance and change. *Dynamic* means having temporally observable movement. But this movement is always along a product vector in that the motion is directed along a path which is the product of a conjuction and interaction between forces for maintenance and forces for change. For every movement or process the product vector is a measured response to the weight or power of one set of forces relative to the weight or power of the opposing set. Depending on the relative strength of each set of forces, the movement will be channeled toward what can be envisaged as a point on a continuum between the poles of absolute maintenance and absolute change. In some cases, forces for maintenance may overpower or effectively neutralize forces for change, and the product vector will track in the direction of the maintenance pole. In other cases, the forces of change will have sufficient strength to counter maintenance forces by variable degrees and swing the product vector toward different points on the continuum in the direction of change.

Our present analytic models for the study of sociocultural dynamics are, by and large, too dependent on and restricted by conceptualizations of process which fail to incorporate some version of the above perspective. A number of reviews of the status of culture-change studies in anthropology indicate the state of art in this respect, mainly by the brevity and diffuseness or omission of discussions concerning the role of maintenance in process (Bee 1974; Spindler 1977; Woods 1975). Until concepts and analytic models of process are consistently developed to guide analyses of the interplay between maintenance and change in process, our failures in theory-building will continue. Despite the considerable research focus on culture and social change since the mid-1950s, the development of theory has, if anything, declined. The emphatic message contained in the 1956 seminar's contributions and in the exercise above is offered as the principal deficiency and cause. Explanations of sociocultural change are unattainable without concomitant explanation of the part played by maintenance forces in giving direction to and structuring the outcomes of the dynamic processes involved.

Bibliography

Aberle, D. F.; Cohen, A. K.; David, A. K.; Levy, M. J.; and Sutton, F. X.
  1950   "The Functional Prerequisites of a Society." *Ethics* 60:100–11.

Acheson, James M.
  1972   "Limited Good or Limited Goods? Response to Economic Opportunity in a Tarascan Pueblo." *American Anthropologist* 74:1152–64.
  1974   "Reply to Mary Lee Nolan." *American Anthropologist* 76:49–53.

Acosta, Roberto
  1949   *Apuntes históricos sonorenses; La conquista temporale y espiritual del yaqui y del mayo.* Mexico, D.F.: Aldina.

Adair, John
  1960   "The Indian Health Worker in the Cornell-Navajo Project." *Human Organization* 19 (2) (Summer):59–63.

Adair, John and Deuschle, Kurt
  1970   *The People's Health: Medicine and Anthropology in a Navajo Community.* New York: Appleton, Century, Crofts.

Adams, John W., and Kasakoff, Alice Bee
  1975   "Factors Underlying Endogamous Group Size." In *Population and Social Organization,* edited by Moni Nag, pp. 147–74. The Hague: Mouton.

Adams, William Y.
    1969   "Ethnohistory and Islamic Tradition in Africa." *Ethnohistory*
            16:277–88.
    1977   *Nubia: Corridor to Africa*. London: Allen Lane.

Aguirre Beltrán, Gonzalo
    1967   *Regiones de refugio: El desarrollo de la comunidad y el proceso dominical en
            mestizo América*. Instituto Indigenista Interamericano, Ediciones
            Especiales 46, Mexico, D.F.

Alland, Alexander, Jr.
    1966   "Medical Anthropology and the Study of Biological and Cultural
            Adaptation." *American Anthropologist* 68:40–51.
    1970   *Adaptation in Cultural Evolution: An Approach to Medical Anthropol-
            ogy*. New York: Columbia University Press.

Arensberg, C.
    1955   "American Communities." *American Anthropologist* 57:1142–61.

Arrington, Leonard
    1958   *Great Basin Kingdom*. Cambridge, Mass.: Harvard University Press.
    1961   *From Wilderness to Empire: The Role of Utah in Western Economic
            History*. Institute of American Studies, Monograph No. 1. Salt Lake
            City: University of Utah Press.

Baer, Gabriel
    1964   "Egyptian Guilds in Modern Times." *Israel Oriental Society, Oriental
            Notes and Studies*, No. 8.

Barclay, Harold
    1964   *Buuri al Lamaab*. Ithaca: Cornell University Press.

Barnett, Clifford R., and Rabin, David L.
    1970   "Collaborative Study by Physicians and Anthropologists: Congeni-
            tal Hip Disease." In *The People's Health: Medicine and Anthropology in
            a Navajo Community*, by John Adair and Kurt Deuschle. New York:
            Appleton, Century, Crofts.

Barnett, Homer G.
    1942   "Invention and Culture Change." *American Anthropologist* 44:14–
            30.
    1953   *Innovation: The Basis of Culture Change*. New York: McGraw-Hill.

Barr, Alwyn
    1973   *Black Texans: A History of Negroes in Texas, 1528–1971*. Austin:
            Jenkins Publishing.

Barth, Fredrik
    1956   "Ecological Relationships of Ethnic Groups in Swat, North Pakis-
            tan." *American Anthropologist* 58:1079–89.

1961   *Nomads of South Persia.* Boston: Little, Brown.

1969   Introduction to *Ethnic Groups and Boundaries,* edited by Fredrik Barth, pp. 9–38. Boston: Little, Brown.

Bartlett, Irving H.

1954   *From Slave to Citizen: The Story of the Negro in Rhode Island.* Providence, Rhode Island: Urban League of Greater Providence.

Beals, Ralph

1946   *Cherán: A Sierra Tarascan Village.* Washington, D.C.: Smithsonian Institution, Institute of Social Anthropology (2).

Bee, Robert L.

1963   "Changes in Yuma Social Organization." *Ethnology* 2(2):207–27.

1974   *Patterns and Processes.* New York: Free Press.

Bennett, John W.

1969   *Northern Plainsmen.* Chicago: Aldine.

1976   "Anticipation, Adaptation, and the Concept of Culture in Anthropology." *Science* 192:847–53.

Berger, Morroe

1964   *The Arab World Today.* New York: Anchor Books.

Black, Donald

1976   *The Behavior of Law.* New York: Academic Press.

Blake, Judith

1955   "Family Instability and Reproductive Behavior in Jamaica." In *Current Research in Human Fertility,* pp. 24–41. New York: Milbank Memorial Fund.

Bloch, Maurice

1977   "The Past and the Present in the Present." *Man* (NS) 12(2): 278–92.

Blu, Karen I.

1980   *The Lumbee Problem: The Making of an American Indian People.* Cambridge: Cambridge University Press.

Boardman, John

1964   *The Greeks Overseas.* Harmondsworth: Pelican Books.

Boas, Franz

1902   "The Ethnological Significance of Esoteric Doctrines." *Science* 16:872–74.

Bohannon, Paul

1963   *Social Anthropology.* New York: Holt, Rinehart and Winston.

Bonfil Batalla, Guillermo

1966   "Conservative Thought in Applied Anthropology: A Critique." *Human Organization* 25:89–92.

Bonney, Rachel A.
    1977   "The Role of AIM Leaders in Indian Nationalism." *American Indian Quarterly* 3:(3):209–24.

Brackett, Jeffrey R.
    1889   *The Negro in Maryland: A Study of the Institution of Slavery.* Select Bibliographies Reprint Series. Freeport, New York: Books for Libraries Press, 1969.

Briggs, Lloyd C.
    1958   "The Living Races of the Sahara Desert." *Papers of the Peabody Museum of Archaeology and Ethnology, Harvard University,* Vol. 28, No. 2.
    1960   *Tribes of the Sahara.* Cambridge, Mass.: Harvard University Press.

Briggs, Lloyd C., and Guède, Norina L.
    1964   "No More For Ever: A Saharan Jewish Town." *Papers of the Peabody Museum of Archaeology and Ethnology, Harvard University,* Vol. 55, No. 1.

Brown, Letitia Woods
    1972   *Free Negroes in the District of Columbia, 1790–1846.* New York: Oxford University Press.

Bushnell, David I., Jr.
    1909   *The Choctaw of Bayou Lacomb, St. Tammany Parish, Louisiana.* Smithsonian Institution, Bureau of American Ethnology, Bull. 48, Washington, D.C.

Castetter, Edward F., and Bell, Willis H.
    1951   *Yuma Indian Agriculture: Primitive Subsistence on the Lower Colorado and Gila Rivers.* Albuquerque: University of New Mexico Press.

Castile, George P.
    1974a   *Cherán: La adaptación de una comunidad tradicional de Michoacán.* Mexico, D.F.: Instituto Nacional Indigenista, Serie de Anthropología Social (26).
    1974b   "Federal Indian Policy and the Sustained Enclave: An Anthropological Perspective." *Human Organization* 33(3):219–28.
    1975   "National Integration and Villages That Progress Chose." Paper read at American Anthropological Association meetings, Dec. 2–6, San Francisco.
    1978   "The Headless Horsemen: Recapitating the Beheaded Community." *Indian Historian* 33(11):38–45.
    1979   *North American Indians: An Introduction to the Chichimeca.* New York: McGraw-Hill.

Clark, Margaret; Kaufman, Sharon; and Pierce, Robert C.
    1976   "Explorations of Acculturation Toward a Model of Ethnic Identity." *Human Organization* 35:231–38.

Clemmer, Richard O.
    1969   "Resistance and the Revitalization of Anthropologists: A New Perspective on Culture Change and Resistance." In *Reinventing Anthropology*, edited by Dell Hymes, pp. 213–47. New York: Random House.

Cohen, Abner
    1971   "Cultural Strategies in the Organization of Trading Diasporas." In *The Development of Indigenous Trade and Markets in West Africa*, edited by Claude Meillassoux, pp. 266–81. London: International African Institute.

Cohen, Fay G.
    1976   "The American Indian Movement and the Anthropologist: Issues and Implications of Consent." In *Dilemmas in Fieldwork Ethics and Anthropology*, edited by Michael A. Rynkiewich and James P. Spradly. New York: John Wiley.

Cohen, Yehudi A.
    1968   Introduction to *Man in Adaptation: The Biosocial Background*, edited by Yehudi Cohen, pp. 1–5. Chicago: Aldine.

Comer, James P.
    1972   *Beyond Black and White.* New York: Quadrangle Books.

Coon, Carleton S.
    1964   *Caravan: The Story of the Middle East.* Rev. ed. New York: Holt, Rinehart and Winston.

Crumrine, N. Ross
    1970   "Ritual Drama and Culture Change." *Comparative Studies in Society and History* 12(4):361–73.
    1975   "A New Mayo Indian Religious Movement in Northwest Mexico." *Journal of Latin American Lore* 1(2):127–45.
    1977   *The Mayo Indians of Sonora: A People Who Refuse to Die.* Tucson: University of Arizona Press.
    1981   "The Mayo of Southern Sonora, Mexico: Socio-economic Assimilation and Ritual-symbolic Syncretism — Split Acculturation." In *Themes of Indigenous Acculturation in Northwest Mexico*, edited by Thomas B. Hinton and Phil C. Weigand, pp. 22–35. Anthropological Papers of the University of Arizona, no. 38. Tucson: University of Arizona Press.

Crumrine, N. Ross, and Macklin, B. June
  1974   "Sacred Ritual Versus the Unconscious: The Efficacy of Symbols and Structure in North Mexican Folk Saints' Cults and General Ceremonialism." In *The Unconscious in Culture,* edited by Ino Rossi, pp. 179–97. New York: E. P. Dutton.

Cruse, Harold
  1968   *Rebellion or Revolution?* New York: William Morrow.

Dabney, Wendell P.
  1926   *Cincinnati's Colored Citizens: Historical, Sociological and Biographical.* Reprint. New York: Greenwood Press, Negro Universities Press, 1970.

DeCell, Harriet, and Prichard, Jo Anne
  1976   *Yazoo: Its Legends and Legacies.* Yazoo City, Mississippi: Yazoo Delta Press.

Despres, Leo A.
  1975   "Toward a Theory of Ethnic Phenomena." In *Ethnicity and Resource Competition in Plural Societies,* edited by Leo A. Despres. The Hague: Mouton.

Devereux, George
  1939   "Social and Cultural Implications of Incest Among the Mohave Indians." *Psychoanalytic Quarterly* 8:510–29.
  1941   "Mohave Belief Concerning Twins." *American Anthropologist* 43:573–92.
  1948   "Mohave Indian Infanticide." *Psychoanalytic Review* 35:126–39.
  1961   *Mohave Ethnopsychiatry and Suicide: A Study of the Psychic Disturbances of an Indian Tribe.* Smithsonian Institution, Bureau of American Ethnology, Bull. 175. Washington, D.C.

De Vos, George
  1975   "Ethnic Pluralism: Conflict and Accommodation." In *Ethnic Identity, Cultural Continuities and Change,* edited by George De Vos and Lola Romanucci-Ross. Palo Alto: Mayfield Publishing.

Dobyns, Henry F.; Ezell, Paul H.; and Ezell, Greta
  1963   "Death of a Society." *Ethnohistory* 10(2):105–61.

Dobyns, Henry F.; Stoffle, Richard W.; and Jones, Kristine
  1975   "Native American Urbanization and Socio-Economic Integration in the Southwestern United States." *Ethnohistory* 22(2):156–81.

Dozier, Edward P.
  1951   "Resistance to Acculturation and Assimilation in an Indian Pueblo." *American Anthropologist* 53:56–66.

1961   "Río Grande Pueblos." In *Perspectives in American Indian Culture Change,* edited by Edward H. Spicer, pp. 94–186. Chicago: University of Chicago Press.

Dunnigan, Timothy
   1969   "Subsistence and Reciprocity Patterns Among the Mountain Pima of Sonora, Mexico." Ph.D. dissertation, University of Arizona, Tucson.

Durkheim, Emile
   1933   *Division of Labor in Society.* Translated by G. Simpson. New York: Macmillan.

Eggan, Fred R.
   1950   *The Social Organization of the Western Pueblos.* Chicago: University of Chicago Press.

Eisenstadt, S. N.; Yosef, Rivkah Bar; and Adler, Chaim, eds.
   1970   *Integration and Development in Israel.* New York: Praeger.

Encyclopaedia Britannica
   1929   *Encyclopaedia Britannica,* 14th ed. Chicago: Encyclopaedia Britannica, Inc.

English, Paul Ward
   1966   *City and Village in Iran.* Madison: University of Wisconsin Press.

Erasmus, Charles J.
   1961   *Man Takes Control: Cultural Development and American Aid.* Minneapolis: University of Minnesota Press.
   1967   "Culture Change in Northwest Mexico." In *Contemporary Change in Traditional Societies,* Mexican and Peruvian Communities, edited by Julian H. Steward, vol. 3, pp. 3–131. Urbana: University of Illinois Press.
   1977   *In Search of the Common Good: Utopian Experiments Past and Future.* New York: Free Press.
   1978   "Culture Change in Northwest Mexico." In *Contemporary Change in Traditional Communities of Mexico and Peru,* edited by Julian H. Steward. Urbana: University of Illinois Press.

Evetts, B. T. A., and Butler, Alfred J., trans.
   1895   *The Churches and Monasteries of Egypt and Some Neighbouring Countries.* Oxford: Clarendon Press.

Fathauer, George
   1951*a*   "Mohave Social Organization." Ph.D. dissertation, University of Chicago.

Fathauer, George *(continued)*
    1951*b*   "Religion in Mohave Social Structure." *Ohio Journal of Science* 51:273–76.
    1951*c*   "The Mohave Ghost Doctor." *American Anthropologist* 53(4):605–7.
    1954   "Structure and Causation of Mohave Warfare." *Southwest Journal of Anthropology* 10(1):97–118.

Faubert, J. B. Edmundo
    1975   "Los indios pimas de Sonora y Chihuahua." Unpublished manuscript. Tucson: Arizona State Museum Library.

Fogelson, Raymond D.
    1961   "Change, Persistence, and Accommodation in Cherokee Medico-Magical Beliefs." In *Symposium on Cherokee and Iroquois Culture,* edited by William N. Fenton and John Gulick, pp. 213–25. Smithsonian Institution, Bureau of American Ethnology, Bull. 180, Washington, D.C.

Forbes, Jack D.
    1965   *Warriors of the Colorado: The Yumas of the Quechan Nation and Their Neighbors.* Norman: University of Oklahoma Press.
    1973   "Nationalism, Tribalism and Self-determination: Yuman-Mexican Relations, 1821–1848." *Indian Historian* 6(2):18–23.

Forde, C. Daryll
    1931   "Ethnography of the Yuma Indians." *University of California Publications in American Archaeology and Ethnology* 28(4):1–278.

Foster, George
    1960   *Culture and Conquest: America's Spanish Heritage.* New York: Wenner-Gren Foundation for Anthropological Research.
    1967   *Tzintzuntzan: Mexican Peasants in a Changing World.* Boston: Little, Brown.
    1969   *Applied Anthropology.* Boston: Little, Brown.
    1974   "Limited Good or Limited Goods: Observations on Acheson." *American Anthropologist* 76:53–57.

Frye, Richard N.
    1963   *The Heritage of Persia.* New York: Mentor Books.

Gadd, C. J.
    1971   Babylonia, c. 2120–1800 B.C." In *The Cambridge Ancient History,* 3rd ed., vol. 1, part 2, edited by I. E. S. Edwards, C. J. Gadd, and N. G. L. Hammond, pp. 595–643. Cambridge: Cambridge University Press.

Gager, John
    1975   *Kingdom and Community: The Social World of Early Christianity.* Englewood Cliffs, N.J.: Prentice Hall.

Gearing, Fred; Netting, Robert McC.; and Peattie, Lisa R.
    1960   *Documentary History of the Fox Project.* Chicago: University of Chicago, Department of Anthropology.

Geertz, Clifford
    1963   *Agricultural Involution: The Processes of Ecological Change in Indonesia.* Berkeley: University of California Press.

Geiser, Peter
    1973   "The Myth of the Dam." *American Anthropologist* 775:184–94.

Gerlach, Luther P.
    1979   "Energy Wars and Social Change." In *Predicting Culture Change,* edited by S. Abbott and John van Willigen. Proceedings of the Southern Anthropological Society, no. 13.

Gilbert, William Harlen, Jr.
    1943   *The Eastern Cherokees.* Anthropological Paper No. 23, Smithsonian Institution, Bureau of American Ethnology, Bull. 133, pp. 169–413. Washington, D.C.

Gluckman, Max
    1954   *Rituals of Rebellion in South-East Africa.* The Fraser Lecture, 1952. Manchester: Manchester University Press.

Gmelch, George
    1977   *The Irish Tinkers: The Urbanization of an Itinerant People.* Menlo Park, California: Cummings.

Gmelch, Sharon
    1975   *Tinkers and Travellers.* Dublin: O'Brien Press.

Gordon, Milton
    1964   *Assimilation in American Life: The Role of Race, Religion and National Origins.* New York: Oxford University Press.

Green, Vera M.
    1970   Field notes, Houston, Texas.
    1978   "The Black Extended Family in the United States: Some Research Suggestions." In *The Extended Family in Black Societies,* edited by D. B. Shimkin, E. M. Shimkin, and D. A. Frate. The Hague: Mouton.

Gregory, James R.
    1976   "The Modification of an Interethnic Boundary in Belize." *American Ethnologist* 3:683–708.

Griffen, William B.

1969   *Culture Change and Shifting Populations in Central Northern Mexico.* Anthropological Papers of the University of Arizona, no. 13. Tucson: University of Arizona Press.

1970   "Procesos de extinción y continuidad social y cultural en el norte de México durate la colonia." *América Indígena* 30(3):689–725.

1979   *Indian Assimilation in the Franciscan Area of Nueva Vizcaya.* Anthropological Papers of the University of Arizona, no. 33. Tucson: University of Arizona Press.

Gropper, Rena C.

1975   *Gypsies in the City.* Princeton: Darwin Press.

Gubser, Peter

1973   *Politics and Change in al-Karak, Jordan.* London: Oxford University Press.

Gulick, John

1967   *Tripoli: A Modern Arab City.* Cambridge, Mass.: Harvard University Press.

Harding, Vincent

1976   "The Black Struggle for Freedom: 1875–1914. Reflections on the Post-Reconstruction South." Paper read at the Annual Meeting of the Association for the Study of Negro Life and History.

Harman, Robert C.

1974   *Cambios médicos y sociales en una comunidad maya tzeltal.* Colección de antropología social 28. Mexico, D. F.: Instituto Nacional Indigenista.

1975   "Personal Names of the Maya in Oxchuc." *Behavior Science Research* 10:101–29.

Harris, B. Dwight

1904   *The History of Negro Servitude in Illinois and the Slavery Agitation in That State, 1719–1864.* Chicago: A. C. McClurg.

Harris, George L.

1958   *Iraq.* New Haven: HRAF Press.

Harris, Marvin

1968   *The Rise of Anthropological Theory.* New York: Crowell.

Hawkes, Jacquetta, and Woolley, Leonard

1963   *Prehistory and the Beginnings of Civilization.* New York: Harper & Row.

Heiken, Diane Bray

1978   "The Hutterites: A Comparative Analysis of Viability." Ph.D. dissertation, University of California at Santa Barbara.

Herskovits, Melville J.
    1945   "The Processes of Culture Change." In *The Science of Man in the World Crisis,* edited by Ralph Linton, pp. 143–70. New York: Columbia University Press.
    1958   *Acculturation: The Study of Culture Contact.* Gloucester, Massachusetts: P. Smith
    1964   *Cultural Dynamics.* (Abridged from *Cultural Anthropology,* New York: Alfred Knopf, 1955). New York: Alfred Knopf.
    1966   "The New World Negro." In *Selected Papers in Afro-American Studies,* edited by F. S. Herskovits. Bloomington: Indiana University Press.

Hertzberg, Hazel W.
    1971   *The Search for an American Indian Identity: Modern Pan-Indian Movements.* Syracuse: Syracuse University Press.

Hill, Mozell, and Ackiss, Thelma D.
    1943   *Culture of a Contemporary All-Negro Community.* Langston, Oklahoma: Langston University Press, Langston University Bulletin.

Hinton, Thomas B.
    1981   "Cultural Visibility and the Cora." In *Themes of Indigenous Acculturation in Northwest Mexico,* edited by Thomas B. Hinton and Phil C. Weigand, pp. 1–3. Anthropological Papers of the University of Arizona, no. 38. Tucson: University of Arizona Press.

Hodge, William H.
    1969   *The Albuquerque Navajos.* Anthropological Papers of the University of Arizona, no. 11. Tucson: University of Arizona Press.

Hoetink, Hermanus
    1967   *The Two Variants in Caribbean Race Relations: A Contribution to the Sociology of Segmented Societies.* Institute of Race Relations. London: Oxford University Press.

Holland, William R.
    1963   *Medicina maya en los altos de Chiapas: Un estudio del cambio sociocultural.* Colección de antropología social 2. Mexico, D.F.: Instituto Nacional Indigenista.

Hostetler, John A.
    1963   *Amish Society.* Baltimore: Johns Hopkins Press.
    1968   *Amish Society.* Rev. ed. Baltimore: Johns Hopkins Press.
    1970   "Transcript of Testimony in Wisconsin v. Yoder." Wisconsin Circuit Court, Green County, Wisconsin. Mimeographed.

Hourani, A. H.
    1947   *Minorities in the Arab World.* London: Oxford University Press.

Howard, James
    1968   *The Southeastern Ceremonial Complex and Its Interpretation.* Memoir
            No. 6, Missouri Archaeological Society.
    1970   "Bringing Back the Fire: The Revival of a Natchez-Cherokee
            Ceremonial Ground." *American Indian Crafts and Culture* 4(1):9–
            12.

Instituto Nacional Indigenista
    1964   *Realidades y proyectos: Dieciseis años de trabajo.* Mexico, D.F.: In-
            stituto Nacional Indigenista.

Jordan, Janet E.
    1974   "Politics and Religion in a Western Cherokee Community: A Cor-
            porate Struggle for Survival in a White Man's World." Ph.D.
            dissertation, University of Connecticut.

Jorgensen, Joseph
    1972   *The Sun Dance Religion.* Chicago: University of Chicago Press.

Kanter, Rosabeth M.
    1972   *Commitment and Community: Communes and Utopias in Sociological
            Perspective.* Cambridge, Mass.: Harvard University Press.

Kasakoff, Alice
    1974   "Levi-Strauss' Idea of the Social Unconscious: The Problem of
            Elementary and Complex Structures in Gitksan Marriage Choice."
            In *The Unconscious in Culture: The Structuralism of Claude Levi-Strauss
            in Perspective,* edited by Ino Rossi, pp. 143–69. New York: E. P.
            Dutton.

Keesing, Roger M.
    1974   "Theories of Culture." In *Annual Review of Anthropology,* edited by
            Bernard Siegel, vol. 3, pp. 73–97. Palo Alto: Annual Reviews,
            Inc.

Kelly, Marsha
    1972   "The Society That Did Not Die." *Ethnohistory* 19(3):261–65.

Khuri, Fuad I.
    1975   *From Village to Suburb.* Chicago: University of Chicago Press.

Kilpatrick, Jack Frederick, and Kilpatrick, Anna Gritts
    1964a   "The Foundation of Life: The Cherokee National Ritual." *American
            Anthropologist* 66(6) Pt. 1:1386–91.
    1964b   *Friends of Thunder: Folktales of the Oklahoma Cherokees.* Dallas: South-
            ern Methodist University Press.

1965   *Walk in Your Soul: Love Incantations of the Oklahoma Cherokees.* Dallas: Southern Methodist University Press.

1967*a*   *Muskogean Charm Songs Among the Oklahoma Cherokees.* Smithsonian Contributions to Anthropology, vol. 2, no. 3. Washington, D.C.

1967*b*   *Run Toward the Nightland: Magic of the Oklahoma Cherokees.* Dallas: Southern Methodist University Press.

Kirchoff, Paul
1954   "Gatherers and Farmers in the Southwest: A Problem in Classification." *American Anthropologist* 56(4):529–60.

Kroeber, Alfred L.
1920   "Yuman Tribes of the Lower Colorado." *University of California Publications in American Archaeology and Ethnology* 16(8):475–85.

1925   *Handbook of the California Indians.* Smithsonian Institution, Bureau of American Ethnology, Bull. 78. Washington, D.C.

1939   "Cultural and Natural Areas of Native North America." *University of California Publications in Archaeology and Ethnology* 38:1–242.

Kushner, Gilbert
1973   *Immigrants From India in Israel: Planned Change in an Administered Community.* Tucson: University of Arizona Press.

Land, George T.
1973   *Grow or Die: The Unifying Principle of Transformation.* New York: Dell.

Lane, E. W.
1908   *Manners and Customs of the Modern Egyptians.* London: J. M. Dent & Sons.

Lapidus, Ira M., ed.
1969   *Middle Eastern Cities.* Berkeley: University of California Press.

Lefley, Harriet P.
1975   "Approaches to Community Mental Health: The Miami Model." *Psychiatric Annals* 5(8) (August):315–19.

Leone, Mark P.
1974   "The Economic Basis for the Evolution of Mormon Religion." In *Religious Movements in Contemporary America,* edited by I. I. Zaretsky and M. P. Leone. Princeton: Princeton University Press.

1977   "The New Mormon Temple in Washington, D.C." *Historical Archaeology* and the Importance of Material Things. *Journal of Historical Archaeology,* Special Publication Series No. 2, pp. 43–61.

1979   *Roots of Modern Mormonism.* Cambridge, Mass.: Harvard University Press.

Levi-Strauss, Claude
    1963   "The Effectiveness of Symbols." In *Structural Anthropology.* New York: Basic Books.

Levy, Reuben
    1965   *The Social Structure of Islam.* Cambridge: Cambridge University Press.

Lewis, Bernard
    1971   *Race and Color in Islam.* New York: Harper Torchbooks.

Liebenstein, Harvey
    1976   *Beyond Economic Man: A New Foundation for Microeconomics.* Cambridge, Mass.: Harvard University Press.

Lindblom, Charles E.
    1977   *Politics and Markets: The World's Political-Economic Systems.* New York: Basic Books.

Linton, Ralph
    1936   *The Study of Man.* New York: Appleton-Century-Crofts.
    1937   "One Hundred Percent American." *American Mercury* 40:427–29.
    1940   "The Distinctive Aspects of Acculturation." In *Acculturation in Seven American Indian Tribes,* edited by Ralph Linton, pp 501–20. New York: Appleton-Century-Crofts.

Lipsky, George A.
    1959   *Saudi Arabia.* New Haven: HRAF Press.

Lurie, Nancy Oestreich
    1966   "The Enduring Indian." *Natural History* 79(9):10–22.

Lutfiyya, Abdulla M.
    1966   *Baytin: A Jordanian Village.* The Hague: Mouton.

Lyman, Stanford
    1972   *The Black American in Sociological Thought: New Perspectives on Black America.* New York: G. P. Putnam's Sons.

Macklin, B. June, and Crumrine, N. Ross
    1973   "Three North Mexican Folk Saint Movements." *Comparative Studies in Society and History* 15(1):89–105.

McNichols, C.
    1944   *Crazy Weather.* New York: Macmillan.

Madsen, William
    1967   "Religious Syncretism." In *Handbook of Middle American Indians,* vol. 6, edited by Robert Wauchope, pp. 369–91. Austin: University of Texas Press.

Malinowski, Bronislaw

    1944   *A Scientific Theory of Culture.* Chapel Hill: University of North Carolina Press.

    1945   *The Dynamics of Culture Change.* New Haven: Yale University Press.

Marcor, Alejandro Carillo

    1976   "Sonora puede cometer genocidio con los mayos." *El Informador del Mayo* 20(6, 895):1, 7. Navojoa, Sonora: Empresa Editorial de Sonora.

Meillassoux, Claude, ed.

    1971   *The Development of Indigenous Trade and Markets in West Africa.* London: International African Institute.

Miller, Carol

    1975   "The American Rom and the Ideology of Defilement." In *Gypsies, Tinkers, and Other Travellers,* edited by Farnham Rehfisch, pp. 41–54. New York: Academic Press.

Miner, Horace

    1953   *The Primitive City of Timbuctoo.* Princeton: Princeton University Press.

Modiano, Nancy

    1973   *Indian Education in the Chiapas Highlands.* New York: Holt, Rinehart and Winston.

Moone, Janet R.

    1973   *Desarrollo tarasco: Integración nacional en el occidente de México.* Mexico, D.F.: Instituto Indigenista Interamericano, Special Publication 67.

Mooney, James

    1891   *Sacred Formulas of the Cherokee.* Seventh Annual Report of the Bureau of Ethnology to the Secretary of the Smithsonian Institution 1885–86, pp. 307–97. Washington, D.C.

    1900   *Myths of the Cherokee.* Nineteenth Annual Report of the Bureau of American Ethnology to the Secretary of the Smithsonian Institution 1897–98, Pt. 1. Washington, D.C.

    1975   *Historical Sketch of the Cherokee.* Chicago: Aldine. Reprinted from James Mooney, *Myths of the Cherokee,* Nineteenth Annual Report of the Bureau of American Ethnology to the Secretary of the Smithsonian Institution 1897–98, Part II, Washington, D.C., 1900.

Mooney, James, and Olbrechts, Frans M.

    1932   *The Swimmer Manuscript: Cherokee Sacred Formulas and Medicinal Prescriptions.* Smithsonian Institution, Bureau of American Ethnology, Bull. 99. Washington, D.C.

Muraskin, William Alan
    1975   *Middle-Class Blacks in a White Society: Prince Hall Freemasonry in America.* Berkeley: University of California Press.

Murphy, Robert E.
    1971   *The Dialectics of Social Life.* New York: Basic Books.

Myerhoff, Barbara G.
    1970   "The Deer-Maize-Peyote Symbol Complex Among the Huichol Indians of Mexico." *Anthropological Quarterly* 43:64–78.
    1974   *Peyote Hunt: The Sacred Journey of the Huichol Indians.* Ithaca: Cornell University Press.

Nader, Laura
    1969   "Up the Anthropologist — Persepectives from Studying Up." In *Reinventing Anthropology,* edited by Dell Hymes. New York: Random House.

Nelson, Cynthia
    1974   "Supports for Ethnic Identity in a Changing Mexican Village." Paper read at American Anthropological Association meetings, Nov. 19–24, Mexico, D.F.

Nolan, Mary Lee
    1974   "The Reality of Differences Between Small Communities in Michoacán, Mexico." *American Anthropologist* 76:47–49.

Norbeck, Edward
    1961   *Religion in Primitive Society.* New York: Harper & Row.
    1967   "African Rituals of Conflict." In *Gods and Rituals: Readings in Religious Beliefs and Practices,* edited by John Middleton, pp. 197–226. Austin: University of Texas Press.

O'Connor, Mary Isobel
    1980   "Ethnicity and Economics: The Mayos of Sonora, Mexico." PhD. dissertation, University of California at Santa Barbara.

Opler, Morris E.
    1972   *The Creek Indian Towns of Oklahoma in 1937.* Papers in Anthropology, vol. 13, no. 1, Department of Anthropology and the Anthropology Club of the University of Oklahoma, Norman.

Patai, Raphael
    1967   *Golden River to Golden Road.* 2nd ed. Philadelphia: University of Pennsylvania Press.

Patterson, Caleb Perry
　　1922　*The Negro in Tennessee, 1790–1865.* Reprint. New York: Greenwood Press, Negro Universities Press, 1968.

Phillips, Ulrich B.
　　1928　*American Negro Slavery.* New York: D. Appleton.

Pratt, Richard Henry
　　1964　*Battlefield and Classroom: Four Decades With the American Indian, 1867–1904.* New Haven: Yale University Press.

Press, Irwin
　　1969　"Ambiguity and Innovation: Implications for the Genesis of the Cultural Broker." *American Anthropologist* 71:205–17.

Pullman, Marc H.
　　1972　"Wisconsin v. Yoder: The Right to be Different — First Amendment Exemption for Amish under the Free Exercise Clause." *De Paul Law Review* XXII: 539–51.

Rabin, David L., et al.
　　1965　"Untreated Congenital Hip Disease: A Study of the Epidemiology, Natural History, and Social Aspects of a Disease in a Navajo Population." *American Journal of Public Health* 55(2) (supplement).

Rattray, R. S.
　　1923　*Ashanti.* Oxford: Clarendon Press.

Redfield, Robert
　　1941　*The Folk Culture of Yucatan.* Chicago: University of Chicago Press.

Rose, Harold M.
　　1971　*The Black Ghetto: A Spatial Behavioral Perspective.* New York: McGraw-Hill.

Rosen, Sheldon B.
　　1980　"Is Worker Management Possible? The Case of the Israeli Kibbutz." PhD. dissertation, University of California at Santa Barbara.

Rousseve, Charles
　　1937　*The Negro in Louisiana.* New Orleans: Xavier University Press.

Sahlins, Marshall
　　1976　*Culture and Practical Reason.* Chicago: University of Chicago Press.

Salem, Elie Adib
　　1973　*Modernization Without Revolution: Lebanon's Experience.* Bloomington: Indiana University Press.

Schensul, Stephen L.
　1973　"Action Research: The Applied Anthropologist in a Community Mental Health Program." In *Anthropology Beyond the University,* edited by Alden Redfield. Proceedings of the Southern Anthropological Society, no. 7.

Schlesier, Karl H.
　1974　"Action Anthropology and the Southern Cheyenne." *Current Anthropology* 15(3) (September):277–83.

Schweri, William F., II, and van Willigen, John
　1978　*Organized Resistance to an Imposed Environmental Change: A Reservoir in Eastern Kentucky,* University of Kentucky Water Resources Research Institute, Report No. 110.

Shaw, George Bernard
　1904　*Man and Superman.* New York: Brentano's.

Sherer, Louise
　1965　*Clan System of the Fort Mohave Indians.* Los Angeles: Historical Society of Southern Caifornia.

Shibutani, T., and Kwan, K. T.
　1965　*Ethnic Stratification: A Comparative Approach.* New York: Macmillan.

Shiloh, Ailon, ed.
　1969　*Peoples and Cultures of the Middle East.* New York: Random House.

Shimkin, Demetri B.; Louie, Gloria Jean; and Frate, Dennis A.
　1978　"The Black Extended Family: Rural Institution and a Mechanism of Urban Adaptation." In *The Extended Family in Black Societies,* edited by D. B. Shimkin, E. M. Shimkin, and D. A. Frate, pp. 25–148. The Hague: Mouton.

Siverts. Henning
　1958　"Social and Cultural Changes in a Tzeltal (Mayan) Municipio, Chiapas, Mexico." In *Proceedings of the 32nd International Congress of Americanists,* pp. 177–89. Oslo.
　1960　"Political Organization in a Tzeltal Community in Chiapas, Mexico." *Alpha Kappa Deltan* 30:14–28.
　1964　"On Politics and Leadership in Highland Chiapas." In *Desarrollo cultural de los mayas,* edited by Evon Vogt and Alberto Ruz, pp. 363–80. Mexico, D.F.: Universidad Nacional Autónoma de México.
　1969　*Oxchuc: Una tribu maya de México.* Special Publication 52. Mexico, D.F.: Instituto Indigenista Interamericano.

Sjoberg, Gideon
　1960　*The Preindustrial City.* New York: Free Press.

Slocum, Marianna C.

1956   "Cultural Changes Among the Oxchuc Tzeltals." In *Estudios an-tropológicos: Publicados en homenaje al Doctor Manuel Gamio,* pp. 491–95. Mexico, D.F.: Dirección General de Publicaciones.

Smith, M. G.

1969   "Pluralism in Precolonial African Societies." In *Pluralism in Africa,* edited by Leo Kuper and M. G. Smith. Berkeley: University of California Press.

Smith, Waldemar R.

1974   "Beyond the Plural Society: Economics and Ethnicity in Middle American Towns." *Ethnology* 14(3):225–45.

1977   *The Fiesta System and Economic Change.* New York: Columbia University Press.

Smock, David R., and Smock, Audrey C.

1975   *The Politics of Pluralism.* New York: Elsevier.

Southall, Geneva

1969   "Contributions of Black Musicians Prior to the Civil War." Afro-American Cultural Institute presentation, University of Iowa, Iowa City.

Speck, Frank G.

1911   *Ceremonial Songs of the Creek and Yuchi Indians.* University of Pennsylvania, Museum Anthropological Publications, vol. 1, no. 2, Philadelphia.

Speck, Frank G., and Broom, Leonard, in collaboration with Will West Long

1951   *Cherokee Dance and Drama.* Berkeley and Los Angeles: University of California Press.

Spicer, Edward H.

1940   *Pascua: A Yaqui Village in Arizona.* Chicago: University of Chicago Press.

1954a   *Potam: A Yaqui Village in Sonora.* American Anthropological Association 56(4, part 2), Memoir No. 77.

1954b   "Spanish-Indian Acculturation in the Southwest." *American Anthropologist* 56:663–78.

1961a   Introduction to *Perspectives in American Indian Culture Change,* edited by Edward H. Spicer, pp. 1–6. Chicago: University of Chicago Press.

1961b   "Types of Contact and Processes of Change." In *Perspectives in American Indian Culture Change,* edited by Edward H. Spicer, pp. 517–44. Chicago: University of Chicago Press.

1961c   "Yaqui." In *Perspectives in American Indian Culture Change,* edited by Edward H. Spicer, pp. 7–93. Chicago: University of Chicago Press.

Spicer, Edward H. (*continued*)

  1962   *Cycles of Conquest: The Impact of Spain, Mexico, and the United States on the Indians of the Southwest, 1533–1960.* Tucson: University of Arizona Press.

  1964a   "Apuntes sobre el tipo de religión de los yuto-aztecas centrales." *Actas y Memorias del XXXV Congreso Internacional de Americanistas,* pp. 27–38. Mexico, D.F.

  1964b   "Indigenismo in the United States, 1870–1960." *American Indigena* 23:349–64.

  1966   "The Process of Cultural Enclavement in Middle America." XXXVI Congreso Internacional de Americanistas, Seville, 3:267–79.

  1969a   "Government Policy and Indian Integration in Mexico and United States." Paper read at annual meeting for the Society for Applied Anthropology, Mexico, D.F.

  1969b   "Political Incorporation and Cultural Change in New Spain: A Study in Spanish-Indian Relations." In *Attitudes of Colonial Powers Toward the American Indian,* edited by Howard Peckham and Charles Gibson. Salt Lake City: University of Utah.

  1969c   *A Short History of the Indians of the United States.* New York: Van Nostrand Reinhold.

  1970   "Contrasting Forms of Nativism Among the Mayos and Yaquis of Sonora, Mexico." In *The Social Anthropology of Latin America,* edited by Walter Goldschmidt and Harry Hoijer, pp. 104–25. Los Angeles: Latin American Center, University of California.

  1971   "Persistent Cultural Systems: A Comparative Study of Identity Systems That Can Adapt to Contrasting Environments." *Science* 174:795–800.

  1972   "Introduction" and "Plural Society in the Southwest." In *Plural Society in the Southwest,* edited by Edward H. Spicer and Raymond H. Thompson. Weatherhead Foundation. New York: Interbook.

  1976   "The Yaquis: A Persistent Identity System." Paper presented at the Singer Symposium, 75th Annual Meeting, November 1976, American Anthropological Association.

  1980   *The Yaquis: A Cultural History.* Tucson: University of Arizona Press.

Spicer, E. H.; Hansen, A. T.; Luomala, K.; and Opler, M. K.

  1969   *Impounded People: Japanese-Americans in the Relocation Centers.* Tucson: University of Arizona Press.

Spicer, Edward H., ed.

  1961   *Perspectives in American Indian Culture Change.* Chicago: University of Chicago Press.

Spier, Leslie

1953 "Some Observations on Mohave Clans." *Southwestern Journal of Anthropology* 9(3):324–42.

Spindler, Louise S.

1977 *Culture Change and Modernization.* New York: Holt, Rinehart and Winston.

Stanley, Sam

1977 "American Indian Power and Powerlessness." In *The Anthropology of Power,* edited by Raymond D. Fogelson and Richard N. Adams. San Francisco: Academic Press.

Steinbeck, John

1939 *The Grapes of Wrath.* New York: Viking.

Sterkx, H. E.

1972 *The Free Negro in Ante-Bellum Louisiana.* Rutherford, New Jersey: Fairleigh Dickinson University Press.

Stewart, Kenneth M.

1947a "Mohave Warfare." *Southwestern Journal of Anthropology* 3(1):257–78.

1947b "An Account of a Mohave Mourning Ceremony." *American Anthropologist* 49:146–48.

1965 "Review of Jack D. Forbes' *Warriors of the Colorado.*" *Ethnohistory* 12(2):187–88.

1968 "A Brief History of the Chemehuevi Indians." *The Kiva* 34(1):9–27.

1969a "The Aboriginal Territory of the Mohave Indians." *Ethnohistory* 16(3):257–73.

1969b "A Brief History of the Mohave Indians Since 1850." *The Kiva* 35(1):1–18.

1973 "Witchcraft Among the Mohave Indians." *Ethnology* 12(3):315–24.

Sturtevant, William C.

1955 "The Mikasuki Seminole: Medical Beliefs and Practices." Ph.D. dissertation, Yale University.

Sutherland, Anne

1975a "The American Rom: A Case of Economic Adaptation." In *Gypsies, Tinkers, and Other Travellers,* edited by Farnham Rehfisch, pp. 1–39. New York: Academic Press.

1975b *Gypsies: The Hidden Americans.* New York: Free Press.

Swanton, John R.

1928 *Religious Beliefs and Medical Practices of the Creek Indians.* Bureau of American Ethnology, Forty-second Annual Report, pp. 473–672. Washington, D.C.

Swanton, John R. (*continued*)

    1931   *Source Material for the Social and Ceremonial Life of the Choctaw Indians.* Smithsonian Institution, Bureau of American Ethnology, Bull. 103. Washington, D.C.

    1946   *The Indians of the Southeastern United States.* Smithsonian Institution, Bureau of American Ethnology, Bull. 137. Washington, D.C.

Sweet, Louise E., ed.

    1971   *The Central Middle East.* New Haven: HRAF Press.

Sykes, Percy

    1930   *A History of Persia.* 3rd ed. 2 vols. London: Macmillan.

Thomas, Robert K.

    1953   "The Origin and Development of the Redbird Smith Movement." M.A. thesis, University of Arizona.

Thompson, Laura

    1976   "An Appropriate Role for Postcolonial Applied Anthropologists." *Human Organization* 35(1) (Spring): 1–8.

Tönnies, Ferdinand

    1957   *Community and Society.* Translated by Charles P. Loomis. East Lansing: Michigan State University Press.

Trens, Manuel B.

    1957   *Historia de Chiapas desde los tiempos mas remotos hasta la caida del Segundo Imperio.* Mexico, D.F.

Turner, Paul R.

    1977   "Intensive Agriculture Among the Highland Tzeltals." *Ethnology* 16: 167–74.

    1978   "Religious Conversion and Community Development." Paper read at the annual meeting of the Society for Applied Anthropology. Mexico, D.F.

Tylor, Edward B.

    1958   *The Origins of Culture.* New York: Harper Torchbooks.

United States Supreme Court

    1972   "Wisconsin v. Yoder." *United States Reports* 405: 205–49.

Van Den Berghe, Pierre L.

    1973   "Pluralism." In *Handbook of Social and Cultural Anthropology,* edited by John J. Honigman. Chicago: Rand-McNally.

van Vollenhoven, C.

    1933   *La découverte du droit indonesien.* Paris.

van Willigen, John
  1971 "The Papago Community Development Worker." *Community Development Journal* 6(2).

Van Zantwijk, Rudolf A. M.
  1967 *Servants of the Saints: The Social and Cultural Identity of a Tarascan Community in Mexico.* Assen, Netherlands: Van Gorcum.

Villa Rojas, Alfonso
  1946 *Notas sobre la etnografía de los indios tzeltales de Oxchuc, Chiapas, México.* Microfilm Collection of Manuscripts on Middle American Cultural Anthropology 7. Chicago: University of Chicago Library.
  1947 "Kinship and Nagualism in a Tzeltal Community, Southeastern Mexico." *American Anthropologist* 49:578–87.
  1962 "El centro coordinador tzeltal-tzotzil." In *Los centros coordinadores,* pp. 51–68. Mexico, D.F.: Instituto Nacional Indigenista.

Vogt, Evon Z.
  1961 "Navajo." In *Perspectives in American Indian Culture Change,* edited by Edward H. Spicer, pp. 279–336. Chicago: University of Chicago Press.
  1969 *Zinacantán: A Maya Community in the Highlands of Chiapas.* Cambridge, Mass.: Harvard University Press, Belknap Press.

Vreeland, Herbert H.
  1969 "Ethnic Groups and Languages of Iran." In *Peoples and Cultures of the Middle East,* edited by Ailon Shiloh, pp. 51–67. New York: Random House.

Wade, Richard C.
  1964 *Slavery in the Cities: The South, 1820–1860.* New York: Oxford University Press.

Wahrhaftig, Albert L.
  1968 "The Tribal Cherokee Population of Eastern Oklahoma." *Current Anthropology* 9:510–18.

Wahraftig, Albert L., and Lukens-Wahrhaftig, Jane
  1979 "New Militants or Resurrected State? The Five-County Northeastern Oklahoma Cherokee Organization." In *The Cherokee Indian Nation: A Troubled History,* edited by Duane H. King, pp. 223–46. Knoxville: University of Tennessee Press.

Wallace, Anthony F. C.
  1956 "Revitalization Movements." *American Anthropologist* 58:264–81.
  1961 *Culture and Personality.* New York: Random House.

Wallace, Jesse Thomas
1927   *A History of the Negroes of Mississippi From 1865 to 1890.* Reprint. New York: Johnson Reprint Corporation, 1970.

Wallace, William J.
1947   "The Dream in Mohave Life." *Journal of American Folklore* 60:252–58.

Weidman, Hazel H.
1975   "Concepts as Strategies for Change." *Psychiatric Annals* 5(8) (August):312–14.

1976   "In Praise of the Double Bind Inherent in Anthropological Application." In *Do Applied Anthropologists Apply Anthropology?* edited by M. Angrosino. Proceedings of the Southern Anthropological Association, no. 10.

Weigand, Phil C.
1978*a*   "Contemporary Social and Economic Structure Among the Huichol Indians." In *Art of the Huichol,* edited by K. Berrin, pp. 101–15. San Francisco: Fine Arts Museum of San Francisco, H. Abrams.

1978*b*   "Prehistoria del estado de Zacatecas: Una interpretación." In *Anuario de historia zacatecana,* edited by Cuauhtemoc Esparza Sánchez, pp. 203–48. Zacatecas, Mexico: Universidad Autónoma de Zacatecas.

Weingrod, Alex
1965   *Israel: Group Relations in a New Society.* New York: Praeger.

Wellin, Edward
1977   "Theoretical Orientations in Medical Anthropology: Continuity and Change Over the Past Half-Century." In *Culture, Disease, and Healing,* edited by David Landy, pp. 47–58. New York: Macmillan.

Westerlind, Peter B.
1978   "From Farm to Factory: The Economic Development of the Kibbutz." Ph.D. dissertation, University of California at Santa Barbara.

Wharton, Vernon L.
1947   *The Negro in Mississippi, 1865–1890.* Reprint. New York: Harper Torchbooks, 1965.

White, Leslie A.
1975   *The Concept of Cultural Systems.* New York: Columbia University Press.

Wilber, Donald N.
1969   *United Arab Republic, Egypt.* New Haven: HRAF Press.

Williams. F. E.

1923 *The Vailala Madness and the Destruction of Native Ceremonies in the Gulf Division.* Anthropology Report No. 4. Port Moresby: Territory of Papua.

1934 "The Vailala Madness in Retrospect." *Essays Presented to C. G. Seligman,* edited by E. E. Evans-Pritchard et al. London: Kegan Paul, Trench, Trubner.

Willis, William S., Jr.

1970 "Anthropology and Negroes on the Southern Frontier." In *The Black Experience in America,* edited by J. C. Curtis and L. L. Gould, pp. 33–50. Austin: University of Texas Press.

Wilson, Byran R.

1975 *The Noble Savages: The Primitive Origins of Charisma and Its Contemporary Survival.* Berkeley: University of California Press.

Wilson, John A.

1951 *The Culture of Ancient Egypt.* Chicago: Phoenix Books.

Wolf, Eric

1955 "Types of Latin American Peasantry: A Preliminary Discussion." *American Anthropologist* 57:452–71.

1956 "Aspects of Group Relations in a Complex Society: Mexico." *American Anthropologist* 58:1065–78.

1959 *Sons of the Shaking Earth: The People of Mexico and Guatemala: Their Land, History, and Culture.* Chicago: University of Chicago Press.

1967 "Closed Corporate Peasant Communities in Meso-America and Central Java." In *Peasant Society,* edited by Jack M. Putter, pp. 230–46. Boston: Little, Brown.

Woods, Clyde M.

1975 *Culture Change.* Dubuque, Iowa: Wm. C. Brown.

Woofter, T. J., Jr.

1930 *Black Yeomanry.* New York: Henry Holt.

Works, John A.

1976 *Pilgrims in a Strange Land.* New York: Columbia University Press.

Zablocki, Benjamin

1980 *Alienation and Charisma: A Study of Contemporary American Communes.* New York: Free Press.

Zeltzer, Moshe

1969 "Minorities in Iraq and Syria." In *Peoples and Cultures of the Middle East,* edited by Ailon Shiloh, pp. 10–50. New York: Random House.

Index

gobernador's role among, 136–38,
144, 146
historical experience of, 135–36
occupational identity of, 136
opposition symbols of, 145
role of fariseos among, 138–44, 147
Myth, and identity, 82–83, 175, 180

National Indianist, Institute, 215–20,
224–26
Navajos, 164–65, 177
Nighthawk Ketoowah movement, 89,
92, 94
North American Indian Ecumenical
Movement, 184–85
Nubians, xvi
adaptation of, 13–14, 23
dispersal of, 11
educational patterns of, 14–15
endogamy among, 20
historical identity of, 9–10
occupational identity of, 8–9, 12,
14, 17
racial identity of, 9, 11–13
religious identity of, 9
resettling of, 8
Nueva Vizcaya, 27–28, 30–31
detribalization in, 30
extent of enclavement in, 37–39
La Juntans in, 34–36
mission Indian groups in, 36
processes of acculturation in, 27–30,
36–39
raiding Indians in, 30
Spanish institutions in, 28–29
Tarahumaras in, 33, 36–37

Occupation, as identity symbol, 9, 12,
14–18
Occupational specialization, 12, 14–16,
21–22, 39
Oneida, 195, 197–99
Opposition, xix–xxi
and anarchy, 193, 196–99
mechanisms of, xx, 44–45, 47–50, 71,
75, 81
between minority and larger society,
xix–xx
as perpetuator of subordination, 81–83

symbols of, 37
terminology of, 55–56, 59
Oppositional process, xix–xx
Order, and change, 228–31, 241

Pan-Indian movements, 178
Pariah groups, xvi, 6–7, 21–22
Pariah occupations. *See* Despised
occupations
Pariahs, 78, 80
People of the Book, 10, 15–16, 19
Pimas. *See* Mountain Pimas
Pluralism, 24–25
and competition, 182
defined, xvii, 37
implications of, 25
and polyarchy, 199
and subordination, 182
Political sphere, 57, 59
Process, role of maintenance in, 228–31,
238–42
Protestant Church, among Tzeltal Maya,
214–16, 220–24

Race, as identity symbol, xvi, 9–13
Racial purity, xvi–xviii
Tarascan myth of, 175
Racism, as opposition mechanism, 69, 71
Rappites, 195–196, 198
"Real people," 94, 96, 104–5
Religion, as criteria of identity, 8–9
Replacement
and acculturation, 239
and assimilation, 239–40
defined, 222
and maintenance, 240
process of, 234–35, 239–41
Reservation cultures
compared to closed corporate
communities, 172–73
as isolation of, 185–86
persistence of, 177, 186
as social type, 177
Reservations
and assimilation, 173, 177, 180–81,
183, 186
as homelands, 186–87
and persistence, 173
Resettlement, 8, 47–49